D1601234

The Moral Self

What do we need in order to have morally sound relationships with others? What does it mean for us to care for ourselves? What is the relationship between self-love and morality?

The Moral Self addresses the question of how morality enters into our lives. Pauline Chazan draws upon psychology, moral philosophy and literary interpretation to rebut the view that morality's role is to limit desire and control self-love. Preserving the ancients' connection between what is good for the self and what is morally good, Chazan argues that a certain kind of care for the self is central to moral agency.

Her intriguing argument begins with a critical examination of the views of Hume, Rousseau and Hegel. The constructive part of the book takes a more unusual turn by synthesising the work of the analyst Heinz Kohut and Aristotle into Chazan's own positive account, which is then illustrated by the use of Russian literature.

The Moral Self offers a dynamic, interdisciplinary slant on the discussion of moral theory, and will be of great interest and use to students of philosophy as well as psychology.

Pauline Chazan lectures in Philosophy at La Trobe University in Victoria, Australia.

The Problems of Philosophy

Founding Editor: Ted Honderich

Editors: Tim Crane and Jonathan Wolff, *University College London*

This series addresses the central problems of philosophy. Each book gives a fresh account of a particular philosophical theme by offering two perspectives on the subject: the historical context and the author's own distinctive and original contribution.

The books are written to be accessible to students of philosophy and related disciplines, while taking the debate to a new level.

The Moral Self

Pauline Chazan

London and New York

First published 1998
by Routledge
11 New Fetter Lane, London EC4P 4EE

Simultaneously published in the USA and Canada
by Routledge
29 West 35th Street, New York, NY 10001

Typeset in Times by Routledge
Printed and bound in Great Britain by
MPG Books Ltd, Bodmin

British Library Cataloguing in Publication Data
A catalogue record for this book is available from
the British Library

Library of Congress Cataloging in Publication Data
Chazan, Pauline, 1948–
The moral self / Pauline Chazan.
p. cm. – Includes bibliographical references.
1. Ethics–Methodology. 2. Moral development.
3. Ethics. I. Title.
BJ37.C43 1998
171'.p–dc21

97–40021
CIP

ISBN 0–415–16861–9 (hbk)
ISBN 0–415–16862–7 (pbk)

I dedicate this book to the memory of my
mother and father, Mira Lipman and Falek Sobol

Contents

Preface

This book began as a Ph.D. thesis, supervised in its early stages by Michael Stocker, and then by Kimon Lycos. I am extraordinarily fortunate to have had the opportunity to work with these two philosophers, and I owe a great deal to both of them.

I thank Michael Stocker for the wonderful work he has done in ethics, for it is this more than anything else which ignited my interest in moral psychology. I also thank him for urging me to begin *The Moral Self*, and for the many stimulating, productive discussions we had in Melbourne prior to his departure for the United States. That departure had left me concerned about the possibility of finding another supervisor as knowledgeable and dedicated as he.

I need not have been apprehensive: Kim Lycos' enthusiasm and love for philosophy infused our discussions with excitement, and I was constantly amazed by the breadth of his knowledge and the depth of his understanding. I am grateful for his generosity with his time, the invaluable comments he made on numerous drafts of my work, and the encouragement he gave me. His death in 1995 dealt a terrible blow, not only to the Australian philosophical community, but to all who knew him.

I would like to thank La Trobe University for granting me a two year Post-Doctoral Fellowship, during which time I was able to prepare this book. I also thank members of the School of Philosophy at La Trobe University for providing such a congenial, friendly atmosphere in which to work.

I am grateful to a number of people who read and discussed drafts of various chapters with me. I would like to thank John Campbell, Christopher Cordner, Graeme Marshall, Behan McCullagh, Dorothy Mitchell, Tim Oakley and Janna Thompson. I also thank my husband, Robert Chazan, for guiding me through the maze of self psychology.

La Trobe University
Victoria, Australia
November 1997

Acknowledgements

Chapters 1 and 2 are modified versions of articles published respectively in *The Canadian Journal of Philosophy* (1992) 22: 45–65; and *The History of Philosophy Quarterly* (1993) 10: 341–54. Material from Chapters 6 and 7 is forthcoming in an article in *Philosophia*, 25. My thanks are owed to the editors and publishers of these journals who gave me permission to use this material here.

Introduction

[The moral philosopher] has to show how and why the moral 'gaze' on life and people is an enriching achievement of human development.

(Lycos 1978: 17)

This work is concerned with providing an answer to the question of how we ought to conceive of the self's entrance into the moral domain, and of morality's entrance into a human life. The account provided here is in some crucial respects different from those offered by contemporary moral theories, and it uncovers a tension between morality and theories about morality.

Within the context of explaining how good agents behave, contemporary theories generally agree that a preliminary prerequisite for a moral orientation is an awareness of being one among many others. In focusing on commitments, obligations and duties, theories as diverse as Kantianism and utilitarianism hold that a moral orientation requires agents to have the capacity to detach from private desires and needs, and to focus instead on the desires and needs of others, no matter what relationship, if any, they have to those others. Some degree of impartiality and objectivity is seen to be required for the very possibility of moral consciousness.

Taken further, this requirement has emerged as a requirement for impersonal, universalisable principles and rules upon which the recognition of duty and the performance of right actions are thought to be founded. The requirement of impartiality can be seen in much moral philosophy to imperceptibly blend with, and in some cases to have been transformed into, the requirement for impersonality and universality. Impartiality ensures that no exceptions are made in favour of the agent herself, while impersonality and universality further ensure that partiality is

1

Introduction

eliminated, putting in place a strong rational influence: moral actions ought to be rationally justifiable; they ought to be performed by any rational agent in similar circumstances; they are actions for which the weight of reason must speak. The combination of impartiality, rationality, impersonality and universality requires moral agents to prescind from particular desires, needs, claims and relationships. Moral philosophy can be seen to have abstracted from the particularity of persons and their lives and to have focused instead on the objective features of actions, states of affairs, and lives. Notwithstanding recent attempts to revise and make modern theories more attractive (e.g. Herman 1996) the private or particular concerns, interests and relationships of the self remain for most theorists morally suspect, as needing moral justification from an impartial and universal perspective, this perspective being regarded as an ethical necessity.

Moral action is viewed by contemporary theories as sitting uneasily with concern for one's own self. Morality and self-interest are portrayed as being diametrically opposed, and each as making irresistible rational demands on agents. In theory, at least, morality has been, in the struggle between morality and self, the overwhelmingly favoured rational option. This is reflected in the fact that a focal point of much moral theorising has been the task of justifying morality to the rational egoist.

Theorists have sought to provide a rationally compelling answer to the question of what the self has most reason to do. Despite being dubious about the possibility of any rationally compelling answer, given the conflict between the demands of egoism and morality, Sidgwick (1929) settled for a universalistic utilitarianism. John McDowell (1978), in claiming that moral reasons, properly appreciated, silence self-interested reasons so that they no longer count as reasons, might be read as giving a direct retort to Sidgwick's uncertainty about what the self has most reason to do. Derek Parfit (1984) has argued that self-interest can be shown to be irrational, since certain considerations lead us to realise that self-interested reasons have no weight, while the weight of reason can be shown to speak for morality. And the Kantian rational intellectual moral motive leaves little room for any considerations pertaining to 'dear self'.

Samuel Scheffler (1982) has allocated some rational weight to the self's personal perspective in moral deliberation, allowing personal and moral concerns to each count as one kind of reason among

2

Introduction

others. Moral thinking has been portrayed by Scheffler as involving a kind of 'weighing up' procedure where the 'rational weight' of different kinds of reasons has central moral importance. This model, consistent with much contemporary theory, conceives of the business of leading a personal life and the business of heeding morality's requirements as being two quite separate affairs. Sharing much common ground with Scheffler, Thomas Nagel (1980; 1986), in arguing that a completely impersonal morality is not a realistic human goal, has allowed the self's personal perspective entry into the objective, moral view. Yet personal concerns and moral concerns remain distinct for Nagel: personal reasons pertain to the business of leading the self's own life, whereas the moral remains co-extensive with the impartial and impersonal.

In contrast to the foregoing, two important conclusions to be drawn from the account presented in this book are, first, that a self's being committed to impartiality and impersonality in the way specified by many moral theories does not sit well with a commitment to what it is that can enable a self to achieve a moral outlook. So instead of regarding impersonality as a standpoint that a self can take, one where 'one does not know who one is and how what one observes relates to one' (Darwall 1983: 153), on the account presented here impersonality is better understood in terms of a certain kind of critical detachment or distancing from values and ends. But this critical distancing does not require the self to ignore the emotional-affective or personal aspects of its own agency in the way that the traditional understanding of achieving an impersonal perspective does.

A second conclusion to be drawn from *The Moral Self* is that a moral theory does not need to make a conceptual distinction between morality and self-interest in order to be coherent. This is to say that the self can act morally well without being motivated by what is widely regarded to be a specifically 'moral' (as opposed to a self-interested) motive. Instead, it will be argued that a certain kind of value that a moral agent places on her own self is of central importance in explaining her moral outlook. My account will suggest that our modern philosophical conceptions of morality fail to account for, or to give high enough value to, elements which encompass aspects of our own selves central to any explanation of the development and existence of our moral orientations. Moreover, we will see that a meaningful account of morality can be given which does not depend on an agent's focusing on impersonal rather than personal considerations, an account where the main dimension of moral assessment is located in the particularity of human relationships and experiences, and in concrete, personal responses to other individuals. Such an account can at the same time preserve the rationality of moral value, judgement and action.

It is an account that will show Susan Wolf's claim (1982) that it is not always better to be morally better as having no foundation. For on my account morality is not a separate option for a person alongside other possible options, but is rather something that permeates the way in which a moral agent goes about all of her activities. Where Wolf says that 'Moral ideals do not make the best personal ideals' (1982: 435), a consequence of my account is that a person's morality is revealed in the very enactment of her personal ideals.

The account presented in this work has certain affinities with Greek accounts since, according to it, an agent is able to respond in a morally appropriate way, not as a result of taking an impartial, impersonal view, but because of her own particular concerns, interests and relationships: because of what she, at the moment of action, has become. My account of the moral life has as its focal point the self's own interests, concerns and values, and so preserves the ancients' connection between morality and the goodness of a human life, between what is good for the agent and what is morally good. My claim will be that the state of a person's self and the moral status of her actions are interdependent: to the extent that a person achieves the unity of thought and desire integral to Aristotelian moral character (the same inner psychic unity that Plato required of his philosopher-kings), so she is able to act morally well.

Also important in my account is the moral self's desire to have the best possible life. It will be suggested that what is morally admirable about an agent also benefits the agent herself. While Aristotelian and Platonic moral agents want for themselves the best possible lives, and while what is constitutive of the best possible life is at the same time what leads them to act in morally good ways, morally good action is not performed in order to achieve for themselves the best possible life. It would be a bad misconstruction of Plato and Aristotle to take them to be telling us that virtue is a means to happiness. Rather, they tell us that happiness, meaningfulness, and the achievement of virtue cannot be separated from each other. Their ethics have no room for the rigid division into the 'moral' and the 'self-interested' of which contemporary moral philosophy is so fond.

Introduction

The account in this book is compatible with the Greek view: the moral agent I will describe acts virtuously because she is the kind of person who has developed a particular type of perception and has come to see the world, herself, and her place in the world, in a certain way. Having this perception, she then has the capacity to achieve a certain critical distancing from those values and ends which are for her of supreme importance, and to reassess whether, given the particular circumstances in which she finds herself, these values and ends are ones she should here pursue.

Where contemporary theories conceive of an agent as remaining in the moral realm by not transgressing certain principles or rules of living, a consequence of my account is that the moral realm ought to be conceived of as consisting of beings who possess certain positive qualities and capacities that entitle them to enter this realm. This does not mean that I am substituting a realm constituted by rules and principles that are accessible to all with a realm constituted by kinds of beings (and so a realm not accessible to all). The account presented here does not contain any moral elitism, since the positive qualities and capacities needed in order to enter the moral realm are ones that are within the grasp of every person.

Among these positive qualities is singled out as crucially important what I (following Aristotle) term 'love of self'. A central thesis of *The Moral Self* is that a certain kind of self-love is foundational for moral agency. This challenges a widespread view of self-love as being vulgar. Apart from being discussed in commentaries on Aristotle, love of self is a relation to the self which has been largely neglected in recent moral philosophy, and the account I will give of this form of self-valuing is quite different from the accounts of self-valuing (e.g. pride and self-esteem) that are found in the modern literature. My account of 'love of self' will show that an agent's moral orientation is grounded in her own desires, interests and values.

Just how far outside the self the ethical ought to be taken to range is a matter of some dispute: '*We* can represent a self-interest as much as *I*' (Williams 1985: 14). Yet the ethical is almost universally assumed to reside at some point outside the self, as a phenomenon that lies, or as a demand that originates from, outside one's immediate concerns and commitments. This is an assumption that my account calls into question. Williams (1985) has made a move in the right direction in arguing that the range of 'the ethical' ought to be broadened to include any concerns that might arise in response to the question of how one should live. However, he still construes 'the moral' in the narrow way, and my account will cast some doubt on whether this is something with which we need to agree.

Another conclusion to be drawn from my account is that the impersonal–personal, universal–particular and objective–subjective dichotomies do not offer a complete description of reasons a person might have for action, and that the account of moral motivation these dichotomies can provide is far too thin. If we conceive of morality on the model of an impartial, impersonal theory of right, a right that is disengaged from the particularity of leading a human life, if moral motivation is grounded in an impersonal, impartial, objective, universal perspective, if morality is a phenomenon that impinges (Scheffler 1986: 537) on one's consciousness and life, rather than a phenomenon that can constitute the very character and quality of consciousness, then any attempt to seek a less demanding theory (Scheffler and Nagel) or to limit the scope of morality or to challenge its authority (Williams 1973; 1981a; 1981b; 1981c) seems to me to be a futile exercise. If 'morality' is fully described by 'impartial morality', if morality requires the pursuit of the impartial, impersonal best, and if moral motivation must be grounded in impersonal universal considerations, then if our actions fall short of fulfilling these requirements, we are morally not very good. Nagel, Williams and Scheffler have tried to make morality more palatable (and, with this, to give a more feasible account of the self's achievement of moral personhood) by providing a rationale for limiting the requirements of impartial morality and by legitimising the pursuit of personal desires and aims. But none of these philosophers has disentangled himself from certain presuppositions regarding the nature of morality and the role it has in thought, feeling and human life. The account in this work shows that morality does not inform a life from a standpoint removed from that life, but that it does so such that the personal aspects of leading a life do not lie at a point external to and removed from the moral sphere. It will be seen that that which leads one to recognise and act on behalf of the claims of others does not lie outside the domain of choosing and leading a good personal life. That is, moral personhood is not separable from the personal aspects of leading a good life; it can be seen, rather, to be definitive of those aspects.

A conception of morality which views the personal as being inherent in the moral life is not a new conception: it was espoused some twenty-eight years ago by Iris Murdoch (1970). She recognises reasons for thought, deliberation and action which are not encompassed by the impersonal–personal division. Her account centres moral significance on the quality of loving attention focused upon another individual, and on the importance of one's personal ties to other individuals. Yet it is an account which simultaneously retains the requirement of the ridding of selfishness in order to achieve an ethical outlook.

I discern in Murdoch's writings the belief that engaging in the endless moral task she describes and finding one's life to be meaningful are one and the same activity. This belief is central to the account in this book. I do not extrapolate from Murdoch's writings though, nor does my account hold, that a lucky consequence of engaging in her moral task is that our lives will be meaningful. Rather, I claim that human flourishing and morality coincide. This is because it is via a Murdochian conception of deliberation and contemplation that the self finds meaning in the day-to-day activities of a life. This conception of morality is one which finds morality to pervade every aspect of a person's life and to condition every encounter they have with the world. Morality, on this view, has an internal relation to the pursuit of our projects and the forming of our commitments; it is constitutive of their meaningfulness.

If morality is conceived of as permeating every aspect of our lives, including the pursuit of our projects and commitments, it does not need to be seen as the threat to our selfhood that Bernard Williams has thought it to be. The limit on what a person is prepared to do in the pursuit of their own ends is not best understood if it is conceived of as the result of an impersonal and impartial recognition of universalisable reasons and principles. I believe this limit is better understood if it is seen as originating from the way in which the agent has come to conceive of the world, of others, and of his own self. It is a limit which originates in the agent's own special understanding of and sensitivity to certain features of the world, and this understanding and sensitivity should be seen as an integral part of the agent's own self, determining his 'being-toward-others'. I will argue in this work that the view the moral agent has of himself is critically important in an explanation of his moral actions, since both the limit beyond which he is not prepared to go in pursuit of his own ends and his 'being-toward-others' are seen by him as inescapable parts of himself. This moral limit, then, is one which can be seen to pertain also to the personal standards of leading a personal life. It will be argued that the limit a person has on what he is prepared to do in pursuing his ends is not only closely connected with his own view of himself, but that it is also causally dependent on the very sense he has of his own worth. We will also see that at the same time the sense of his own worth is vulnerable to transgressions of the limit beyond which he will not customarily go.

Rather than conceiving of moral thinking as involving a 'weighing' of different kinds of reasons, my account holds that if we want to understand a person's moral orientation, we must understand why she has the reasons she has, and why they are reasons *for her*. The claim of this book is that we must look beyond the 'rational weight' of reasons, values and ends, and look rather to the nature and constitution of the moral self. That is, instead of looking at the object of moral understanding (beliefs, values, ends, acts) we should look rather at the subject of understanding. We should look more closely at what it is that makes a self into a moral self.

So a central task of this work is to look at the question of how we should conceive of the moral self. Some crucial differences between the account of morality I present and that of a number of modern moral theories have their source in the way in which the moral self is conceived. Many modern theories take it that there is a theoretical, articulable conception of what a moral self is, from which the limits of action arise. The moral self is conceived of in terms of some determinate pieces of knowledge that it possesses, and the moral limits that confront it emerge because of this knowledge. For a Kantian, knowing that rational nature must be respected in itself and other rational beings, draws the boundaries of what the moral self is and is not permitted to do. For a utilitarian, knowing that the maximisation of utility is the ultimate justification of action presents the self with objective criteria according to which it can be judged whether certain actions are permitted, required or forbidden.

Where for these theories the moral 'must' and the moral 'cannot' are derived from certain determinate pieces of knowledge, my claim in this work is that since moral understanding does not consist in a knowledge of a determinate set of things, the moral 'must' and the moral 'cannot' are not derived from any pieces of knowledge. On my account, the moral self is the self that emerges in the context of certain practices (certain kinds of critical reflection) that display a moral understanding that it must, or that it cannot, do certain

8

things. This experience of 'moral impossibility', and the moral understanding with which it goes hand-in-hand, is on my account constitutive of the moral self, but the understanding in question is not given by any theory. Ethical reflection, on my view, is not theoretical. My account will present moral understanding as depending on the self's own sense of justice which, I will argue, is not something teachable. So where a number of modern moral theories purport to tell us what kind of knowledge the moral self has, the account I will present in this work will refuse to say that the ethical subject has knowledge, where 'knowledge' is understood as something that is teachable.

The limits on thought and action that the experience of moral impossibility presents are (what I term) 'internal' or 'built-in' limits. They are internal or built-in because they do not merely serve as an external guard on action in the way that the intellectually or socially constructed limits of many modern moral theories do, but the critical reflection which gives rise to these limits can be seen to be the context in which the moral self is constituted. I conceive of these limits as being constitutive of the moral self. These limits ensure, not merely that right acts will be done, but they can ensure that we will have a world of people who will not be content to not *be* good. So I believe that the kind of moral limits that I conceive of as being constitutive of the moral self fit better with the nature of human striving for nobility and goodness.

This striving for nobility and goodness should be seen as an integral part of what it is to be human: this is an essentially Aristotelian notion. Aristotle believed that a human being has a determinate nature and that a happy life is one in which this nature is fulfilled. This book shares the Aristotelian beliefs that the proper realisation of human nature consists in a life of virtue, and that a life of virtue and a happy life are one and the same. I discuss Aristotle in Chapter 4.

The first three chapters are devoted to expounding and examining the relationships that Hume, Rousseau and Hegel saw to obtain between the value that a person places on her own self and her moral capacity.

We will see that for both Hume and Rousseau a person could develop a strong self-awareness and self-knowledge, and place considerable value on himself, without ever entering the moral domain. The Humean agent might gain 'knowledge of his own force' by means of the reflected impressions of various particular aspects of himself from the environment without ever correcting his perspective and adopting Hume's 'general point of view'. According to Rousseau's account, if we could counteract the effects of civil society we would still not have a moral being (for this the social contract is needed) but we could have a self with a strong centre of values. Both Hume and Rousseau see the development of a strong self with a centre of values, and the development of moral consciousness as being two quite separate phenomena.

Hegel's account holds that the development of a strong self with a secure centre of values and the development of the moral self are one and the same development. These could not be seen as the same development by Rousseau, since he conceives of the self in the state of nature as an isolated self, while the self of virtue and vice is fundamentally social. When the self enters into a social contract and follows the general will it is transformed from an isolated self into one that sees itself as part of a social body: it is transformed into what is, in essence, the forerunner of Kant's rational beings who are members of a kingdom of ends. And we will see that for Hume the development of the pre-moral self and of the moral self could not be the same development. Further, where Hume sees the self as being constructed from something given (the reflected impressions originating in the social environment), Hegel sees the self as the product of a more complex developmental process. This product is regarded by him as coinciding with the moral self. In this respect Charles Taylor's work (1989) might be seen to be closer to Hegel than to either Hume or Rousseau.

This book holds in common with Hegel a developmental account of the moral self, although it does not see the development of love of self or morality to be necessary or inescapable in the way that Hegel sees the appropriation of the values and reasons of *Sittlichkeit* to be. My account also holds in common with Hegel the belief that significance in human life is to be found in morality, but rejects the Hegelian thesis that a full political community is required for morality.

Chapter 4 looks backward to Aristotle and forward to Heinz Kohut. It shows that the perspectives that Aristotle and Kohut's self psychology have on the relation that the self has to itself and to others converge at important points. Kohut's work is shown to present a modern account of a central Aristotelian claim: that the relation that a virtuous person has to her own self has priority over her capacity to relate to others in the way that a virtuous person does. This sets the groundwork for drawing connections between Aristotelian ethics and the account of the moral self that I present in the last four chapters. The relations between moral goodness, love of self, and the kind of psychic health that Aristotle believed went hand-in-hand with virtue are introduced in this chapter. I rely on Aristotle throughout this book, and references to his work are to the *Nicomachean Ethics*.

I have chosen to discuss the accounts of Aristotle, Hume, Rousseau and Hegel because my account of morality stands in a continuous relation with their writings. Each of them places a great emphasis on the importance of what it is that makes a self moral rather than on some objective content (e.g. what it is right to do). In fact, these philosophers, each in his own way, stand opposed to the modern-day emphasis on objective ethical content, and each focuses instead on the *subject* of moral understanding. My own opposition to the emphasis being placed by many contemporary theorists on the importance of some objective content for the ethical will be made clear in Chapter 8.

In Chapter 5 I begin my account of the moral self by introducing the concept of 'significant' action. It is this class of action to which I conceive moral action as belonging. While moral action is rational action, an understanding of an agent's rationality will be shown to be insufficient for an understanding of her moral actions. It will be argued that the intentionality of 'significant' actions expresses a person's moral aspirations in a way that the intentionality of merely rational actions does not. 'Significant' action will be distinguished from 'non-significant' action in order to highlight certain elements that I consider to be important in the emergence of a person's moral orientation. These elements include the values an agent holds, her understanding of what is entailed by her commitment to these values, and her capacity to re-assess this commitment in the light of her understanding of the particular circumstances in which she finds herself.

In retrieving some strands from the discussion of Aristotle and Kohut in Chapter 4, Chapters 6 and 7 extend the discussion in that chapter of the psychic health that is required for virtue, and show that the performance of 'significant' actions and the exercise of moral agency involve a certain kind of self-valuing. I term this self-valuing 'love of self', but my account of this relation to the self goes beyond what can be found in Aristotle. While I borrow the term 'love of self' from Aristotle, my use of this term makes it quite akin to what Plato called 'caring for the soul'. These two chapters contrast the kind of self-valuing involved in contemporary conceptions such as self-esteem and pride, with the relation that I call 'love of self'.

If the moral value of love of self is as great as I will suggest, then it must exclude evil action. I take up this issue in Chapter 8, where I show that an objection which is justified when directed at the Hegelian account of morality is not justified when directed at my account. I argue that Hegel's thesis regarding the constitutive relation between the self and the state must be rejected, and that the moral self is not constituted in terms of some 'other', but that it is rather a self for which each individual person is solely responsible. This chapter defends the view that the development of love of self should be seen as an important aspect of what it is to be human, as well as being central to answering the question of how a person constitutes himself or herself as a moral subject.

CHAPTER I

Hume on self-valuing and moral selfhood

Our reputation, our character, our name...[our] virtue,
beauty and riches...have little influence, when not seconded
by the opinions and sentiments of others.

(Hume 1978: 316)

INTRODUCTION

The history of moral philosophy reveals that philosophers have
responded differently to the question of whether the constitution of
the self and its valuing of itself as an ethical being is generated
individually, socially, culturally or psycho-socially. Hume, Rousseau
and Hegel share with Aristotle the view that in order to sustain the
capacity for unified decision-making and action, the self must value
itself as an autonomous centre. Even though each of these
philosophers offers a different account of what makes a self moral,
they would agree that the self must esteem itself as an entity capable
of acting in accordance with what it deems to be important and
worthwhile if it is to be constituted in the world as a moral self.
While each of these philosophers would agree that some degree
of self-consciousness and unified agency is required for self-
constitution, self-valuing and the achievement of virtue, they
give quite diverse accounts of the nature, origin and maintenance
of these. This chapter will show that for Hume the object of the
moral self's self-valuing is the self *qua* how other people see it, and
this object can be promoted by the positive regard and esteem that
others provide. We will see that Hume replaces the psychic harmony
that for Aristotle goes hand-in-hand with virtue with a certain
bundle of impressions and ideas.

The account that Hume presents[1] of how the self enters the
moral domain and comes to a consciousness of itself as a moral

13

being is one that is superimposed upon his account in the *Treatise*, Book Two, of the constitution of the non-metaphysical self.[2] This primordial[3] self is for Hume constructed out of the passions of pride and humility, which are themselves in turn constructed out of certain feelings of pain and pleasure, these feelings being worked on by memory and imagination, and converted back and forth into series of ideas and impressions. In presenting this account of how we achieve a coherent self-awareness and self-knowledge such that we 'know our own force' (T 597), Hume employs a radical psychology which he must discard once the moral self comes into view. Once we understand the implications of this psychology we will be able to dispel the confusion that some have found in his story.

A grasp of Hume's psychology will enable us to remove the kind of confusion that has puzzled John Passmore:

> If what really happens is that pride 'produces' the idea of self, that idea will be its effect, not its object; if, on the other hand, pride *itself* views the self, this will involve a complete revision of Hume's epistemology. The consequences will be no less far-reaching if pride somehow provokes the mind to have an idea of itself; and in this case, too, that idea is in no sense the 'object' of pride, but only an idea which regularly occurs *later than* pride.
>
> (Passmore 1968: 126–7)

In the following section I will present a reconstruction of Hume's account according to which the idea of the self is not, strictly speaking, the effect of pride; we will see that pride does not, according to Hume, '*itself* view the self'; nor is the idea of the self an idea that 'regularly occurs *later than* pride'. Instead, we will see that for Hume pride and the idea of the self come into being simultaneously: both will be shown to be the joint effects of a certain train of perceptions.

Confusion is the charge that has also been directed at Hume's account of the boastful guest at the feast who is proud of the feast even though he was merely present at it and had nothing to do with its production (T 290). Gabriele Taylor refers to Hume's account as

> a story that allows us to accept both that some relation is not close enough for pride and that nevertheless pride can be based on it.... The boastful guest ... is allowed to be proud of

the feast, though we are meant to infer that he is not at all
sensible in being proud, that he has no reason for his pride.

(Taylor 1980)

Taylor also accuses Hume of not having 'kept his promise to offer
points that will distinguish pride as such from joy or pleasure'
(1980: 388). Hume does indeed keep his promise, and the points
that distinguish pride from joy or pleasure are quite apparent once
we understand the psychology he is employing.

By examining Hume's radical psychology, we will see that while
Hume grounds both the self for which we care and are concerned
and the moral self in a bundle of impressions and ideas, the nature
of the bundle in the case of the moral self is so transformed that the
psychological framework from which the self of virtue and vice
emerges is a far less radical one. It is not merely the case that the
difference between pride which grounds the self for which we care
and are concerned and virtuous pride is that the latter 'is a social
passion, and a bond of union among men' (T 491); the latter is also
a passion felt as a result of the kind of correction which transforms
the original psychological mechanism on which the construction of
the Humean primordial self rests.

THE CONSTITUTION OF THE HUMEAN
NON-METAPHYSICAL SELF

While in Book One of the *Treatise* Hume denies the existence of any
'uniting principle' among our perceptions which could give us an
intellectual self-consciousness or an intellectual idea of self-identity,
in Book Two he proceeds to present an account of the self for which
we care that is grounded in the properties of pride and humility.
These properties are a dependence on pleasure or pain caused by the
perception of something related to us, and a dependence on our
capacity to transform another's pleasure or pain in something
related to us, so that it is felt by us as pride or humility. While we
make an error concerning our 'personal identity as it regards our
thought and imagination' because we mistake diversity for identity,
when it comes to personal identity as it regards 'our passions or the
concern we take in ourselves', the problem surrounding this mistake
disappears. For, according to Hume, the self-consciousness and self-
knowledge of the self about which we are concerned are traceable to
the passions of pride and humility, and while these, like all passions,

15

are reflexive impressions,[4] they do not require intellectual contemplation, judgement or understanding. They require, rather, a reactive sentiment which centres on a relation between impressions and ideas and which issues in a non-intellectual rather than an intellectual self-consciousness.[5] It is the relation between impressions and ideas involved in the construction of pride and humility which provides the foundation for the constitution of the Humean self, and for Hume this relation explains the communication of self-worth. We sustain our pride, and so our self-consciousness of who and what we are, by means of a continued perception of qualities and attributes related to the self, perceptions reflected back to us by the regard and esteem of others. Our pride, our self-consciousness and, ultimately, our moral selfhood are for Hume dependent on others.

Since the idea of the self originates from an impression of reflexion,[6] this idea refers to, and is preceded by, a series of impressions and ideas consisting of an impression of sensation (which is pleasurable or painful), a copy of that impression taken by the mind (an idea), and an impression of reflexion: a series which may be the source of further impressions and ideas. Since it originates from an impression of reflexion, the idea of the self is largely the result of memory and imagination. Hume presents it as being bound up with those pleasures and pains that concern our own qualities and attributes, i.e. as intimately connected with pride and humility.

Now pride and humility are for Hume indirect passions, which are felt according to the favourable or unfavourable circumstances in which the person finds herself. The perception of some admirable quality which would naturally cause a feeling of pleasure is felt as pride when the admirable quality is attributed to the self. The cause of pride is something (e.g. an admirable quality) related to the self, and the object of pride is the self as possessor of the admirable quality. On being perceived, the admirable quality causes a feeling of pleasure, not merely in the self which possesses it, but also in other observers when they perceive it. When an admirable quality is perceived by others, the feeling of pleasure is love, and in the case of a loathsome quality, the feeling is hate. Other selves are the objects of love and hatred, while pride and humility are directed towards their object, which is one's own self.

We extrapolate from Hume's account that pride, in order to be sustained, depends on a continued perception of qualities and attributes related to the self.[7] And it is on such a continued perception that the idea of the self depends in order for *it* to be sustained. Even though the human mind 'resembles a string-instrument, where after each stroke the vibrations still retain some sound' (T 440), the sound does, after all, 'gradually and insensibly decay[s]' (T 440–1). Without a continued perception of qualities and attributes we would end up without 'that succession of related ideas and impressions of which we have an intimate memory and consciousness' (T 177), and so the idea of the self, together with the passion of pride, would fade away.

This does not mean that one needs to continually inspect one's own positive qualities and attributes oneself in order for pride to endure. For other minds serve as mirrors to reflect the assessments one makes of one's own qualities and attributes (T 365). For pride to endure we need, not constant self-inspection, but constant feeding, and we get this from the impressions of pleasure and esteem others have on perceiving our admirable qualities and attributes, which are then reflected back to ourselves. If feeding is not available, comparison with others, or others' envy of our qualities, attributes and possessions, can also sustain pride and, in this case, pride is again dependent on others. Since neither pride nor humility will endure unless 'seconded by the opinions and sentiments of others' (T 316), for Hume our self-consciousness and self-worth are socially dependent and socially generated.

We must now take note of the new and radical thought that emerges from Hume's thesis. According to Hume's account, it does not seem to be required, in order for you to feel pride, that I convey to you my felt pleasure as pleasure that takes *you* as an object; all that seems to be needed for you to feel pride is that I communicate my felt pleasure on my perceiving some pleasing quality or attribute that is connected to you. Yet you construct my pleasure as being pleasure in *you*. You feel proud of *yourself*, as possessor of the pleasing quality, not of the pleasing quality that, as it happens, is yours.

HUME'S RADICAL PSYCHOLOGY

According to Hume's account, an acrobat's perception of the audience's pleasure on viewing her display of suppleness and agility, and the audience's subsequent applause, would cause the acrobat to feel proud. But the audience's felt pleasure, and its manifestation in applause, may in actuality be a response to *the suppleness and agility* that has been displayed. Unless we tell a special story, it can be an unimportant fact for the audience that these qualities happen to belong to the particular acrobat on stage. Let us assume the audience values the acrobatic skills that have been displayed, not the fact that these skills belong to *her*. The audience's pleasure need not be felt in response to *her* possessing that suppleness and agility (as might be true of the pleasure felt by the acrobat's mother on perceiving her only daughter's acrobatic skills). The same suppleness and agility displayed by someone else would elicit from the audience the same response of pleasure, yet the acrobat feels proud, not of suppleness and agility (that happens to belong to her) *per se*; she feels proud of *herself* as one who is supple and agile. She feels proud because *she* is supple and agile, and most other people are not. Her pride, but not the audience's pleasure, is essentially possessive.

In interpreting the audience's response as a valuing of *her*, and not merely as a valuing of suppleness and agility, the acrobat carries in her imagination a picture of herself as one who is supple and agile and, insofar as her self-worth depends on her acrobatic skills and on her capacity to cause an audience to feel pleasure and to applaud, these skills and this capacity become essential to her self-conception. They are now specially valued by her: the value she places on them will be disproportionately high if she sees them to be crucial to her self-worth.

But, as we will see in a moment, according to Hume her self-conception is not prior to her pride: the audience's pleasure is not taken by her as pleasure directed at a self that pre-exists her feelings of pride. What is radical about Hume's thesis is that pride comes into being as the self comes into being. One does not precede the other.

Hume does say at T 278 and T 287 that pride produces the idea of the self. If we take what Hume says at face value and understand him to be asserting a linear causal relation between pride and the idea of the self (according to which the acrobat's pride would be prior to the idea of herself as a supple and agile acrobat), we get the incoherencies that philosophers have found in his account (Passmore 1968; Neu 1977).[8] The reconstruction that I present below of Hume's thought sees it as advanced and quite radical for his time. My reconstruction will present Hume, when he says that pride produces the idea of the self, as claiming that the relation between these two is not a one-way causal relation (whether 'causality' is taken in a Humean or non-Humean sense) but, rather, that there exists between these two a relationship of mutual construction. We will see that pride produces the idea of the self because we cannot have the former being constructed without the latter also at the same time being constructed.

Furthermore, both pride and the self will be seen to depend on a psychological contingency. The audience's pleasure is taken by the acrobat in a certain way: she constructs it as pleasure in a self that is in turn constructed only because the pleasure is taken in that way. The pleasure is 'taken as' or 'seen as' pleasure directed at her self. We will see that in making the object of the pleasure her self, the acrobat simultaneously constructs this object.[9]

Yet there is nothing in the nature of the case that necessitates this 'taking as' or 'seeing as': both pride and the self are for Hume contingent constructs. Of course, he so entrenches the self in the passion of pride that it is difficult to see how one could fail to feel proud on perceiving another's pleasure in something connected to oneself. Nevertheless, as we will see below, Hume will need to deny that we are unable to offer descriptions of prideless persons.

What from a commonsense point of view seems to be a basic emotion (pride) can be seen to become, on Hume's account, a non-basic passion which must be constructed. We can have neither pride nor the self without the other, yet neither one is for Hume a given. What is given the acrobat is the audience's pleasure, but she is proud of something which may not correspond with what we might take to be the reality of this pleasure (i.e. pleasure on viewing the acrobatic display). For she is proud of the fact that it is *she* who is supple and agile. Both her pride and her self are her own constructs, and Hume can quite easily account for both of them. He notes that

> the transition of the affections and of the imagination is made with the greatest ease and facility. When an idea produces an impression, related to an impression, which is connected with an idea, related to the first idea, these two impressions must be in a manner inseparable, nor will the one in any case be unattended with the other. 'Tis after this manner, that the particular causes of pride and humility are determined.
>
> (T 289)

On Hume's account, our acrobat passes easily from

0 (An impression of the audience's pleasure and applause when she puts on the display of suppleness and agility)

I place this impression in parentheses because Hume's story in the above quotation begins after it. This impression gives rise to

  1 An idea that the audience is pleased and is applauding the display of suppleness and agility (put on by her)

This is the first idea to which Hume refers in the above quotation, and it produces

  2 An impression of the audience being pleased and applauding her suppleness and agility

This impression is connected to

  3 An impression of the audience being pleased and applauding *her* (this impression, Hume says, is inseparable from 2: one will not 'be unattended with the other')

This impression is connected to

  4 The idea that *she* is, by virtue of possessing suppleness and agility, the cause of the audience's pleasure and applause.

It is this idea that becomes part of her self-conception, and its construction causes pride. It is related, as Hume says, to the first idea in 1. At the same time, her pride reinforces this idea of herself as a self with such-and-such qualities.

Both this idea of her self and her pride are systemic effects of the system of perceptions: neither can be separated from each other or from the system. So when Hume says that pride produces the idea of the self, we do not need to take him to mean that there exists a metaphysical linear causal relation between these where pride is independently describable from, and prior to, the self; but we should take him to mean instead that there exists between them a relationship of mutual construction. He says that pride produces the idea of the self because one cannot have pride coming into being without the idea of the self simultaneously coming into being: in effect, each dynamically constructs the other. When we understand Hume in this way we can remove the seeming incoherencies in his account. We can, for example, put together the fact that he needs the self for pride with the fact that at the same time pride constitutes the self.[10]

In the process of the acrobat passing easily from 1 through to 4, she imagines herself as, and wants to be one who is, supple and agile. Suppleness and agility and the cause of audience pleasure and applause become part of her self-conception: in the process of constructing the passion of pride she simultaneously constructs the idea of her own self.

Now we can see why Hume says 'these two impressions [2 and 3] must be *in a manner* inseparable' (my emphasis). For while Hume says they are inseparable, as an empiricist he must deny that there is any *necessary* connection between these impressions. So he does not say (as common opinion would say) that the impressions are inseparable in thought. For if 2 and 3 are converted into ideas and put into propositional form, the logical implications of each are quite different. The radicalness of his thesis emerges when we consider that it involves a certain kind of psychological contingency which allows for cases where 3 will be missing. While of 2 and 3 Hume says that one will not be unattended with the other, he does not hold that pride and humility are inescapable. Both require certain causes: certain impressions which are related to each other. But these impressions give rise to ideas that are logically distinct; while they are connected, there is no *conceptual* connection between them. This being so, a person might not have *both* impressions. The consequence of this for Hume is an account of pride as being contingent, and *a fortiori* of the self as contingent. If the acrobat moves from certain impressions to certain ideas, she will feel pride, but the necessity is constructed in the midst of contingency.

We can well imagine a case where, for example, an acrobat puts on an excellent performance and is aware of the audience's pleasurable response, but, having her mind on other and more pressing matters, does not 'take the pleasure as' or 'see the pleasure as' pleasure which *she* has caused. There is nothing in the nature of her being aware of the audience's pleasure that necessitates her taking the pleasure in this way. There is a clear difference between suppleness and agility being taken to be the object of the audience's pleasure, and *she* being taken as its object. As Hume knew, the imagination can easily put these together, but he would need to concede that there will be times (e.g. when one is preoccupied with other matters) when one's imagination may simply fail to do so.

In such a case, the performer is aware of her display on stage having caused the audience pleasure (she has 2), but does not have the impression of 3. So she fails to feel pride because she cannot get to 4 without 3. Of course, were a person never to pass from 2 to 3, we would then be describing one who completely lacked a sense of personal self, and such a case would be an extreme and possibly pathological one. For such a prideless person would be one who might take pleasure in her many wonderful accomplishments, but never pleasure in her self.

When our acrobat does move from 2 to 3, she then also has 4: an idea of *herself* as one who is supple and agile and who causes the audience pleasure. Being derived from an impression, this idea has the vivacity of an impression and is what explains the acrobat's pride in the fact that *it is she* who is supple and agile, even though the original impression was merely of the audience's pleasure on perceiving the display.

Yet attaining her pride and her sense of self-worth has involved the acrobat, via the double relation of impressions and ideas, in arriving at an idea which may not correspond with the original perception. From the mere fact of the audience's display of pleasure, it does not necessarily follow that she does in fact have the fine acrobatic skills to which she aspires: if the audience happens to be a poor judge of acrobatic skills, her pride may be quite misplaced.

So long as the audience displays pleasure, she can feel proud, and this despite the fact that her performance may have been an inferior one.[11] This elaboration of what Hume's account seems to imply is consistent with his account of the mechanism of pride being dependent on the double relation between impressions and ideas. For the implications of Hume's account are that pride can be felt without being grounded in the reality of one's actual possession of particular attributes, and without the pleasure of another having as its object one's own self. One might here easily compare the Freudian view that the ego can function in such a way as to enable a person to deal with reality, and may utilise fantasy to do so rather than operate solely on the basis of considerations pertaining to reality.

Although the Freudian view of the formation of the ego has its own theoretical assumptions, a general continuity can be found between it and the Humean account. For a consequence of Hume's account seems to be that pride can be generated willy-nilly according to the perceptions of pleasure had by others, so long as that pleasure is in some way related to ourselves. Let us call this 'proto-pride'.

Proto-pride involves a projection of the self, conceived of as possessing certain particular qualities and attributes; a projection which takes place in order that the self be the object of another's pleasurable response to something one has, does, or to which one is related. It refers to a piece of psychological reconstruction of someone else's pleasure, one which does not require an exercise of judgement. Proto-pride involves a reconstruction which consists in, for example, my taking your pleasure in my fine piano-playing as if it were directed at *my being the owner* of certain musical skills. The reconstruction consists, not in my taking your pleasure as pleasure in the fact of my *having* the skills, but in my taking your pleasure as pleasure in the fact of *my* having the skills. The reconstruction thus involves the projection of a self that interposes between your pleasure and its object. In an important sense, I, the biological individual, am the location of these skills, but while the idea of myself as owner of the skills overlaps the biological unit which I am, this idea of myself as the owner of these skills is not similarly located. It is instead a projection which makes possible my reconstruction of your pleasure.

What differentiates proto-pride from pride proper is not its object: in both cases the object is the self. Rather, proto-pride represents a stage in the construction of pride proper, the latter being a more sophisticated version of the former. Proto-pride is primitive and basic: it is indiscriminate and latches onto any feelings of pleasure that are connected with something about oneself.[12] There is an 'as if' quality about proto-pride: one interprets another's pleasurable response *as if* that response were directed at *one's being the owner* of some excellent quality or attribute.

This reinterpretation is accounted for by Hume by means of a radical psychology where proto-pride is a *constituted* result of the conversion from impressions to ideas, but which need not have any objective validity. The conversion involves a kind of illusion which becomes possible only on the hypothesis that a projective act has taken place. One projects the idea of one's self between another's pleasure and its object, and one then has the illusion that another is pleased in the fact of *one's* possessing certain qualities, causing one to feel proud of oneself. In other words, one simply latches on to what one takes to be pleasure directed at one's possession of certain pleasing qualities,[13] and one *makes* one's possession of them the object of the other's pleasure. The perception of pleasure is thus regarded by one, or functions as, self-enhancing. Certain attributes are seen not merely as being worthwhile attributes, but as attributes that swell up one's self. Judgement (e.g. judgement regarding possessed attributes) is merely contingently associated with the passion of pride; judgement is not embodied in, or integral to, the passion. Passions for Hume are not dependent on evidential beliefs; the passions of pride and humility are dependent on a conversion from impressions to ideas, and the mechanism involved in this conversion utilises imagination rather than judgement and evidential belief.

On Hume's account of pride, what is given us is the feeling of pleasure, and by nature we are unable to distinguish the pride (which we construct) from the pleasure: becoming civilised and adopting conventions causes us to form an articulate conception of pride, and now, as a matter of convention, we may not be entitled to feel pride. Now Hume's boastful guest who was merely present at the feast is not entitled to feel proud of it. Once we are socialised beings and articulate our pride, we distinguish pride from mere pleasure or joy, and our feeling proud needs to be objectively valid. Now Hume's 'limitations' apply: the relation between subject and self must be closer than joy requires (T 291); the agreeable thing must be peculiar to ourselves, or common to us with a few persons (T 291); it must be obvious to ourselves and others (T 292); and it must be constant and durable (T 293). Taylor's complaint that if 'being present at' is a relation close enough for pride to be felt then Hume fails to distinguish pride from joy or pleasure, is overruled since Hume's boastful guest has the capacity to feel proud even though (according to social convention) he is not entitled to these feelings. He is not irrational (G. Taylor 1985: 22), but merely contravening convention. What distinguishes proto-pride from joy or pleasure is not the pre-existence of 'a close relation', but rather a projective act of self-construction. When proto-pride is felt, one *makes* the relation a close one: one makes the object of pleasure one's own self (together with its real or imagined attributes) and in so doing simultaneously constructs this self (as a self with such-and-such qualities).

While we may feel joy at merely being present at a feast, the master of the feast 'beside the same joy, has the additional passion of self-applause and vanity' (T 290). Yet Hume writes: ''Tis true, men sometimes boast of a great entertainment at which they have only been present; and by so small a relation convert their pleasure into pride' (T 290). This concession makes it clear that he thinks it is *by nature* possible to feel proto-pride by means of a conversion from perceptions of pleasure. A visitor at the feast may feel proud at having merely been present at the feast even though he had nothing to do with its production. He would like to be master of the feast, perhaps. And maybe in his imagination he is. We might want to say that his pride is misplaced,[14] but this is for Hume a matter of convention and has nothing to do with the fact of his capacity to feel proud at being merely present. Hume goes on to explain that even though men might boast (i.e. be proud) of being at an entertainment where they have merely been present, 'it must in general be own'd, that joy arises from a more inconsiderable relation than vanity' (T 290). Yet the closer relation to ourselves which is required for pride (rather than joy) to be felt is a matter of convention, not one of nature. So long as a person feels pleasure on perceiving something pleasing connected to himself, he has the capacity for proto-pride. This capacity is not grounded in some mistaken belief of his which is 'no proper basis for pride' (G. Taylor 1980: 389)[15] but it is a capacity which is guaranteed so long as the double relation between impressions and ideas holds. Proto-pride is grounded in the projection of a self between the perception of pleasure and pleasure's object. It is in fact a capacity 'common to all creatures... since the causes... operate after the same *manner* thro' the whole animal creation'. The psychology Hume is working with 'supposes so little reflexion and judgement, that 'tis applicable to every sensible creature' (T 328).[16]

It follows that on Hume's view, prior to the self's entrance into the moral domain, there is nothing to stop it from feeling proud of qualities that would be regarded by many moral theorists to be evil. So long as another conveys to us their feelings of pleasure on perceiving something related to ourselves, we may feel proto-pride. Your felt pleasure conveyed to me on your viewing my courageous daring in hijacking the aeroplane may be felt by me as pride, and this with no consideration being given to the moral status of the actions and qualities for which I feel proud. So long as there is an audience to convey feelings of pleasure on viewing something connected to myself, I may feel pride (i.e. proto-pride) for what would be regarded by many theorists as evil qualities. The account given by Hume of the constitution of the self prior to becoming conscious of itself as a moral being is one that is essentially of an infantile being that can randomly latch on to feelings of pleasure and pain, convert these into proto-pride and proto-humility and, utilising these feelings as a foundation, construct itself. But on the self's entrance into the moral domain, proto-pride does not, and cannot, remain. While the non-metaphysical self can be constructed from attributes that are evil, the moral self is for Hume precluded from being formed in that way.[17]

THE HUMEAN MORAL SELF

Pleasure is for Hume 'the very being and essence of pride' (T 286). But for the pleasure of pride to be confirmed by the moral sentiment and so play its role in constituting the moral self, the pleasure of pride must be 'well-founded', and therefore felt only after having been 'corrected'. The constitution of the Humean moral self requires the taking of a 'general point of view', this view being required for us to have a sense of our own moral worth and moral personhood.

Although Hume says that 'To have the sense of virtue, is nothing but to feel a satisfaction of a particular kind from the contemplation of a character' and that 'The very feeling constitutes our praise or admiration... in feeling that it pleases after such a particular manner, we in effect feel that it is virtuous' (T 471), to have 'the sense of virtue' is not merely to feel pleasure on the contemplation of some action or character. The pleasure must be the kind of pleasure had after taking an impartial view. To have the sense of virtue and so enter the moral domain we must correct our perspective and 'form some general unalterable standard'. If we did not do this, we would see things only from our own particular point of view and other people 'cou'd never converse with us on any reasonable terms, were we to remain constantly in that situation and point of view which is peculiar to us' (T 603). To take our proper place in society, to be able to communicate in a common language with others, and to enter the moral domain, we must correct our own perspectives and sentiments so that they are in line with everybody else's. The moral sentiment is felt from 'the point of view of humanity' (E 272), and this is the point of view from which we speak the language of morality. To speak this language we must go beyond our own private point of view and take account of everybody's interests. As a moral being it is not enough to feel proud of one's own moral character and actions: the pride must be felt after having taken 'general views'. The capacity to take such general views is explained by Hume in terms of the universal propensity for sympathy.

Now sympathy is for Hume not itself impartial, and its lack of impartiality must be counterbalanced by being corrected before it can be regarded as a morally significant sentiment. Sympathy is for Hume corrected when it arises out of a concern for, or involves itself with, the interests of society as such. When corrected, it is, according to Hume, a principle of human nature by means of which we are able to judge actions and characters as good and bad, right and wrong. Sympathy must be corrected if the agent who experiences it is to be regarded as operating within the moral domain. For it is corrected sympathy which explains our capacity to judge an action to be right even though the good consequences that flow from it do not originate with, and have no effect on, our own selves. The thoughts we have regarding those who are caught up in war or who suffer from disease or famine are painful ones because of 'an unavoidable sympathy, which attends every conception of human happiness and misery' (T 222). Yet such sympathy needs to be corrected if it is to be directed at persons unrelated to ourselves or in distant places. Since judgements made, and sentiments felt from our own point of view are ones which may not be shareable, in order to judge of goodness, badness, rightness, wrongness, virtue or vice, it is necessary that we take a general point of view so that our judgements are ones which others can understand and with which they can agree. Moreover, since 'we can form no wish, which has no reference to society' (T 363), 'He must ... depart from his private and particular situation, and must choose a point of view, common to him with others' (E 272). Sympathy is not a mere feeling: in order to qualify as the moral sentiment it must result from the exercise of judgement.[18]

When pride receives confirmation from the moral sentiment, we have corrected pride. Since 'No one can well distinguish *in himself* betwixt the vice and the virtue, or be certain, that his esteem of his own merit is well-founded' (T 597–8), some correction is needed in order that pride in one's own virtue not be in actuality an over-valuing, ill-founded vanity or conceit. *Proto-pride is no longer sufficient.* My perception of another's pleasure felt in response to something virtuous about me needs to be had from a general, corrected point of view rather than from the private vantage-point of my own desires and imagination. Correction is needed in order to ascertain the real, rather than the merely imagined, value of what we take to be our moral merit. For pride to be confirmed by the moral sentiment, it is necessary that we consider our own character 'in general, without reference to our particular interest' (T 472), but with reference to the interests of society as such. I am no longer entitled to merely project the idea of myself between another's pleasure and its object so that I feel proud. After having corrected my sentiments and perspective, I know that the other's pleasure is pleasure felt on viewing a particular kind of action or character: the kind that I happen to exemplify. When I take an impartial view, I am no longer so ego-oriented that I take the other's pleasure to be pleasure in *my particular possession* of a certain kind of character or in *my particular enactment* of virtue. When pride is corrected in this way by the taking of an impartial view, it becomes one with the moral sentiment itself.

There is for Hume, in effect, a two-tiered account of the development of the moral self and its ethical self-valuing. The first tier consists of the random taking of perceptions of pleasure and pain related to oneself that are converted into proto-pride and proto-humility. Here, judgement and objective validity are unimportant; the pre-moral self and the value it places on itself have a definite primitiveness. The second tier involves a 'correction', and the adoption of a view which takes in everybody's interests, a view which the rest of humanity can share. Now, both judgement and objective validity are crucial. Moreover, the view of humanity for Hume is not the view of a particular society. Being a humanist, and having inherited a Ciceronian background, the view of humanity is for Hume the view of all the citizens of the world. Despite social differences, we are nevertheless sharers of a common human nature, so the aim for Hume is to be a citizen of the world, not a citizen of a particular society. As a citizen of the world, objective validity is crucial to one's virtuous pride.

As citizens of the world, not just any pleasure may count as the type of pleasure which can be transformed into and constitute virtuous pride in us, or which can contribute to the construction of our moral personhood. The construction of the Humean moral self parallels the construction of the self for which we care and are concerned only to a certain point. The former demands that there be a continuous adjustment to what is civilised,[19] for now we must be aware, not merely of another's felt pleasure in something related to us (for it may be pleasure felt merely from our own perspective or from a perspective shared by only a few), but we must be aware of another's felt pleasure in something related to us that is *in fact* admirable. We must, in other words, be aware of another's corrected pleasure.

According to Hume, we all have the capacity to correct our

sentiments and take a general point of view, and so the capacity for virtuous pride is given to all of us. Insofar as we correct our sentiments and take the general point of view, we will enter the moral domain, speak the language of humanity, and have a sense of our own moral personhood. As moral agents we are reflected-upon, self-assessed persons, this self-reflection and self-assessment only being possible for Hume from a perspective that identifies with the party of mankind, for it is for Hume definitive of taking this perspective that partiality is dropped.[20]

Once an impartial view is taken, the Humean moral self continues to be constituted, and to sustain self-worth, quite passively. In order to enter and remain in the moral domain a person must become and remain ready to present her own character and actions for judgement, and have an ever-present readiness to accept the judge's verdict. It is in the felt pride that results from her own corrected self-observations and from the reflected observations of others, that her moral selfhood is grounded. The constitution of the Humean moral self and the maintenance of its self-valuing requires that it be receptive to certain sets of perceptions. It requires a monitoring of how the self appears to an audience: in order for the Humean agent to enter the moral domain it must become an object for approval. Only if it is pleasing to others will it feel virtuous pride and gain a sense of who and what it morally is. The Humean moral self is thus dependent on others for its sense of self-worth, and it is constituted socially.

Custom and experience determine for Hume what is valuable, useful and pleasant. In detaching from one's own point of view and taking a general view, one must take account of society's opinions and sentiments. Adjusting one's perspective does not require effort or strength of will: we are motivated to take an impartial view because we desire our own well-being. Certainly, what motivates our taking an impartial view for Hume is not an adherence to non-contingent values or any deep-seated commitment. There is, for example, no value to which we are deeply committed and which is internal to taking an impartial view which, on Hume's view, motivates us to take it despite contrary inclinations. An impartial view is not adopted for the sake of reason, as it is in Kant. Our own well-being is Hume's ultimate motivator. If we want to live in society, if we want to be able to communicate with others in a common language, and if we want to be well-thought of by others and so think and feel positively about our own selves, we need to take an impartial perspective. Taking a general point of view is, at base, in the interests of our own long-term well-being. This view is, then, not one for which we must actively strive in the face of much difficulty in order to achieve it.

Whether our own long-term well-being is a goal worthy of pursuit or whether we want to be the sort of person who pursues her own well-being cannot be questions that the Humean moral self asks. For the desire for our own well-being is not for Hume a desire that reason may examine. Nor does the constitution of the Humean moral self depend on the result of such intellectual introspection. A bundle of impressions and ideas can exist in the absence of non-contingent values and in the absence of deeply held commitments to values. A bundle of impressions and ideas is constituted in just the way Hume describes: via the source of the reflected impressions received from the environment.

Thus we have Hume's complete story about ourselves: what constitutes the Humean non-metaphysical self is proto-pride, while corrected pride constitutes the Humean moral self. The radical psychology employed in the former must give way to a definite conservatism once we are moral and social beings. Yet the bundle remains for Hume as grounds upon which the idea of ourselves as moral beings rests. The account is in many ways extremely persuasive, and the radical psychology Hume employs has great explanatory power. Yet we ought not to forget that we can accept Hume's dismissal of the Cartesian ego as being a mere fiction, while still holding that a bundle of impressions and ideas provides inadequate grounds upon which to base an account both of the self for which we care and are concerned and of the moral self.

In the next chapter we will look at Rousseau's collective account of what is required for a self to become a moral being, in order to see whether the grounds he provides for the emergence of the moral self and its ethical self-valuing are more adequate than those presented by Hume.

CHAPTER II

Rousseau

The generators of self-valuing and the constitution of the moral self

> Self-love is always good...the tender and gentle passions spring from self-love.
>
> (Rousseau 1969: 174)

INTRODUCTION

In Rousseau we find not merely a disparagement of Hume's 'How I am reflected in others' eyes', together with the sharp distinction that is drawn by him between *amour de soi* and *amour-propre*.[1] We also find that the very structure with which Rousseau operates stands in stark contrast to the structure of Hume's account. While Hume works with a straightforward two-tiered structure, where the emergence of the moral self must await a 'correction' of perceptions had by the pre-moral primordial self, Rousseau operates with a somewhat ambiguous three-tiered structure where the highest level (morality) does not merely supersede but also incorporates the previous two. It is in this aspect of his thought that he might be seen as a precursor of Hegel. This feature makes the accounts of Rousseau and Hegel quite unlike the account I will present in the second half of this book.

The distinction between *amour de soi* and *amour-propre* is central to Rousseau's account of what is required for a self to become moral. This distinction is grounded in his three-tiered structure of innocent goodness, deterioration at the hands of civilisation, and a return to a lost, but transformed, goodness. The development of the right kind of self-love and the living of a moral life require, for Rousseau, not that the self be constituted by Hume's 'How I appear to others' or by Hegel's binding oneself to the political state, but that people be freed from the artificial external forces imposed by society which have impeded the natural development of the

31

passions. Instead of developing what Rousseau regarded to be a false self which thrives on the regard of others, man, according to him, needed to be self-sufficient and possess an inner unity, resilience and wholeness; he needed to have a strong unified centre which was his true self. For Rousseau this centre was achievable by the exercise of individual will which enabled one to resist the dictates of one's passions and the opinions of others. It is the exercise of individual will, and this will's relation to a political community, that marks the third tier of Rousseau's account.

His account seems to leave open the possibility of an engagement in what many moral philosophers regard as evil[2] being involved in the development of the moral self. It would seem that for Rousseau moral selfhood is regained only at quite some cost.[3] This charge will be considered below.

In examining his account and the conclusion that is reached – that the right kind of political and social institutions are creative of moral consciousness – three related points concerning Rousseau's use of the distinction between *amour de soi* and *amour-propre* will be exposed.

First, it is not a distinction that Rousseau first makes, *and then applies*, to his account of innocent goodness, deterioration and reparation. Rather, without the particular three-tiered structure that he employs, he would not have arrived at this distinction in the first place. We will see that the three-tiered structure of his account *is* the distinction between *amour de soi* and *amour-propre*. While commentators usually separate Rousseau's theory concerning *amour de soi* from his theory of society as a corrupting influence, no separation should in fact be made between these.

Second, *amour-propre* is not merely the name of a passion that Rousseau thinks we would do better to be without, or one which has a proper place in our lives so long as it does not become disordered (Dent 1988); rather, *amour-propre* operates as a technical term in his writings. When we understand the role that the concept of *amour-propre* plays in his work, and what the logic of this concept requires, we will realise that, third, as a technical term that is itself the name of a disorder or distortion, *amour-propre* has, according to Rousseau, no rightful place in our lives at all.

As a psycho-social moralist, Rousseau diagnoses people in civil society to be suffering from a universal psychological illness; for this he prescribes a political 'cure' which involves not merely a move from *amour-propre* back to *amour de soi*, but a complete obliteration of *amour-propre* together with the kind of self-conception had by a person under its influence. The 'cure' thus involves a complete transformation of the psychology of the self.

Amour de soi is usually translated as 'self-love' or 'love of self',[4] but Rousseau employs this term to refer to the pre-reflective self's self-conception and the desire it has for its own self-preservation (Rousseau 1955a: 192). He conceives of *amour de soi* as being an innate possession of the self in the state of nature, and it is in this sentiment that he sees virtue to have its origins.[5]

Amour-propre[6] (conceived of by Rousseau as being the first vice), refers to the sentiment of existence and self-worth had by the self of civil society. It refers to a self-conception that is given by, and depends on, the esteem and regard of others. Rousseau uses this term to highlight the social self's preoccupation with how it appears in others' eyes.

Rousseau's *amour-propre* is akin to Humean pride: it thrives on the opinions and regard of others, being dependent for its existence on a constant feeding from a source external to the self.[7] But where Hume sees pride, when corrected, to be the self-making virtue which makes the constitution of the moral self possible, Rousseau sees dependence on *amour-propre* to be the very antithesis of moral development and as compromising the attainment of a strong unified centre.

Where for Hume society is necessary in order for pride or self-esteem to be generated, and where (as we will see in the next chapter) Hegel places supreme moral importance on the community, Rousseau presents society as having weakened and enslaved the self that confronts and is confronted by others. He observes that civil society consists of people who live 'outside themselves', basing their lives on what society expects of them rather than on the unimpeded progress of their natural selves which society has distorted. Where the self in the state of nature is self-sufficient, having needs in proportion to its abilities to satisfy them, the social self's desires and needs are unrestrained, developed in response to social pressures. This results in the social self striving to be 'more than it is', its strength being insufficient for its 'needs'. Man in civil society is unfree since he is at the mercy of his own passions which beckon him to procure a never-ending list of items – property, fame, honour, superiority – that can never be properly satisfied. A man whose actions are performed in response to his *amour-propre* is a man whose actions are dictated by his appetites, and such a man can be neither free nor moral (Rousseau 1969: 48).[8]

The seeds of *amour-propre* are sown in society, and it 'leads each individual to make more of himself than of any other, [and] causes all the mutual damage men inflict one on another'. By contrast, man in the state of nature knew 'neither hatred nor the desire for revenge, since those passions can spring only from a sense of injury' (Rousseau 1955a: 182). Society, dividing self and other, negates nature's goodness. Where in the state of nature man was in harmony with the outside world as well as with himself, in the civilised world there is only disharmony: both between man and the world, and between man and his own self.

Amour-propre thrives in society because it is here that man compares himself with others and wants to be superior. Self-preference and egoism become the hallmarks of a self whose very sense of its own existence and worth depends on, and fluctuates according to, the recognition bestowed by others. In society *amour de soi* cannot follow its natural course of development because a person under the influence of *amour-propre* has a sense of his own existence given, and so is guided, by an ever-changing public opinion (Rousseau 1969: 47). Who and what the social self will be is determined by the changing mood and fashion of the particular society in which it finds itself.

Rousseau believed that the source of social man's wretchedness lay in the fact that his fundamental concerns revolved around how he appeared in others' eyes. In moulding himself to public opinion, he developed a 'false self':

> Social man...only knows how to live in the opinions of others...he seems to receive the consciousness of his own existence merely from the judgment of others...everything being reduced to appearances, there is but art and mummery in every honour, friendship, virtue...we have nothing to show for ourselves but a frivolous and deceitful appearance.
>
> (1955a: 220–1)

If he is to be happy, free and moral, man must be reunited both with the world and himself. The second tier of Rousseau's account (culture and civilisation) must be transcended, yet Rousseau does not recommend that this tier be completely obliterated, but rather that certain of its elements be incorporated together with the first into the third (and highest) tier (morality and a return to *amour de soi*). It is in the context of this three-stage account of innocent goodness, corruption and degradation, and reparation, that his crucial distinction between *amour de soi* and *amour-propre* emerges.

Let us look at the move from *amour de soi* to *amour-propre* and at the nature of the cure that this move demands.

THE MOVE FROM *AMOUR DE SOI* TO *AMOUR-PROPRE*: THE DEMAND FOR A CURE

In his 'Discourse on the origin of inequality' Rousseau presents an idealised portrait of the self in the state of nature. This is the stage of uncontaminated *amour de soi*: a time of innocence, spontaneity, confidence, unity, happiness, peacefulness and changelessness. Life here is analogous to childhood, lived in the present moment only, with no need to look either to the future or beyond the bounds of the self. Perception is undistorted and consciousness is uncontaminated by the need to transform the world to satisfy needs and desires. Yet while there is no difference between people's appearances and the way things really are with them,[9] and while they do not live in conflict, either with the world or with themselves, their lives are infused with a pre-moral naiveté, leaving them unable to distinguish between good and evil (Rousseau 1955a: 180). The second tier – the advent of culture and society – brings a distortion of nature and a corruption of the natural self. Here evil enters the world: man loses the authenticity he had in the state of nature, becoming a slave to material possessions, prestige and fame. Selfishness, envy, vanity, isolation, inequality and false appearances are the manifestations of society and civilisation.

There is to be discerned in Rousseau's writings a personal yearning to return to a lost innocence, and a passionate desire to reacquire a lost goodness and genuineness. As a child his own innocence was destroyed when he was falsely accused by those whom he loved of breaking a comb, and punished for a crime of which he was not guilty (Rousseau 1967: 28–30). His accusers were taken in by the false appearances of his guilt, rendering his own innocence quite impotent.

Just as he yearned to return to the happy state of his own stolen innocence, so the third tier of his account of the self's achievement of morality is a return to a condition of which the self has been deprived. But since a return to the state of nature is neither possible nor desirable (not desirable because such a return would not render the self moral), Rousseau imposes a further level of artificiality (a certain political structure) in order to reacquire the goodness and genuineness of the natural self and to achieve morality.

Commentators have pointed to the paranoia in many of Rousseau's writings, particularly in his revelation of the universal plot against Jean-Jacques. There is, in addition, in Rousseau's three-tiered structure of advance and return, or deterioration and progress, a certain *structural* paranoia. With regard to the comb incident, it is precisely the people whom he loved and respected who *took away from him* his innocence and goodness. The world failed to see him as he really was (innocent and good) and only a return to what he really is could compensate for what he has suffered. Likewise, social man must return to what he really is.

The loss at the hands of civilisation must be made good if social man is to achieve morality. Having inflated needs, his reason is no longer guided by natural sentiments, but combines with *amour-propre*, and so with uncontrolled and uncontrollable passions. Rather than being in possession of '*la raison naturelle*', social man is under the control of the 'reason that turns man's mind back upon itself, and divides him from everything that could disturb or afflict him' (Rousseau 1955a: 184). People under the sway of reason that combines with *amour-propre* are less affected by the plight of others and so are less capable of experiencing and expressing compassion than is uncivilised man.

Becoming a social self, bowing to social pressures, and encountering the falseness of appearances and the evil that these bring, is for Rousseau constitutive of a loss of self. The self must be regained in its original purity and goodness. Selfhood must be restored: the aim being the realisation of the self as an object of love in order that the self's morality be able to be completed. Man's primitive goodness and his *amour de soi* still exist in civil society, but these are 'hidden, veiled, shrouded in artifice' (Starobinski 1988: 15). The task is to cure the corruption by removing this veil and returning, not to the state of nature, but to a higher stage of moral self-consciousness that incorporates the previous two stages.

The strength and exercise of individual will, and the will's relation to a political community, mark the third tier of Rousseau's account, as well as representing the cure for man's move from *amour de soi* to *amour-propre*. While Rousseau had a conception of an individual as a being who is fundamentally good and simple, and while he conceived of uncivilised man as having the capacity to experience a pre-reflective pity for others, he argued that the individual needed to leave the state of nature in order to live 'as an intelligent being and a man', since in that state he was 'a stupid and unimaginative animal' (Rousseau 1955b: 16). Unlike Hobbes, Rousseau conceived of the 'natural' self as pre-moral since it was not properly aware of other selves. So certain elements of the second tier of his account needed to be retained: the completion of morality required the self to remain social. Rousseau believed that if the self autonomously conceded that its own private will be replaced with the general will,[10] it would be freed from its enslavement to the many particular wills and public opinion, enabling it to resist the dictates of its own passions and make a return to *amour de soi* and the achievement of morality possible.

So the third tier of his account marks the completion of the cure, the completion of morality, and a radical change in the nature of the self's self-conception since its self-knowledge is freed of the debilitating dependencies plaguing the social self. Yet for man to be reunited with his own self so that he is free of these dependencies, it is not enough that he recognise the advantages of following the general will; rather, he must find a perfect coincidence between his own private individual interests and the interests expressed by the general will. If he does not do so, he must (presumably) either be 'forced to be free' or he must act in accordance with what he recognises his duty as a citizen to be (Rousseau 1955b: 15–16).[11]

The cure for the self's psychological ills thus involves a radical change in the nature of its self-conception and in the way it is to derive feelings of self-worth: it must move from the dependencies, comparisons and illusions of *amour-propre* to the authenticity of 'what it really is'. In other words, it must become a being that has a non-comparative self-conception, a self-determining being whose sense of its own existence and worth is independent of public opinion, given instead by the determinations of its own self. In becoming 'what it really is', it becomes an autonomous, self-legislating, rational citizen capable of acting on principle.

When fully spelt out, we find that to be cured of his psychological illness, social man must not merely become a citizen, but must surrender or suppress his personal self and private will, and agree to conform to the general will even if this means sacrificing his own private interests. For he must become a being that conceives of itself as 'nothing and [one which] can do nothing without all the others' (Rousseau 1955b: 32–3). The cure prescribed by Rousseau involves the self's sense of its own existence and worth being given by the whole community from which it is (now, as a citizen) inseparable. The veil is thus lifted from the self's *amour de soi*: if every person conceives of himself as 'nothing and [as a being who] can do nothing without all the others', if each person's will is the same as every other person's will in virtue of everybody's will conforming with the will of the whole community, there are no longer any private individual wills being exercised (a consequence being that *amour-propre* is obliterated). This means that the self's sense of existence and worth comes, not from the recognition of other private wills, but from its own self. But since it is 'nothing and can do nothing without all the others', the self's self-understanding is now given in terms of its being part of a collective entity. This is the cost that must be paid to undistort the self of *amour-propre*.[12]

Yet Rousseau's distinction between *amour-propre* and *amour de soi* represents far more than merely different ways in which the self conceives of itself and gains feelings of self-worth. For the logic of the concept of *amour-propre* and the three-tiered structure that Rousseau employs cannot be disentangled from each other. A failure to see this is, I believe, a cause of much of the confusion that has occurred in interpreting Rousseau's distinction, as well as being a cause of an inability to appreciate the real depth of Rousseau's original insight that society *constitutes* selves.

THE LOGIC OF *AMOUR-PROPRE*

Rousseau's exposition of *amour-propre* rests on his original insight that civilisation *constitutes* selves; *amour-propre* is the concept with which he articulates this insight. Civilisation produces selves that depart from what is natural, selves that are distorted in a variety of ways. In his writings, this insight regarding civilisation being the creator of selves is never differentiated from the concept of *amour-propre* itself. This might be seen to be a weakness in the account, for it is what leads him to offer a political solution to what he sees to be in actuality a widespread psychological scourge.

As a distortion, *amour-propre* is for Rousseau itself already an excess, and the claim that for Rousseau *amour-propre* is bad only in its excesses (Dent 1988) does not take note of this. *Amour-propre* is the name of a distortion of the natural sentiments, a distortion that is widespread because social pressures generate a new psychic fact. Rousseau reveals the ways in which what he sees to be a social psychosis (*amour-propre*) is alienating for those afflicted by it. People in society who take *amour-propre* to be an absolute value can, and need to be, psychically undistorted: for Rousseau, *amour-propre* is *an historically generated distortion of a self that needs to be cured.*

That *amour-propre* is for Rousseau the name of a distortion means that this concept carries with it certain logical commitments. The very logic of *amour-propre* points to *a something that is not distorted*: being the name of a distortion, *amour-propre* logically requires that there be something there that is not distorted.[13] The logic of *amour-propre* points to the subjunctive mode which asks 'What would things have been like if civilisation had *not* produced distorted selves?' This manoeuvre allows Rousseau to arrive at the concept of *amour de soi* and so to make his important distinction. That is, if we remove Rousseau's observation that the history of civilisation has produced a widespread artificial sentiment, he would not have the crucial distinction between *amour de soi* and *amour-propre*. In effect, Rousseau's three-tiered structure of primitive innocence, deterioration, and return to a lost innocence and goodness *is* this distinction.[14]

Without the primordial goodness, the loss and degradation inflicted on the individual by society, and his return to a former (but transformed) goodness, Rousseau could hardly have made this distinction. What makes the distinction possible for Rousseau is his taking civilisation seriously as a self creating force. Where for Hume civilisation is merely a yardstick by means of which we can judge of good and bad, right and wrong, for Rousseau there is a psychological reality that corresponds to civilisation. Civilisation has produced the ills of a certain kind of psyche; it has created false, distorted selves that are psychologically ailing. One of the consequences of civilisation is that factitious selves have actually usurped or taken the place of true selves when they should not have done so. The remedy of lessening the impact of civilisation is to psychologically undistort these selves and make them free so that the real, true selves can emerge. A person influenced by Freudian (and some of the neo-Freudian) psychoanalysis would be likely to say of Rousseau's account that, according to it, civilisation is the cause of all the natural force of *amour de soi* being appropriated by its substitute (*amour-propre*), and that Rousseau offers a social/ political theory as a solution to the problem of how to restore the energy to its proper object (*amour de soi*).

There is a built-in normativeness in Rousseau's three-tiered account of the goodness of the natural self, its deterioration and substitution at the hands of society, and the regaining of its inherent, but lost, goodness through the remaking of the social/ political world. For the structure presents man as not only *having the power* to transcend *amour-propre*, but presents stages through which man *must* pass to become a moral being. The widespread distortion Rousseau sees in society is, in effect, a catastrophic excess that must be corrected. Rousseau sees what he takes to be the social realities: that the progress of history must be repudiated and reversed in order for the self's morality to develop.

What he offers, in effect, is a political palliative as a psychological cure. On his account, we cannot have a civilised moral being that has completely escaped *amour-propre* and its ills. For a moral being *amour-propre* is inescapable, but its ill effects are able to be counterbalanced through the social contract and by involving people in legislation.

Rousseau can be seen to have run together the question of the alleviation of the psychological malaise suffered by members of society with the question of how a moral self develops, in such a way that the answer to both questions was for him the undistortion of the self. And an undistorted self is explicated by him in terms of the absolute moral limits that confront the self on its conforming with the general will. Rousseau's account of what makes a will into a moral will is thus given by him in terms of its conforming with the general will. On conforming with the general will, an undistorted self shows that it is autonomous, self-determining, free of both the tyranny of other individual wills and of its own passions and, most importantly, completely free of its *amour-propre*.

THE STATUS OF *AMOUR-PROPRE VIS-À-VIS* HUMAN LIFE

Since *amour-propre* was seen by Rousseau as the feature peculiar to social man that depraved and perverted him (Rousseau 1969: Book 4), it needed to be completely expelled and replaced with a return to *amour de soi* where the self could achieve a non-competitive, non-comparative self-conception. For Rousseau, *amour-propre* has no rightful place whatever in our lives.

It has been claimed that *amour-propre* has for Rousseau a proper place in man's living with others, and that he is critical of it only when it becomes disordered, inflamed, and gives rise to perverse forms of dependency. Nicholas Dent writes:

it is not alien to our own proper constitution to need... some forms of... recognition from others. To require *any* such thing is *not* automatically to have become abandoned... to the control and direction of others.

(1988: 32)

If we ignore the logical demands of the concept of *amour-propre*, we could readily agree with Dent. For needing some form of recognition from others is not in itself alienating. But some things have been missed in Dent's exposition.

First, there is a contrast that needs to be made between the *appreciative* and the *constituting* gaze of the other. While Dent would be right to claim that for Rousseau we all need and like the appreciative gaze of the other, it would be wrong to make such a claim with respect to the other's *constituting* gaze. Perhaps Rousseau does not distinguish these properly himself, and it might even be the case that he would have resisted the clarification between them since it would probably have undermined the force of his own rhetoric. There may be an irremovable ambivalence in Rousseau with respect to this clarification. Yet since he is so set against the alienated selves that are constituted by society, one cannot take him to hold that the constituting gaze of others is not alienating. It is precisely the constituting gaze of others that produces the alienated, psychologically ailing selves that, on his account, need to be cured.

Second, we must remember that *amour-propre* is used by Rousseau to refer, not merely to the *need* for some form of recognition from others, but to the social self's complete *dependence* on public opinion for the very sense of its own existence and worth, and this is indeed self-alienating. For in the presence of such complete dependence, every time there is a shift in regard from outside, there is a shift in one's sense of self. With an accumulation of these shifts, there is an inevitable accompanying sense that one's self is not one's own.[15]

Furthermore, if, as we have seen, *amour-propre* operates as a technical term in Rousseau's writings, and is itself the name of a disorder, it can have no place at all for Rousseau in man's living with others. This is to say that for Rousseau *amour-propre* cannot exist among men in society *without* being what Dent refers to as 'inflamed'. As a distortion of the natural self, Rousseau conceived of *amour-propre* as being itself already malign, cruel and a source of self-estrangement, giving rise to alienation from both self and others. So a 'little bit of *amour-propre*', but not enough so that it becomes 'inflamed' or disordered, makes no sense.

One can agree with Dent that there is nothing wrong with wanting and needing others' praise and recognition. But this is not to admit that there is for Rousseau nothing amiss with a person who *depends completely* on the regard and esteem of others for her self-conception and feelings of self-worth.[16] The self that is completely dependent in this regard, the self of *amour-propre*, is the self for whom 'seeming' is far more important than 'being' (Rousseau 1955a: 202). For such a self, esteem is far more important than virtue, and this is for Rousseau the distorted self created by civil society: the self that is incapable of morality.

Dent fails to see that Rousseau's use of *amour-propre* buys into a certain logic. If we admit the concept of *amour-propre*, then, necessarily, there must have been something in society or in the individual that conspired to generate that state to which *amour-propre* refers. The notion of what it is to be free of *amour-propre* gives rise to the notion of *amour de soi*. Since in order to be in possession of *amour de soi*, one must be free of *amour-propre*, there is no sense in which *amour-propre* might be seen to have a place in our moral lives. Rousseau's psychological cures through political action necessarily involve a ridding of the morally unsatisfactory, malformed self of civilisation together with its *amour-propre*.

ROUSSEAU'S PSYCHOLOGICAL CURES

Rousseau assumes that evil, as a product of civilisation, belongs to the artificial self that civilisation has produced. To escape this evil man could avoid society and its conventions by turning to the isolated life of the solitary walker. Yet since this avenue was possible for very few, Rousseau's cure involves instead a psychological transformation incorporating the collectivism of a communal self-identity.

Human evil could be overcome by putting in place the right kind of social institutions: 'Good social institutions are those best fitted to make a man unnatural, to exchange his independence for dependence... so that he no longer regards himself as one, but as part of the whole, and is only conscious of the common life' (Rousseau 1969: 7). The evil of mutual personal dependence could be overcome if men acted, not as separate individuals, but as a single unit.

On Rousseau's account, evil exists because people see themselves and others through a kind of filter, the filter being civilisation, where the self of *amour-propre* dominates. We have here a new theory of human evil. Evil no longer consists in the transgression of divine commandments, or in a failure to act in accordance with certain principles. Instead, corruption of the soul (caused by dependency on others), with its attendant psychic disunity, lies at the heart of human evil.[17] To become a citizen and a moral being, the social self needed to be free of this dependency and psychic disunity.

The morally unsatisfactory self of civilisation needed to be educated in a certain way so that it could follow the general will and become public-minded. Just as Emile achieves real freedom when he obeys his own true will, subordinating his 'lower' to his 'higher' self, so people in civil society are free when they obey the general will which is the true will of each citizen. The aim of Rousseau's cures was to prevent and/or ameliorate the alienation, dependency and psychic disunity engendered by *amour-propre*. Being educated in the right way and willing in conformity with the general will were both conceived of by Rousseau as being incompatible with the self being under the sway of *amour-propre*.

What was needed, ideally, was for pre-reflective *amour de soi* to be allowed to develop according to nature without interference from private human wills. It would then become more complex and be directed towards others (Rousseau 1969: 174). Emile's education is therefore designed to protect him from the many private wills of others. The moral education provided for Emile would, Rousseau believed, produce the kind of self-consciousness needed for citizenship. The rational consent required for Rousseau's version of the social contract demands that individuals have the kind of psychology that enables them to follow their own true wills, rather than be guided by appetites developed in response to the social pressures of many private wills. This psychology is envisaged by Rousseau as being the end-product of the educative syllabus to which Emile is exposed.

The central idea behind Emile's education was that he be independent of others' opinions and judgments. This would guarantee real autonomy. By being artificially protected from other human wills for as long as possible, he would develop an inherent sense of his own worth, freeing him from the need to be well-thought of by, and to conform to the desires of, others. So he would have no need for false appearances.

As a self creating force, Rousseau saw civilisation and the *amour-*

propre that it produced as being incompatible with the development of a self that could be conscious of itself as a source of motivation and action. Rather, the self of civilisation was conscious of being motivated by forces external to itself. For Rousseau, the consciousness of the self of *amour-propre* and the consciousness of the self of *amour de soi* (and *a fortiori* the consciousness of the self of morality) could not be one and the same consciousness. *Contra* Dent (1988), there was for Rousseau a definite discontinuity in moving from the psychology of *amour de soi* to the psychology of *amour-propre*.

The kind of freedom that Rousseau saw as being inextricably connected with a moral consciousness was the kind that would enable the self to become a source of moral and political obligation. Of course, individual autonomy was reduced by the will being moulded into a faculty which would strive for the achievement of the common good. And while the result of Emile's education is that he achieves autonomy, this autonomy is limited by the fact that he consents to the authority of his teacher (Rousseau 1969: 435). The form of freedom is preserved, but since Emile's teacher has heeded the advice 'Let him think he is master while you are really master' and since at the end of his education Emile consents to be what his master has made him into, one might well be left wondering about the real substance of Emile's freedom and autonomy. Yet Emile's education, in shielding him from social demands and pressures, 'forces him to be free': free of the constraints and demands of social existence, leaving him immune from the source of his own 'inner disunity and wretchedness'. So long as *amour-propre* remained, this freedom was impossible.

Emile beseeches his teacher: 'make me free by guarding against the passions which do me violence; do not let me become their slave; compel me to be my own master and to obey, not my senses, but my reason' (Rousseau 1969: 290). Here again, we find that individual freedom requires that the individual be free, not merely of the influence of others' wills, but also of his own 'lower nature'. And Rousseau regarded there to be a close connection between these: the influence of others' wills sowed the seeds of *amour-propre*, making individuals susceptible to submitting to the demands of their lower natures.

While Emile's insulation from personal dependence was promoted by the right kind of education, it was his own will's consenting to the continuation of the restrictions imposed by that education on his own passions that crowned his autonomy and *amour de soi.* So what appears to be a curtailment of individual autonomy is presented instead, in virtue of individual consent, as the achievement of what Rousseau took to be real autonomy: freedom from personal dependence on others' wills. This is, in effect, freedom from *amour-propre.*

The will's consent is for Rousseau crucial, and this element is transferred by him into the political arena in order that the self be able to complete the transformation involved in becoming a moral being. When natural liberty is surrendered in favour of a civil liberty limited by the general will, which is each citizen's real will, man acquires moral liberty: 'for the mere impulse of appetite is slavery, while obedience to a law which we prescribe to ourselves is liberty' (Rousseau 1955b: 25). Just as obeying one's own real will is to be free, so is being compelled to follow the general will. For following the general will protects against the many particular wills whose aim is self-aggrandisement and inequality. Following the general will is incompatible with the presence of *amour-propre* where one is, by definition, susceptible to the influence of the many particular wills. Following the general will represents a capacity to will what is in everyone's interests: it is a capacity to autonomously order one's own will in accordance with rational principles. Being susceptible to the changeability of public opinion where *amour-propre* thrives cannot coexist with the development of this capacity.

In rationally ordering its own will by conforming to the general will, in deciding what it 'really wills' while detached from the pressures of other wills, the self could determine the meaning of its own existence, its own worth as an independent agent, as well as enter the moral realm as a free moral agent. This is the final achievement of this three-tiered account, and while each of the three stages is necessary for the achievement of morality, the second stage (the substituted self whose nature is given and determined by society, together with its *amour-propre* where the private will reigns free) must be replaced with the autonomous and principled self whose sense of existence and worth is no longer vulnerable to the fluctuations of public opinion. This is the self which, in freely giving itself over to the whole community, is fit to be a citizen and a moral being.

CONCLUSION

We have seen that for Rousseau the bad effects of society could be counterbalanced, not only by the development of individual strength of will, but also by a particular remaking of the social and political world. The self's participation in social and political institutions involves, for him, a certain kind of self-imposed regulation of desire and impulse so that a person's actions are governed by rules which the person has himself established. What was necessary, according to Rousseau, in order to avoid being governed by the will of others, was that each person frame rules applicable to, and acceptable by, all.

In doing this, a person could have an *amour de soi* which would leave him independent of the wills and opinions of others. We have here a forerunner of the Kantian autonomous rational will which obeys its own self-given laws: to obey the general will is to aim at a general universal object (the good of all), to obey oneself and to strive for the good.[18] Yet, where for Kant as long as one's will is good one operates as a moral being, for Rousseau moral personhood requires the right development of *amour de soi*. Given the effects of society, to *be* moral beings, persons needed to have as the ground of their existence a participation in a collective will. What was crucial for moral personhood for Rousseau was the nature of the person's self-identity. Though quite differently conceived, it is this emphasis on self-identity which my own account of the moral self will be seen to share with Rousseau's.[19]

Hume gives an account of the moral self as socially dependent, and of pride or self-esteem as being socially generated. For Rousseau, while valuing and loving oneself as a moral being, together with the exercise of virtue, are dependent on social and political associations, these are generated by, and very much the achievements of, an individual self. It is as a result of what *man is himself able to do* that determines morality and the right kind of self-valuing. We have in Rousseau the important notion that there is a self for which each person is solely responsible.[20] Both in the sphere of individual education and in the formation of the right kind of political community, man has the power to counteract the evil effects of civilisation and restore what history had deprived him of. To account for this process of restitution Rousseau employs the three-tiered account, the structure of which enables him to make the crucial distinction between *amour de soi* and *amour-propre*.

The contrast between Hume and Rousseau is not simply to be put in terms of Rousseau's having made this distinction and Hume's not having made it. Hume's account also has much less theoretical baggage to carry. For Hume, what corrects pride can be left to what counts as civilised, and this is accounted for in terms of historically evolved conceptions. While the concept of the party of mankind carries very little theoretical baggage, the cost for Hume is that he is unable to explain what Rousseau sees as a widespread distortion in society that needs to be corrected. Where Rousseau sees the social realities, Hume sees only uncorrected perceptions. While Hume is able to exclude fixed beliefs regarding the content of the ethical from being the ultimate determinant of actions – what is civilised might be mistaken (what is civilised is both changeable and correctable) – we might want to criticise his faith in the party of humanity as being qualified to represent the limits of moral thought and action.

Though each philosopher has different theoretical commitments, they hold in common a belief that there is theoretical articulable conception of what a moral self is, from which the limits of moral thought and action arise. For Hume the moral self is the self that corrects its point of view so that it is in line with that of society in general. For Rousseau it is the self that aligns its will with the general will. This view of the moral self will be contrasted with my account in the last four chapters.

Different theoretical commitments lead Hume and Rousseau to different accounts of the moral self as well as to quite different conceptions of moral limits. Where for Hume a correction or adjustment of perceptions in line with the view of the party of mankind is needed in order for virtuous pride and morality to be possible, for Rousseau the progress of history must actually be repudiated and reversed in order for *amour de soi* and morality to develop. In Hume's two-tiered account the addition of the general point of view serves to correct perceptions and judgements, and virtuous pride ever being the result of an adherence to fixed beliefs regarding the determinate content of the ethical is excluded, since taking the general point of view ensures that the interests of humanity are taken into account, and these interests may always be subject to revision and change.

The point of view of civilisation is for Hume something to be seriously reckoned with; it is this point of view that is a measure of the moral limits on thought and action. One might say that for Rousseau civilisation is taken even more seriously, since for him there is a psychological reality that corresponds to civilisation: it has produced factitious, distorted selves which suffer psychic ills.

The real weakness in Rousseau is that the cost of 'undistorting' these selves is that persons must (paradoxically) become essentially public-minded. A consequence of his account is that if I, as a moral being, see another person suffering, this must be seen by me as a call upon my public self, and my response must be filtered through considerations that refer to the general will. *Qua* public person, Rousseau's citizen gravitates towards being a passionless being. A response to another's suffering must be filtered through a consciousness of being a citizen, and this leaves little room for an agent to exercise her own reflective evaluation in order to understand the particularities of the circumstances before her, or to arrive at an understanding of the significance of a range of human values. There is little room in Rousseau's account for an agent to reassess or reorder those values (including values given by the general will) according to a conception of human good to which he is non-contingently committed. An agent's own understanding of what would be just can get little hearing in deliberations whose conclusions must conform to the general will.[21]

Moreover, Rousseau's general will is not rational in the way in which Kant's good will is rational. The general will is rational in its generality and universality, but there are in the general will no absolute rational canons. It aims at the common good, yet the common good is for Rousseau the good of a particular society, and it may well be the case that promoting the common good will need to involve the performance of acts *vis-à-vis* members of some other society which individual members would judge to be unjust.

The will of the state is for Rousseau 'the rule of what is just or unjust' (Rousseau 1955c: 237). In other words, the consent of the members of the state is the yardstick according to which what is just and unjust is to be judged. Apart from the collective will of the members, there are no standards of justice and injustice.[22]

While the general will furthers the good of all the members of the state, there seems to be nothing to prevent the general will from being tyrannical in its relations to other states. While the associates will treat each other as moral beings, the question of how they will treat outsiders (e.g. in a time of war) is left open. In following the general will, a person may need to form what he sees to be unjust intentions *vis-à-vis* those who are not members of his particular state. The values pursued by a particular society are contingent on the promotion of the common good of that particular society.

Rousseau's account, in conceiving of the moral self as an inseparable part of a collective unit, fails to pay attention to the self's own motivation to (fairly or justly) understand the particular circumstances in which it finds itself, or to understand the significance of a range of human values, a commitment to which might serve to block certain kinds of responses. Given Rousseau's collective account of what makes a self moral, an agent's own understanding of what would be just could not generate an ethically significant self-valuing. So we ought not to lose sight of the fact that even though we can accept Rousseau's thesis that a world of beings whose sense of existence and worth is independent of private wills and public opinion is in many respects a better world than one pervaded by *amour-propre*, this does not mean that we need also to accept a collective account of the moral self and of what constitutes the good of particular individuals.

The question of whether an agent's own understanding of what would be just could generate an ethically significant self-valuing will be most pertinent in my consideration of Hegel in the next chapter.

CHAPTER III

Hegel
Ethical self-valuing and the constitution of the moral self

Since the state is mind objectified it is only as one of its members that the individual himself has objectivity, genuine individuality, and an ethical life.

(Hegel 1942: 156)

INTRODUCTION

Hegel shares with Rousseau the view that a person is only able to enter the moral domain as a member of a political community. Yet while Hegel follows Rousseau in requiring individual participation in the social/political arena for the completion of the moral self, and while he shares with Rousseau a structural similarity in that his account incorporates contradictions between stages which result in a higher synthesis being attained, there is in his account nothing of the Rousseauian need to regain something that has been lost. Hegel's view that the self can only enter the moral domain as a member of a community is a consequence that flows from his conception of an individual self, of the relation that he sees an individual to have to his community, and of the conditions he believes must be fulfilled for an individual to pass through the stages of those social and cultural forms which constitute his striving for and achieving the self-consciousness, self-realisation and freedom that fulfil his essential nature.[1]

Hegel's account of the constitution of the moral self is shaped by his ontological vision of man as a primitive being needing to undergo certain transformations in order to be raised to the universal and serve as an adequate medium for *Geist*'s attainment of self-consciousness and self-knowledge.[2] We will see that the possibility remains in Hegel that acts *vis-à-vis* other states, that might be judged by individual members of the state to be unjust (particularly during war) will need to be performed, although this possibility is not as great in Hegel as it is in Rousseau.

In describing the succession of those forms of life by means of which individuals achieve self-consciousness, self-realisation and ethical self-valuing,[3] Hegel posits *Geist* as a universal cosmic spirit whose necessary embodiment is the whole world. Hegel's view of an individual self as a mere moment in the life of *Geist* grounds his account of the moral life. Thus he distinguishes *Sittlichkeit* from *Moralität*: the latter refers to the concept of individual obligation and, in particular, to the autonomous agent of Kantian ethics whose own resources provide what is needed for morality. *Sittlichkeit* refers to morality in a community setting, and this reflects the idea of *Geist*: an objective spirit that goes beyond the *Moralität* of the singular individual. To conceive of oneself as moral is for Hegel to conceive of oneself as embedded in a social matrix. The true or essential self is the self as universal consciousness.

For Hegel, morality and significance in human life cannot be had without being bound to the political state. While the account I will present in the last four chapters of this book holds in common with Hegel the view that we can find significance in our lives by being moral, on my account, significance, meaningfulness and integrity are not socially constituted, but arise out of an individual's own sense of justice, his desire for understanding, his own reflective evaluation, and his affective attachment to certain values.[4] Even though the values to which an individual is affectively attached have their source in a particular culture and society, morality on my account will be seen to relate to an inner state, and to the very nature of the individual's approach and response to circumstances in the world. By contrast, morality is presented by Hegel as relating to a complex of social practices, customs and activities.

Where I take the generators of ethical self-valuing and morality to be the product of individual reflection, evaluation and action, these are both for Hegel socio-cultural manifestations constituted by the progress of the dialectic.

THE PROGRESS OF THE DIALECTIC: A MORAL BEING AS A MEMBER OF AN ACTUAL STATE

Hegel's conception of the development of a self, its ethical self-valuing and its attainment of universal self-consciousness, is inseparable from the dialectic by means of whose progression he takes a person to bind himself to communal institutions and so partake in ethical life. For Hegel the moral self and its ethical self-valuing are socially and politically constituted.

Where Kant thought that a moral being must locate his moral precepts in his own will, Hegel believed moral precepts flowed from the relation between an individual and *Geist*. Since *Geist* is necessarily embodied in the state, Hegel believed that both an individual's essence and his final goal were the state.[5] Moreover, an individual was the particular individual he was because of his membership in the state: 'All the worth the human being possesses, all spiritual reality, he possesses only through the state' (Hegel 1944: 39).

Yet not just any state will do. It has to express the ontological structure of things: 'the Idea' (the goal of all human endeavour: the Truth) (Hegel 1942: 155). The state needs to be an external realisation of rational will, and therefore a fully rational state. This is for Hegel (among other things) one which protects individual rights and fosters the self-realisation of its members. If the state is not rationally organised, individuals experience its morality and laws as being in opposition to themselves, as conflicting with their own convictions, and so as imposing a limit on their freedom.

Since Reason means for Hegel an identification of the individual with universal spirit embodied in the state, a fully rational state is for Hegel one where the customs and norms with which its citizens identify themselves are expressed.[6] We have here a several-layered account of the development of the moral self: it is only at the highest level of the dialectic (Reason) that the self enters and becomes part of *Sittlichkeit* and is able to value itself as a moral being.

For Hegel, universal will is not merely the individual's real will (Rousseau), but the individual's will as a rational being. While conforming with Rousseau's general will means that the common good is thereby promoted, this may in fact be conformity with something that is judged by individual members to be unjust *vis-à-vis* other communities. Rousseau's general will is not based on rational principles as Hegel's universal will is, so it seems that more room is left for an unjust self to be involved in the development of morality.

For Hegel it is a conceptual matter that the state is rational. Reason is realised in a free state because its members choose in accordance with rational principles which are embodied in it (Hegel 1931: 378). Choosing rationally, members of the state fulfil their own selves by aligning themselves with the state and its *Sittlichkeit*:

this requires a perfect coincidence between private interests and social values. Reflective individuals, guided by their own reason, break their ties with *Geist* and leave the ethical domain, entering the domain of *Moralität*, but man's realisation does not lie in the morality which pertains to us as rational wills. To break with *Sittlichkeit* is to leave morality without a content (this is the accusation Hegel directs at Kant):[7] only a political community could provide a content and a reality for the dictates of a person's own reason.

It is by means of the progress of the dialectic that Hegel presents a person as simultaneously achieving universal self-consciousness (recognising other selves as being distinct from and also unified with himself) and becoming bound up with his fellow men.[8] Where for Rousseau the development of the moral self requires a process incorporating a return to an earlier stage, for Hegel this is a product of a process whose stages reflect the attainment of selfhood at levels which are regarded by him as stepping-stones leading to the realisation of ethical life. Ethical life is a social and political realisation.

ETHICAL LIFE: A SOCIAL AND POLITICAL REALISATION REQUIRING A SURRENDERING OF INDIVIDUALITY AND OF INDIVIDUAL CONSCIENCE

While Hegel wants to preserve an individuality of sorts (individual self-realisation and self-determination are furthered by bonding to the customs of the state) and while he seems to leave some room for individual conscience (his admiration of Socrates and Luther indicates that he did not believe that people ought simply to comply with values and laws with which they disagreed), morality for Hegel ultimately requires a surrendering of individual conscience.

He at first appears to escape the criticism which seems devastating for Rousseau – that the state might be made up of selves that behave unjustly *vis-à-vis* other states – in virtue of the fact that what is in the state, described by Hegel as 'actual', is based on reason.[9] Being rational will rather than general will, the Hegelian universal will bypasses subjectivism (and a capacity to will unjustly), and concurs with the rationality of the state's institutions.

Setting aside the problem of recognition, and so of the acceptance, of the rationality of the universal, it seems that Hegel, in presenting morality as a social and political realisation, succeeds in preserving individual will as a moral guide while at the same time ridding it of the subjectivism that brings with it the willing of, and consent to, injustice. Individual conscience, it seems, might be able to gain a foothold in such an account. Yet Hegel writes:

> any state may be shown to be bad... The state is no ideal work of art; it stands on earth and so in the sphere of caprice, chance, and error, and bad behaviour may disfigure it in many respects. But the ugliest of men, or a criminal, or an invalid, or a cripple, is still always a living man. The affirmative, life, subsists despite his defects, and it is this affirmative factor which is our theme here.
>
> (1942: 279)

Just as a criminal or a cripple is still a living man, so a corrupt state is still a state. If we take Hegel to be saying that we should therefore obey the laws of *any* state, adhering to the state now appears to require a surrendering of individual conscience,[10] since we might well be led to intentionally do what we recognise to be unjust. There seems to be a definite ambiguity in his thought, since the conception of rationality he presents (and its role in the state) is one which could, at least *prima facie*, overcome this problem of injustice being involved in adhering to the laws of the state.[11]

Since individuals 'are conscious within themselves of being these individual independent beings through the fact that they surrender and sacrifice their particular individuality', so '[the] labour of the individual for his own wants is just as much a satisfaction of those of others as of himself, and the satisfaction of his own he attains only by the labour of others' (Hegel 1931: 376–7). It is a person's conceptual connections with others, rather than the individual person himself, which is of ultimate importance.[12] In unifying with *Geist*, the individual's selfhood and freedom are fulfilled rather than surrendered, but his individuality[13] appears to be annihilated:[14] 'the individual cannot preserve himself... the good can only be performed through the sacrifice of the individual' (Hegel 1931: 382). Subjective conscience (the reliance on which Hegel regards as an evil) must take a back seat.

While we must concede that it is not clear that Hegel's state is a totalitarian one where individual interests count for nothing in the face of the state's interests, it is arguable whether individual will and individual interests are, as Hegel claims, 'contained and preserved'

(1942: 164). For when Hegel writes that 'To these powers [ethical powers which regulate the life of individuals] individuals are related as accidents to substance' (1942: 105), he seems to divest persons of individuality and ascribe a reality to them only insofar as they partake in the Absolute. Individuality, understood as involving singularity and uniqueness, seems quite obliterated in an ethic where all values are of necessity universal values and therefore necessarily shareable, and where individuals, by being embodied in the state, are stripped of subjectivity. There are no criteria, apart from *Sittlichkeit*, according to which an individual might judge a principle or rule regarding its goodness or rightness. The universality of the self, not the inner state of the singular individual, is of moral significance (Hegel 1931: 424).

Since for Hegel an individual is in essence the product of a particular society's customs and traditions, it is difficult to say what Hegel would make of the notion of a 'personal self'. I take it that Hegel could not agree with Socrates' view that the good man cannot be harmed, which I take to be a claim for individual moral invulnerability. For Hegel the good man could be harmed if the state were to disintegrate.

In the case of morality, just as in the case of science, Hegel believes that precepts must have interpersonal validity (Hegel 1942: 91). So the notion of a person adhering to personal standards of a personal life, or of following the dictates of an individual's own moral conscience, cannot get a grip in Hegel's account. One can be a moral being only by fulfilling one's role in the social matrix.

In identifying public and private interests and goals, a moral being is portrayed as achieving the good in realising the good of others as his own good (Hegel 1931: 479). The moral will is accounted for in terms of its willing what the state wills. Hegel's account shares with Hume's and Rousseau's the absence of a commitment to a range of ultimate human values. So also missing in this account is any re-assessment or re-ordering of values in light of the agent's own understanding of the particular circumstances. Morality is for Hegel a social construct, and the singular, unique individual drops out of his account.

HEGELIAN ETHICAL SELF-VALUING, MORALITY AND FREEDOM: A SOCIAL CONSTRUCT OF A PARTICULAR KIND

Hegel goes beyond Hume's 'how I appear to others' in his account of the mutual recognition which provides the foundation for his account of self-consciousness, ethical life and ethical self-valuing. This mutual recognition gives rise to the kind of self-consciousness necessary for morality: a self-consciousness that is grounded in taking the perspective of the state.

The dialectic of the master and slave (Hegel 1931) illustrates Hegel's contention that freedom, self-consciousness and ethical self-valuing can only be attained within a social context where each person sees others as ends rather than as means. Through this dialectic Hegel seeks to establish the conceptual preconditions and presuppositions of self-consciousness. The Hegelian thesis is clearly revealed here: the moral self is the result of the development of a certain kind of self-consciousness.

There is for Hegel an essential connection between self-consciousness and the recognition of others. 'How I appear to others' may give the Hegelian agent some sense of personal self,[15] but the consciousness of his own moral personhood and worth is only attained by realising his constitutive bonds to others. Self-consciousness presupposes interpersonal experience and, Hegel argues, mutual recognition.

By enslaving the other, the master enjoys the fruits of the slave's labour but is unable to find a definition of his own self: in the eyes of the slave or in any contrast with the otherness of the world. For the slave is made by him into a mere means; a consequence is that the slave cannot serve as an appropriate mirror for the master and confirm his selfhood. And, not needing to work, the master is not aware of the otherness of the world by means of whose contrast he might define himself. Not working on objects in the world, the master is alienated from them.

By contrast, the slave is able, through his own labour and by imprinting his own ideas on objects, to objectify himself: his ideas find a permanence in the external world and so he becomes aware of his own consciousness. He is, to some extent, independent of the master. And since the slave fears for his life (he knows that at any time he might be killed by the master) he has an additional sense of independence: the knowledge of the possibility of his own death gives him the sense that he is not completely in the master's control. He can, at any time, take his own life.

Yet the slave's self-consciousness is incomplete since he cannot find a reflection of his own autonomy and personhood in the master's eyes: 'Self-consciousness exists in and for itself, in that, and by the fact that it exists for another self-consciousness, that is to say, it *is* only by being recognised' (Hegel 1931: 175).[16] Nor does the slave enjoy the product of his own labour, which is, in Marx's words, 'alienated'. Master and slave both desire to regain the independence which they lost with the arrival of the other on the scene. Each requires acknowledgement as a person by the other, this being necessary for each to recognise himself as a person. And being recognised as an independent and autonomous agent requires that one recognise others as such too (Hegel 1931: 176). Full self-consciousness requires that one see oneself as one agent among others. Master and slave both need to 'bring their certainty of themselves, the certainty of being for themselves, to the level of objective truth' (Hegel 1931: 231–2). So long as they remain in the master–slave relation where they are unaware of their bonds to *Geist*, neither can recognise the other and so neither can achieve full self-consciousness.

Only when both master and slave renounce the 'life and death struggle', recognise each other as independent and autonomous beings, and align themselves with the state and its *Sittlichkeit*, will they find mutual recognition, achieve self-realisation and freedom, and so enter the moral realm. Complete self-consciousness, moral personhood, ethical self-valuing and freedom are thus for Hegel social constructs: they are consequential upon there having taken place a certain opposition and conflict.

Since the moral will is not for Hegel an individual will, but is a socio-cultural construct,[17] morality cannot be for Hegel the result of individual striving. Yet as we have seen, ethical self-valuing, freedom and morality are not merely social constructs; they also depend on the development of the kind of self-consciousness that develops out of the mutual recognition described by Hegel. So they depend on the adoption of the perspective of the state and participation in *Geist*'s plan.

THE INDIVIDUAL'S PARTICIPATION IN *GEIST*'S PLAN: THE END OF ALL HUMAN STRIVING

It is through his conception of the self as an expression of *Geist* that Hegel portrays an individual's achievement of the kind of integrity and unity that can transcend the Kantian separation of reason from sensibility. The overcoming of this separation is central to Hegel's account of ethical life which is not experienced as something imposed by an authoritative reason, identified by Kant as the 'true self', but rather as an expression of the essential nature of members of the community. Yet Hegel is led to a position where acts judged by individuals to be unjust may contribute to morality and ethical self-valuing. He is led to this, not by his refusal to accept the Kantian picture of the self as constantly at war with itself and incapable of being perfectly moral, but as a consequence of his comments concerning the importance of war.

When acceptance of the state wanes, as it does during times of peace, war is seen by Hegel to be ethically important, while 'corruption in nations would be the product of prolonged, let alone "perpetual" peace' (Hegel 1942: 210). Individualism is the result of lengthy periods of peace, while war imposes the wider aims of the state (the good of all) on its citizens. Moreover, the ethical significance Hegel attributes to war makes it clear that the singular individual is not of much import: 'War is the spirit and form in which the essential moment of ethical substance...is manifestly confirmed and realised...war...stands out as that which preserves the whole in security' (Hegel 1931: 475). The individual being sacrificed in war for 'ethical self-consciousness' presents no problem for Hegel.[18]

Rejecting Kant's ideal of everlasting peace, Hegel points out that war fosters patriotism and the willingness for personal sacrifice in favour of universal principle. Moreover, he thinks that the very concept of war is necessary for our understanding of the nature of the state. In the same way that facing danger and the possibility of death play crucial roles in the construction of self-consciousness, war (and its demand for self-sacrifice) intensifies the identification of members of the state with it (see Thompson 1987: 110).

Commentators have pointed out that Hegel's view of war must be distinguished from that of the fascists. Further, 'we should not confuse Hegel's estimate of the wars that had occurred up to his own time with a celebration of war as we know it today or imagine it in the future' (Kaufmann 1972: 53). Yet while these points are well taken, and while we can concede that Hegel does not believe that war is 'good in itself', as Popper (1973: 68) claims he does, Hegel does believe uninterrupted peace to be ethically undesirable. Of course, one ought not to take a philosopher out of his historical and cultural context and submit his writings to criticism from a perspective that would be quite alien to the philosopher's own experience. Yet in criticising Hegel's view of war, one need not criticise anything that is peculiar to his particular cultural or historical circumstances, but one can criticise his metaphysics because of the disastrous implications these have for his ethical views.

His view concerning the ethical importance of war can be seen to be a consequence of his belief that the self-manifestation of *Geist* is of supreme importance, being the end of all human striving. If history has a purpose (the self-fulfilment of *Geist*), anything which contributes to this purpose can be justified even though individual actions, for example during war, may be found by the state's members to be morally abhorrent. Such justification flows from Hegel's metaphysical account of history and the role he envisages an individual self to play in history. If 'The History of the World is none other than the progress of the consciousness of freedom' (Hegel 1957: 361), an individual's role in the history of the world is a constituent of the self-consciousness of *Geist* in its freedom.

It is in Hegel's comments concerning the ethical importance of war, rather than in his concepts of rational will or of the political state and its *Sittlichkeit*, that one might charge his account with allowing what is judged by individual members of the state as unjust to be a possible generator of morality and ethical self-valuing. If an individual's role in the history of the world is a constituent element in the coming to full self-consciousness of *Geist* in its freedom, any actions which, when taken out of this wider context, are seen by an individual agent to be unjust, may be justified as necessary parts of *Geist*'s plan.

For Hegel, personal morality must be subordinated to the rationality of the state (Hegel 1942: 91), while 'To have a conscience... is simply to be on the verge of slipping into evil' (Hegel 1942: 92). Against the state, private conscience is for Hegel of no ethical import. If all human striving is directed towards realising the Idea, if 'the History of the World is nothing but the development of the Idea of Freedom', if 'the glory of the Idea mirror[s] itself in the History of the World', if 'the History of the World, with all the changing scenes which its annals present, is this process of development and the realisation of Spirit', if 'what has happened, and is happening every day... is essentially His (Spirit's) Work' (Hegel 1944: 456–7), then any actions whatever, no matter how individuals might judge them, are to be assessed in relation to their role in history and the part they play in the development of Spirit. The development of Spirit and the progress of history are for Hegel inescapable, while all actions can be justified with reference to them. And, most tellingly, for Hegel 'The history of the world... is the world's court of justice' (Hegel 1942: 216).

The implications of all this seem clear: it is according to the success or otherwise of the state in history that the state and the actions of its members are to be judged. These are not to be judged on the basis of moral principles or standards which are external to, or disengaged from, the 'concrete existent' itself. And they are certainly not to be judged on the basis of an individual's own sense of justice (Hegel 1942: 215). Since 'The state is the actuality of the Ethical Idea', there can be no challenge at all to the authority of the state.

In the case of conflict between states, there is no appeal to be made either to moral principles or to any individual member's understanding of what would constitute a just response: for Hegel states do not stand to each other in moral relations. War is for Hegel the answer to disputes between states (Hegel 1942: 214) because moral relations, and relations involving rights, do not bear on states: 'States are not private persons but completely autonomous totalities in themselves, and so the relation between them differs from a moral relation' (Hegel 1942: 297). We must ask whether there can be, according to Hegel, restrictions of any kind on what one state is permitted to do to another.

Janna Thompson has argued that Hegel allows that the relations between states can be ethical: there is a limit placed by Hegel on what one state can do to another state in war since other states are required for ethical life to be possible. The state needs other states with which to contrast itself in order that the consciousness of its citizens be properly 'united and elevated' (Thompson 1992: 111–12).

Yet one can allow that the Hegelian state needs the existence of other states for its own ethical life without holding that the actions of the state *vis-à-vis* other states are morally bound in such a way that what individuals might regard in the particular circumstances to be unjust responses are excluded by a limit that is placed on what one state can do to another. Thompson herself writes

> So long as individuals have a state to be loyal to, does it really matter what state it is? There seems no reason why Hegel should be opposed to stronger states swallowing up weaker states, or to the establishment of a system of regional states.
>
> (1992: 125)

If 'the history of the world is the world's court of justice', it would seem that the only restrictions that might be brought to bear on the treatment one state gives to another are ones pertaining to success or failure. Since for Hegel 'It is the absolute interest of Reason that this moral whole (the state) should exist' (Hegel 1957: 388), the justification of an action lies in the continued existence of the state. This might require the *existence* of other states, but it says very little about how other states may be treated. Thus: 'herein lies the justification and merit of heroes who have founded states – *however rude these may have been*' (Hegel 1957: 388, my emphasis).

It does not seem to be an exaggeration to say that for Hegel the end (the sovereignty of the state) justifies the means, with no attention needing to be paid to how any private individual judges or understands these means. That a state should 'seek and create a sphere of activity abroad' is justified, in Hegel's view, since 'long domestic peace' fosters individuality and so renders the state susceptible to 'injury' (Hegel 1942: 214). What is commonly regarded to be a morally important distinction between attack and defence is here completely blurred by Hegel. The distinction that an individual might want to make between just and unjust wars is also disregarded.

An Hegelian might claim that since the state is rational, it will not require people to do anything that is unjust, and that if the state mistakenly requires that a member should be unjust, this is an indication that the state is in a condition of deterioration. A state in deterioration is not a rational state and is not a realisation of universal will. The aim for Hegel is that the individual should identify his will with universal will, so unjust action might seem to be excluded in virtue of universal will being based on rational principles. Since conformity with Rousseau's general will is not conformity with rational will, we can see that the possibility that unjust acts might contribute towards ethical self-valuing and the constitution of the moral self does appear to be stronger in Rousseau's account than it is in Hegel's.

Yet even though Hegel, along with Hume and Rousseau, can exclude an agent's acts being determined by a set of fixed beliefs regarding a determinate content that is taken to describe the ethical (since rational will can vary according to the particular historical context), he does not completely escape the charge regarding unjust acts. It is during times of war with other states (or during civil war) that the state (despite being based on rational principles) may require the performance of actions which individuals find to be morally abhorrent. Since the furtherance of the 'ethical substance' has complete priority, the Hegelian moral self might well need to be an unjust self. This is a conclusion that we should not be willing to accept.

Yet if we accept Hegel's thesis regarding the constitutive relation between the self and the state, we have no grounds for rejecting this conclusion. Hegel shows that war (and the acts that war requires) is good for the health of selves that are completely constituted entities.[19] Activities that are good for the state are automatically good for the health of such selves. There are for the Hegelian self, so conceived, stakes that are far more important than justice: the achievement of the Ethical Idea and the Truth.

In Chapter 8 we will see that it is simply false that the moral self is constituted socially or politically. If Hegel were right on this, as moral selves we would have no moral worries: these would merely be a stage in moral development that needed to be transcended. Given that we have moral worries that are not merely contingencies of alienation or of social processes, we must reject the Hegelian conception of the moral self. Furthermore, if we were to accept Hegel's thesis, we would lose what is so valuable in Rousseau's auto-oriented concern: the sense that there is a self for whose well-being I am solely responsible. If we are to preserve this important notion, we must reject the conception of the moral self as being a socio-politically constituted entity.

In the next chapter I leave Hume, Rousseau and Hegel behind. I look forward to Heinz Kohut's contemporary self psychology and backwards to Aristotle in order to prepare some groundwork for my own account of the moral self in the last four chapters.

CHAPTER IV

Aristotle and Kohut
Converging perspectives

the extreme of [character-]friendship is likened to one's love for oneself.

(1166b2)

there are various forms of narcissism which must be considered . . . as forerunners of object love.

(Kohut 1966: 269–70)

INTRODUCTION

The thesis of *The Moral Self* is that a certain kind of self-love is foundational for moral agency. Some may find the claim that virtue requires self-love difficult to comprehend, yet it is a central Aristotelian claim (1168a28–1169b3).[1] Aristotle holds that the relation that the self has to itself has priority over its relations to others: virtuous conduct depends on the relation to the self which Aristotle terms 'love of self', and the best kind of friendship, of which only virtuous people are capable, depends on a person's love of self:

Friendly relations with one's neighbours, and the marks by which friendships are defined, seem to have *proceeded from* a man's relations to himself.

(1166a1–3, my emphasis)

He also writes of the good man's relation to himself that 'he is related to his friend as to himself (for his friend is another self)' (1166a30–1). A good human life requires both friends and the right kind of self-love. Thus love of self is placed firmly into the ethical domain: a virtuous person is one with the right kind of self-love,

Aristotle and Kohut

while wicked people, 'having nothing lovable in them... have no feeling of love to themselves' (1166b17–18).

Following Aristotle, the account of the moral self in the following chapters centrally involves the right kind of self-love. A self that loves itself in the required sense has a particular view of its own rational agency: it wants its acts to be guided, not by opportunities that the circumstances happen to present, but by its own clear and just understanding. When the self seeks such understanding, it wants to 'act for the sake of its reasoning part', this being the part that it loves more than any other part of itself (1169a2–3). Moreover, it is from a virtuous person's love of self that the right kind of relation between self and others flows (1166a1–9): this is mirrored in my own account of the relation between the moral self and others.

Aristotle holds that only if a person relates to himself in the way in which a lover of self does, will he be able to relate to others in the way in which a virtuous person is able. Interestingly, the work of contemporary self psychology has presented similar claims that emphasise the importance of the nature of a person's psychic life for the kinds of relationships that she will be able to have with others. Heinz Kohut's self psychology will be shown in this chapter to take a perspective on the self that is in important respects similar to Aristotle's, and we will see that Kohut's work presents us with a modern account of why the right kind of self-love is something good and foundational for human beings.

Contemporary self psychology addresses the critical nature of emotional self regulation for the constitution of cohesive selves capable of leading healthy human lives. In various ways, Aristotelian virtue resembles the kind of health postulated by self psychology: Aristotle held that a certain kind of emotional regulation was consistent with virtue, and that emotional disregulation was typically found in the psychic lives of vicious characters:

> both fear and confidence and appetite and anger and pity and in general pleasure and pain may be felt both too much and too little... but to feel them at the right times, with reference to the right objects, towards the right people, with the right motive, and in the right way, is what is both intermediate and best, and this is characteristic of virtue.

> (1106b17–23)

Virtue for Aristotle is 'a state of character concerned with choice, lying in a mean' (1106b36–1107a1). A person with the requisite state of character has an emotional-affective life that enables her to feel in accordance with a rational principle, one 'by which the man of practical wisdom would determine it' (1107a1–2). We will see below that the theory of the self that self psychology presents can elaborate these Aristotelian claims by explaining why some people are able to contain and modulate their emotions and affects so that these are experienced appropriately, while some experience them as uncontrollable external impingements, and others must not allow themselves to experience them at all.

Aristotle's explanation of people's containment and modulation of emotions and affects is given in terms of a certain kind of habituation, upbringing and education. Just and temperate acts are not merely acts that are done in the same way and for the same reasons that just and temperate people do them (1105b5–10); they are also acts that flow from the kind of psychic state and character that is able to modulate emotions and affects, and finds pleasure in the right things (1104b5–6). There is something about the non-rational process of habituation and upbringing, rather than reasoned arguments, that can change what gives a person pleasure and pain. Self psychology is consistent with Aristotle in also holding that the process by which some people become able to contain and modulate their emotions and affects, and control what gives them pleasure and pain is a non-rational one.

While for Aristotle virtue is acquired in a non-rational way, the exercise of virtue centrally involves the exercise of reason. A person who lives a *eudaimonic* life does what her reason tells her to do. This does not mean that she does what is rationally justifiable (even though what she does may *be* rationally justifiable) but that she has an active power of moral discrimination. Rationality is understood by Aristotle substantively rather than procedurally: a person is rational if she has 'correct vision', if she has the capacity to see and understand the circumstances in the way that someone with moral wisdom would. A person who is rational wants to act virtuously and takes pleasure in it. The right emotional response is inseparable from right judgement and correct understanding.

So while for Aristotle moral choice does not take place without reasoning and reflection, two central Aristotelian claims are that 'moral excellence is concerned with pleasures and pains' (1104b8), and that there is a very close relationship between love of self and virtue. Self psychology, as a theory of the subjectivity of the self and its emotional-affective life, will be seen to be quite consistent with these claims.

Aristotle introduces love of self in the context of a discussion of friendship. Only virtuous people are capable of 'character-friendship' (1156b8–25) where the friend, being attracted by the other's goodness, responds to the otherness of the other. The inferior pleasure- and advantage-friendships are maintained only so long as the friend stands to gain by way of pleasure or advantage. Aristotle claims that a person will be capable of character-friendship only if he has a certain kind of psychic capacity or inner strength. To understand the claim about the priority of the relation to the self over its relations with others, it is important to understand what it is about this psychic strength that differentiates virtuous people from people who are not capable of character-friendship.

THE PSYCHIC STRENGTHS OF CHARACTER-FRIENDS

Aristotle's account suggests that a person who is incapable of character-friendship suffers from a certain type of psychic deficiency, manifesting in the fact that the conceptions of 'the other' under which pleasure- and advantage-friendships, on the one hand, and character-friendships, on the other, are formed and maintained are quite different. Only a character-friend has the capacity to relate to and love the other person because she is the person she is, that is, she has the capacity to relate to the other's 'self as such', rather than needing to focus on aspects of the other that fulfil her own needs (1156a16–19): 'Those who are friends for the sake of utility part when the advantage is at an end; for they were lovers not of each other but of profit' (1157a14–16). Moreover

> There is nothing strange in breaking off a friendship based on utility or pleasure, when our friends no longer have these attributes. For it was of these attributes that we were the friends; and when these have failed it is reasonable to love no longer.
>
> (1165b1–5)

A person who, despite the presence of suitable character-friends, is incapable of character-friendship, is one who seeks the friendship of those whose attributes will fulfil his own needs. Such a person's hunger for pleasure or advantage suggests that there is something lacking in his own psychic life that, were it present, might give him the kind of psychic strength that would enable him to relate to the whole breadth of another person instead of only to that aspect that fills a deficit in some aspect of his own self.

A twentieth-century suggestion informed by some of the work of recent psychoanalysis is that a psychically weak or enfeebled self is far more likely than a self that has inner strength and resilience[2] to become preoccupied with pleasure- and advantage-seeking aims, a psychically weak self being one for which pleasure and/or advantage brings it a satisfaction that its own life and way of being is unable to provide for it. By contrast, a virtuous person does not need to seek pleasure 'as a sort of adventitious charm' (1099a15–16) since a virtuous life is pleasant in itself. Having a life that is pleasant in itself, she is not confined in her relationships with others to gaining pleasure or advantage from them.

The psychic strength that enables a person to form character-friendships is the same strength that enables her to relate to herself in virtue of something lovable in herself. Aristotle gives us an example of what a self might have 'in it to love' so that it stands in this relation to itself: a person who is capable of character-friendship is aware of her own virtue.[3] The subjective experience she has of her own self is of one that strives to be virtuous, one with the self-confidence in her capacity to remain virtuous. This is a person who does not need to engage in certain activities in which other less virtuous people feel the need to partake. For in becoming virtuous, she has acquired a certain character and psychic structure[4] so that her perceptions of, and attitude to, the world, as well as her behaviour, have a number of firm, enduring characteristics: she is temperate, able to delay, is flexible, trusting, calming, courageous and consistent.[5] This is a person who is able to accept misfortune with a quiet pride rather than with resignation and hopelessness. Having the inner strength and resilience to cope with the various contingencies of human life, she is able to retain a stability to her character, demeanour and behaviour, and to 'hit the mean', desisting from the addictions, excesses and destructive behaviours and relationships that provide unvirtuous people with pleasure, advantage and feelings of self-worth. Her confidence in her own virtue provides her with something 'in her to love', and this means that she has the right kind of self-love:[6] she is able to love herself *qua* virtuous being. Only if she stands in this kind of relation to herself will she have the requisite psychic strength to relate to others in the way that a character-friend does.

Aristotle says that character-friendship is 'self-dependent' (1164a12–13): it depends only on the nature of a character-friend's self – its goodness and psychic strength. Even if things do not turn out the way that a character-friend had planned that they should, he is still able to retain the knowledge and experience of himself as a good person. He 'bears with resignation many great misfortunes, not through insensibility to pain but through nobility and greatness of soul' (1100b31–2). A good person does not easily lose the relation in which he stands to himself, 'for he will never do the acts that are hateful and mean' (1100b32–4). We may be reminded here of Plato's claim that a good man cannot be harmed (*Gorgias*, 527c–d; *Apology*, 41d). While Aristotle says that only a person maintaining a thesis at all costs could call a life filled with suffering and misfortune a happy life (1096a1–2), he also says that 'the good [is] not easily taken from [one]' (1095b25–6), that virtue is more permanent and durable than knowledge (1100b11–15), and that a good person does not fear the possible evil eventualities feared by those who are not good since he is not bothered by things 'that do not proceed from vice and are not due to the person himself' (1115a17–18). While a man will not reach blessedness if he meets with the fortunes like those of Priam, Aristotle insists that a good man can never become miserable (1101a6–7). A virtuous person retains the psychic strength he has acquired in becoming virtuous and in leading a virtuous life; virtue is not something easily lost.

When Aristotle says that a virtuous man 'will bear the chances of life most nobly and altogether decorously, if he is "truly good" and "foursquare beyond reproach" ' (1100b20–1), and that 'no happy man can become miserable' (1100b34), it seems clear that he thinks that a good person's goodness provides the kind of psychic strength that can insulate him from the impact of misfortunes that the contingencies of the world might bring, misfortunes to which bad people are especially vulnerable. This does not mean that a good person is invulnerable to misfortune, but that, while he may be disappointed and, indeed, traumatised by many misfortunes that befall him, these will not diminish his psychic strength, or what he morally is. With his moral self intact, his capacity to relate to others in the way a good person is able can remain unaffected.

Nevertheless, there can come a point at which the impact of

misfortune and pain is so great that his resilience is overwhelmed. If the experience of trauma is sustained and great enough, a good person may be forced into a position where he must constantly *react*, and so be prevented from being able to *respond* to the world. For the experience of trauma may cause him to become vigilantly focused on external stimuli, and this may replace the previous emphasis on his inner life and his capacity to be attuned to his own self. Aristotle rightly saw that there could come a point at which catastrophe was so great that a certain threshold – 'beyond human strength' (1115b8) – was reached such that a person's psychic resources and, with this, his ability to relate to others in the way that a good person does, could become overwhelmed by the subjective experience of trauma. When this happens, a person may lose his underlying capacity to connect with what he has 'in him to love', and could only be called happy by one who was 'maintaining a thesis at all costs'. Yet this does not mean that under extreme trauma a good person loses his underlying capacity for goodness. Rather, in face of his inability to be attuned to his own inner life, his love of self is now insufficient to facilitate the expression of that goodness, which remains latent.

In the absence of extreme trauma, Aristotle insists that the capacity that virtuous agents have to form and maintain stable, enduring relationships with others is very closely connected to a certain kind of inner strength and resilience. For the right kind of self-love enables a person to relate to and value others in a way that treats those others as whole, complete individuals, instead of needing to relate to and value those aspects of others that fulfil his own needs or desires. The nature of the self's psychic life (and so the way in which it relates to itself) determines the kind of relations with others that the self will be capable of forming.[7]

This notion that the nature of the self's psychic life determines the nature of its relations with others is central to contemporary self psychology. The next section looks at the work of self psychology in order to gain some further insight into why psychic strength and inner cohesion are so closely connected to the possibility of living a virtuous life.

SELF PSYCHOLOGY AND CONCEPTIONS OF SELF AND OTHER

Heinz Kohut's self psychology might be seen as serving as a counterpoint for traditional psychoanalysis. Beginning within the classical Freudian tradition, Kohut addressed a particular aspect of the clinical situation which led him to radically modify the then existing metapsychological constructs. While not exclusive of Freudian formulations, his ideas facilitate a psychology of emotional deficit and give an account of the subjectivity of the self (hence 'self psychology') rather than the structure of the mental apparatus.

Self psychologists conceive of the self metaphorically as being constituted by a psychological 'structure': this 'structure' refers to a certain cohesiveness, as if the structure were well-glued, or to fragmentation, as if the structure could fall apart easily. A self with a 'well-glued' self structure is referred to as a 'cohesive self', while a fragmenting self is regarded as fragile, one that is regressing towards a lessened cohesion. Ernest Wolf defines 'self' as that psychological structure which makes its presence evident by providing one with a healthy sense of self, of self-esteem and well-being (Wolf 1988: Chapter 3).

All we can know about these structures are the phenomena to which they give rise. The self's stability can be lost, gradually or suddenly, and there may be rapid changes in function and manifestation such as an altered sense of self, lowered self-esteem, and a lost feeling of well-being. So it is conceptualised that structure has been lost or altered: this is what is meant when it is said that a self is 'fragmented'. The subjective experience of a regressing, fragmenting self is so painful in anxiety and loss of self-esteem that emergency measures may be instituted to reverse the process: individuals with fragile selves use others to shore up fragile self-esteem and make themselves feel stronger. When they do this, they use others as 'selfobjects' (Kohut 1971; 1977; 1984).

Selfobjects are the subjective aspects of a function performed by a relationship with another. The function is to maintain the person's sense of integrity, cohesion, competence and well-being. A selfobject refers to 'that dimension of our experience of another person that relates to this person's shoring up of our self' (Kohut 1984: 49). The selfobject function is to provide 'something necessary for the maintenance of a stable, positively toned sense of self' (Lichtenberg 1983: 166). For Kohut it is the self's conscious and unconscious experience of the relationship with another which determines the cohesion, vigour, harmony and self-esteem of the self.[8]

Kohut noticed that many of his patients did not merely relate to him in a way that was consistent with the classical transference (a

70

repetition with the therapist of key past experiences), but treated him as though he were an alienated part of their own selves. He initially referred to this phenomenon as a 'narcissistic selfobject transference', and later as a 'selfobject transference'. Rather than viewing narcissism as being the result of conflict pathology, in the way that classical psychoanalysis had, Kohut saw pathological narcissism as a developmental deficit that arose from the accumulated trauma of failures within the earlier child–caregiver selfobject relationship. Where, on the classical view, childhood experiences determine the therapeutic relationship, for Kohut the yearnings he noticed in patients for certain kinds of transferences resulted from deficits in psychic structure caused by an absence of certain subjective experiences. He noticed that it was by means of the satisfaction of these yearnings (i.e. by means of selfobject transferences) that a person was able to support a fragile self, to soothe herself, to feel strong and capable, and to feel 'complete'.

There is a developmental line in selfobject relationships ranging from archaic to mature forms. When A and B have an immature selfobject relationship, then from A's perspective, B's self completely disappears since all that is important for A is A's self function that B facilitates. The relationship between A and B here is based on, and exhausted by, the selfobject function that B provides for A. A selfobject relationship at this level of immaturity is extremely narcissistic, and while it may be all-consuming, it can be formed on the basis of a merely partial intimacy. This means that an immature selfobject relationship can be formed on the basis of knowing another person only in one context, or only in a certain way. When this happens, only one aspect of the other may be seen and related to by the person: that aspect that facilitates his own self function. Some examples of aspects of another that might be seen in this way are the other's appearance, their manner, their behaviour at work, or a certain talent they possess.

In a slightly less immature selfobject relationship there remains for A some degree of awareness of B's self, and there may be several, rather than merely one, aspects of B which function as selfobjects for A. So when one selfobject function is withdrawn by B, A may then rely on another aspect of B for his own self function. If we imagine a progression of maturity, we imagine a progression where gradually the whole self of the other comes into focus with all of its personal and idiosyncratic characteristics.

In a mature selfobject relationship, the selfobject function that B provides is no longer crucial to A's self function: the relationship is no longer based on or exhausted by it. This means that the behaviour of a person in a mature selfobject relationship is stable because she can successfully function without depending on the external selfobjects that the other provides: the withdrawal of a selfobject function does not cause her to change her behaviour, her character, or to engage in activities aimed at shoring-up her own self.[9] Instead, such a person has sufficient inner resources to sustain her: these being comprised of a range of selfobject sources, including ones provided by her own psychic structure. This means that she has the capacity to delay, to choose deliberately (rather than being guided by the opportunities that circumstances happen to present) and to be flexible.[10]

For Kohut, a self with its own self function is the result of 'transmuting internalisation': when minor non-traumatic failures in external selfobjects occur, the self tries to repair the violations, performing the selfobject function for itself, so laying down its own internal organising principles, and developing its own self-regulating functions. A person who has transmuted selfobject functions into her own psychic structures has a cohesive self structure, one not prone to fragmentation on the withdrawal of external selfobjects. Self psychology replaces Freud's developmental theory of growth from narcissism to maturity, i.e. from dependence to independence, with a developmental theory where the self grows from infantile, archaic dependence, via the internalisation of selfobject functions as psychic structures, to mature dependence. Failure in the laying-down of psychic structures leads to narcissistic psychopathology manifested in a defective sense of self, an inability to maintain a steady level of self-esteem, and immature selfobject relationships. Activation of selfobject transferences is the attempt on the part of the self to fill a deficit, i.e. to repair an archaic selfobject failure.[11]

The conception of 'the other' under which selves form friendships will be different according to the level of maturity or immaturity of the selfobject relationship involved. A fragile, fragmenting self will have great difficulty in relating to the whole breadth of another person, needing instead to focus on that aspect of the other that serves to shore up its own self. For its deficiency in self functioning leaves it dependent on external selfobjects to compensate for its own internal self deficiency.[12] The conception of the other under which such a self forms relationships is the other *qua* satisfier of archaic selfobject needs.

A cohesive self that has enough of its own self function to sustain it is able to form friendships with others where what is related to and loved is not some particular aspect of the other, but the other's self as such. Since its sense of self is independent of external selfobject satisfactions, it can relate to and love the whole breadth of another person. Having, as a result of psychic structuralisation, the subjective experience of 'a nourishing, sustaining presence inside' (Lee and Martin 1991: 244), the conception of the other under which it is able to form friendships can be the other *qua* the person he is. In a way that is consistent with Aristotle, self psychology holds that the nature of the self's psychic life determines the kinds of relations with others that the self is capable of forming.

In the next section I will point to some more interesting parallels that exist between the Aristotelian account and the work of contemporary self psychology.

ARISTOTLE AND SELF PSYCHOLOGY: SOME PARALLELS

According to the work of self psychology, what must be true of a self in order that it be capable of relating to the whole breadth of another person is that it have sufficient psychic structure and self function of its own so that it is not dependent on particular aspects of another for immature or archaic selfobject satisfactions. We may be reminded here of Aristotle's claim that character-friendship is 'self-dependent': it depends only on the self's own virtue, and so on the psychic strength that it provides for itself. A virtuous person has the psychic capacity to 'remain what he is' independently of anything persons or external events might have to offer him. But we would not be entitled to assimilate these claims and conclude that a person who engages in a pleasure- or advantage-friendship must relate to the other in the way she does because, lacking psychic strength, she depends on the other for external selfobject satisfactions. From the fact that a person forms a friendship only on the basis of advantage or pleasure, it does not follow that she depends on the other for a selfobject function. There will be plenty of cases where a person, in forming friendships, is merely seeking pleasure or advantage, but not necessarily selfobject satisfaction.

Yet if a person were *only* capable of relating to others in the way that pleasure- and advantage-friends do, and were *incapable* of relating to the whole breadth of another person, from a self psychological point of view we would be given cause to wonder about the level of maturity of her self functioning. On Aristotle's account, certain kinds of people are incapable of relating to and loving another person in virtue of her being the person she is because of the relation in which they stand to their own selves: not having anything 'in them to love', they seek advantage and/or pleasure to fill deficits in their own psychic lives. The story Aristotle can present to explain why a person who is not a self-lover is unable to love another in virtue of her being the person she is, is very similar to the story self psychology presents: 'initially the self does not seek tension reduction or instinctual expression but relatedness, attachment, connection to others. If there is severe injury to the self and its relations... there is a deterioration to pure pleasure-seeking' (Greenberg and Mitchell 1983: 360–1). An injured, fragmenting self is not capable of the kind of intimacy of which Aristotelian character-friends are capable since, needing to repair its own psychic life, it is unable to empathise with the subjective experience of the other.

Kohut regarded the empathic bond (involving awareness of the subjectivity of the other) as a centrally important tool for the exploration of another's subjective world. This is consistent with Aristotle's reference to a character-friend as 'another self'. When I recognise my friend as 'another self', I recognise someone 'just like me', someone with whom I can easily empathise, understand, and share my life with. In addition, I recognise that my friend is not simply an extension of me, but is a discrete other self of whose subjectivity I am very much aware. Self psychology has similar things to say about the relation between selves who are able to form mature interpersonal relationships. As 'another self' a character-friend fulfils the requirements of Kohutian empathic attunement – 'the recognition of the self in the other, the expansion of the self to include the other, and the accepting, understanding human echo evoked by the self' (Lee and Martin 1991: 114). Just as a Kohutian mature self has the capacity to relate to the otherness of the other, so an Aristotelian character-friend, as 'another self', is able to maintain an intimate relationship with his friend as a discrete, other self.

The intimacy of immature selfobject relationships involves a specific kind of blurring of boundaries between selves, where one person is used as an extension of the other to support her own self. So long as this function is provided, this intimacy remains and the relationship, which depends on the other's ability to provide a means for the person to maintain her sense of self, can continue. If such a person is to feel competent, complete, able to make decisions or to take risks, etc., she must be provided with certain external selfobject functions in the absence of which she is prone to fragment. Her self-confidence, being the result, not of her own psychic life, but of the selfobject function that another provides, is distorted. And the intimacy of her relationships is only partial, meaning that only one aspect (or few aspects) of the other forms the basis of her relationships.

Similarly, only those aspects of the other providing advantage or pleasure form the basis of the intimacy in Aristotelian advantage- and pleasure-friendships. Such partial intimacy is similar to the intimacy of immature selfobject relationships in that it involves relating to the other only in a certain context or in a certain way, and it is often associated with a sense of need or yearning, and sometimes also with a desperate striving to fill a gap. In these friendships, the whole breadth of the other is not related to or loved, and if a person were always confined to a merely partial intimacy in this way, this would be a good indication that the person is only capable of immature selfobject relationships.

Both self psychology and the Aristotelian account insist on the priority of the relation that the self has to itself over its relations with others. For both, in order to relate to others without seeking to fulfil some need had by the self, the self first has to be in a certain state: for self psychologists it must be a self whose self cohesion is not disturbed when an external selfobject is withdrawn; for Aristotle it must be a self that has the capacity to be independent of pleasure- and advantage-seeking aims. For Aristotle, a person's virtue is something that can provide the requisite independence,[13] while self psychologists would regard Aristotelian virtue as being able to provide a self with an internal selfobject that enables it to relate to others without being preoccupied with external selfobject functions that others provide.

The *acquisition* of virtue, as described by Plato and Aristotle, would also appear to self psychology to confer the requisite psychic strength by providing internal psychic structures that support self function. Aristotle points out that 'moral excellence is concerned with pleasures and pains' (1104b8), and Plato held that the right kind of upbringing was conducive to the acquisition of virtue since it would ensure that we would delight in and be pained by the things that we ought (*Laws*, 653aff; *Republic*, 401e–402a). Consistent with

Plato's views, Aristotle held that virtue is acquired by means of the right kind of habituation and training. This does not mean that virtue can be acquired through blind imitation that forms certain habits, but it involves the transformation of desire and affect so that the person takes pleasure and pain in the right things (1104b9–13). Only if pleasure and pain is taken in the right things will the person have the appropriate dispositions to love the noble and hate the base (1105a6–7). Self psychology would hold that the Aristotelian process of coming to take pleasure and pain in the right things must involve a certain psychic structuralisation involving the acquisition of a certain way of perceiving and responding to (as well as a certain set of beliefs about) the external world. For self psychology, a basically bad set of experiences with a care-giver will lead an infant to a radically different set of beliefs about, and attitude to, the external world than will another infant's basically good experiences. These invariant features of experience become *organising principles* (principles according to which the external world is psychologically organised). In an adult, experience is shaped by these: they determine what will be seen as important and salient in a situation, how a situation is emotionally responded to, and how other people will be related to.[14]

Living with virtuous people would seem to be a good way, not only to learn how to act justly and temperately (1105b7–8), but also a way in which the requisite psychic structuralisation would be acquired. A person who lives with virtuous people would be treated with respect by them; he would experience them as empathising with his own subjective experiences (both of the world and of himself), and these are people who would have the capacity to respond to him with empathic attunement.[15] An infant whose care-givers respond to its needs and upsets with empathic attunement experiences itself as being connected to a source of strength and understanding, allowing him to become attuned to, and to accept, his own emotions which he experiences as affects that can be contained and dealt with. Such an individual will not only allow himself to feel appropriately, but, as an adult, will also have the inner strength and confidence to act on his vision of human good.[16] Plato writes that 'A child's first infant consciousness is that of pleasure and pain; this is the domain wherein the soul first acquires virtue or vice' (*Laws*, 653a). The capacity for emotional modulation is stressed by Plato as being of crucial importance for the development of virtue (*Laws*, 653b–c). Self psychology holds that in the presence of unempathic caregivers who, for example, either ignore, respond with panic to, or mirror the infant's upsets, anxiety or anger, the infant experiences his own emotions as sources of frustration or as frightening, uncontrollable experiences. Such caregivers chronically undermine the infant's self function, failing the infant as selfobjects. The infant learns it is better not to feel certain emotions, and disavows them. Not having internalised a capacity to accept and modulate desires and emotions, the infant will, as an adult, be unable to regulate these.

Such adults resemble Aristotle's intemperate people. Aristotle presents an intemperate person as being unable to control his own desire for pleasant sensations: 'That is why a certain gourmand prayed that his throat might become longer than a crane's' (1118a33–1118b1). A person is intemperate because he feels an undue amount of pain at missing out on pleasures. By contrast, a temperate person is not pained when he misses out on pleasures, for the virtuous life is pleasant in itself and so 'has no further need of pleasure as a sort of adventitious charm' (1099a15–16). Similarly, Kohutian mature selves have their own self function to sustain them when they miss out on pleasures. Aristotelian virtuous agents and the mature selves of self psychology share the feature of being less prone to resentment when they miss out on some pleasure offered by the external world.

The sorts of pleasures people seek, and the nature and intensity of their emotions, says a lot about the kind of people they are. Irascible people get angry more than is right (1126a14), while choleric people are angry about everything (1126a19). Aristotle believes these kinds of characters are incapable of virtue. Self psychology would say that these are characters who have failed to internalise a capacity to contain and deal with their own emotions. People who have not internalised the capacity to accept and modulate desire and emotion, and who experience these as uncontrollable, are not able to take pleasure and pain in the right things. Where for a virtuous person, the non-rational part 'obeys the rational principle' (1102b27–8), the vicious people Aristotle describes experience conflict between the rational and non-rational parts of the soul. Self psychology would regard such people as having archaic selfobject needs, as being dependent on external selfobjects to maintain emotional and self regulation. These are people who are likely to seek pleasure and excitement by, for example, acting out or making use of artificial stimulants: not having a life that is in itself pleasant, they are stimulus-bound, looking to external selfobjects for pleasure.

This does not mean that making use of external selfobjects *per se* is either pathological or immature. Non-pathological, mature adults derive a range of selfobject experiences in a variety of ways, but they do not relate to others in ways that fail to regard them as persons in their own right. The use of selfobjects becomes pathological in cases where all goodness or worthlessness is attributed to the other, these being split off from the wholeness of the other, and then related to as though they represented the totality of the other. Also pathological is a total merger with the other so that nothing remains of the merging person's own self. These pathological uses of selfobjects are avoided in people whose selves have developed in a healthy way.

Self psychology holds that in order for the self to develop in a healthy way, it must extract from the environment responses that match the three poles of self development postulated by Kohut (1977). These poles represent potentialities that are present at birth. It may be hypothesised from Kohut's work that a child is born with innate psychological needs, or selfobject needs, such as the need to be mirrored, to be listened to, to be cared about, to be understood, to be treated with positive regard, to be treated genuinely, to have someone to idealise as a source of calming strength. The three poles represent three major aspects of the way a baby relates to parents, and three major ways in which parents can fulfil its selfobject needs. The selfobject functions (that parents provide) become internalised within the child as regulating capacities, giving him the ability to soothe himself and to modulate both excitement and depression. So the capacities provide a source of inner strength. Care-givers who reflect back an appreciation and valuing of the infant's grandiosity as well as provide security, protection, warmth and a sense of belonging, facilitate the development of a strong, healthy, mature narcissism.

In health, another person may provide a selfobject function, but the other can be related to as a person in her own right, and be regarded as having a unique value and worth of her own, rather than be related to as though she were merely a means to the person's own narcissistic ends. This is consistent with Aristotle's account: character-friends, like Kohutian mature selves, are not completely independent of each other. Yet the nature of their dependency is quite different from the nature of the dependency involved in immature selfobject relationships.

Aristotle and Kohut

Aristotle says that man is a social animal, and so needs friends (1169b17–22). A virtuous person's life is enriched through interactions with his character-friends. In virtue of the fact that he may well gain psychic lifts through participating in a variety of activities with his friends, there is a kind of dependency involved in character-friendship. Yet this is fundamentally different in nature from the dependency of advantage- and pleasure-friendships. These friendships depend on the pleasure or advantage that the other provides, the other being replaceable because all that is related to and loved is the particular feature of the friend that provides pleasure or advantage. It is also fundamentally different in nature from the dependency of immature selfobject relationships where the other is replaceable because all that is related to or loved is the cohesive self function that the other provides.

As a social animal, a character-friend also depends on certain interactions with others to realise what he is. It is through demands made on his self by others (e.g. for advice or assistance) that he reinforces his sense of what he is. Yet this is a far cry from a dependency on the continued availability of pleasure, advantage or selfobject functions that others provide. So while character-friends are not completely independent of each other, their dependency is not of the immature narcissistic kind that self psychology believes needs to be transformed into more mature forms.

Kohut rejected Freud's account of narcissism (as being the result of conflict pathology and needing to be replaced by object love) and saw narcissism and object love as developing along two separate but parallel continua, ranging from archaic to mature forms. He believed that ridding of narcissism was not only impossible, but also undesirable. The clinical task for self psychology is to harness narcissism for constructive purposes. For example, creative work is seen by self psychology as a transformation of archaic narcissism: a creative individual experiences the external world on which she works as part of her internal life, so the external world is experienced by her with greater intensity and sensitivity, as belonging to what she is. The capacity to love and the capacity to work (Freud's definition of normality) would both be regarded by Kohut as legitimate, mature selfobjects: the selfobject function for a person does not ever disappear, but undergoes transformation and maturation so that a person can maintain an adequate level of grandiosity. The feeling of being competent, of being 'good enough', of being able to cope well, and of being likeable or lovable are all signs of what Kohut would regard to be normal grandiosity[17] or healthy narcissism, and this sustains a person so that she does not need to engage in activities aimed at shoring up her self.

Self psychology would view many of the Aristotelian vices as being the result of deficiencies in grandiosity (or of a failure to transform archaic narcissism into mature forms). Aristotle writes of inirascible people that 'to endure being insulted and put up with insult to one's friends is slavish' (1126a7–8). From a self psychological point of view, these people display deficiencies in grandiosity, not having a secure sense of their own worth. Other vicious types that Aristotle describes suffer from the same kind of condition: the coward, the obsequious flatterer, mock-modest and boastful people have precarious, unstable selves. Boastful and mock-modest people depend on the good opinion of others, and so, from a self psychological point of view, depend on mirroring selfobjects[18] for a sense of self. The flatterer aims to gain favour with privileged people in order to improve his own position (1127a7–9), while vain people seek honour although they are not worthy of it (1125a27–31). By contrast, cantankerous and churlish people are contemptuously independent of others' opinions, not caring enough about others and their views: their behaviour is explicable by self psychology in terms of their seeing others as threatening or hostile, this being the result of their own psychic insufficiencies. They do not experience themselves as being able to cope with what they perceive to be a threatening world unless they behave in a cantankerous or churlish way.

The Aristotelian paradigm of virtue, the *megalopsychos*, has the right attitude toward self and others (1123a34–1125a16), and self psychology would view him as possessing mature narcissism. He wants the esteem, not of just anybody, but of other virtuous individuals whose judgements of him are sensitive to the truth. His narcissism is mature because his passion for truth is far stronger than his desire to be well thought of and admired by others (1124b26–7). While the *megalopsychos* wants others' esteem, self psychologists would say that the self function provided by his own virtue means that he can 'remain what he is' even when the esteem of others becomes unavailable. He is not dependent on external selfobjects for a sense of what he is. At the same time, he is not contemptuously independent of how others see him. Being in possession of mature narcissism, he has the inner resources to be both selfless and trustful of others.

It is not being suggested that Aristotelian 'love of self' and Kohutian 'healthy narcissism' should be seen as co-extensive, but that the acquisition and possession of virtue might be seen as providing the internal self function and self-cohesiveness that manifests itself as the healthy narcissism that Kohut describes. Virtue would seem to be precisely what can provide a person with the healthy narcissism that interests self psychologists. And it is only through virtue that Aristotelian love of self develops.[19]

We have seen that the very psychic strengths that enable character-friends to form friendships that are not distorted by their own psychic insecurities, are the same strengths that are missing from the selves of people who are dependent on the pleasure, advantage or archaic selfobjects that others can provide. In the next section I will show that many of the observations of self psychology regarding a healthy, mature self, have direct relevance to Aristotle's account of character-friendship and virtue. This discussion will show that what must be true of a self, in order that it be capable of relating to another in the way that a character-friend does, is that it be a self that has no need to develop strategies to avoid self fragmentation, and that it have the flexibility of response to the world and to others that precludes the development of a 'false self'.

CHARACTER-FRIENDSHIP AND VIRTUE: WHAT THESE REQUIRE

There are five defining features of character-friendship, according to Aristotle, which can be found in a good man's relation to himself (1166a2–10), and the former proceed from the latter (1166a2). The first – wishing what is good for one's friend, for the friend's sake – is inconsistent with using friends as selfobjects to shore up a fragile self. Such use suggests a deficiency in the self's stability: where the self is prepared to adapt its character to external expectations and demands, so long as its own fragile sense of self is thereby repaired. Such changeability makes a person unstable, and Aristotle insists that a good person's character is stable and enduring.

According to the second defining feature of character-friendship when found in relation to the self, a virtuous person wishes, not merely that his friend should stay alive, but also that he himself should stay alive. For a life of virtue and *eudaimonia* make his life choice-worthy, and without being alive he is unable to strive for nobility and goodness. The other defining marks of character-friendship when found in relation to the self refer to a virtuous person's unity: he wishes to live with himself since he is free of inner conflict; he has the same tastes and makes the same choices as himself – this means that his soul is cohesive and free of the inner turmoil that plagues wicked people; he 'grieves and rejoices' with himself – this indicates that he is not alienated from his own emotions, but very much in touch with his own emotional-affective life.[20]

Since a character-friend's life is noble and good, he has all the inner strength and 'wholeness' he needs to feel 'complete', and this without depending on external selfobjects for self support. By contrast, the deficiency of self that plagues a person who is completely dependent on others for selfobject functions to make her intact may be evidenced in her engaging compulsively or desperately in selfobject transferences.

Kohut describes three distinct kinds of selfobject transferences (1971; 1984) that correspond to the three poles of the self structure, as conceptualised by him. The mirroring selfobject transference occurs when another provides a person with a reflection of her positive qualities, attributes or talents, confirming the sense she has of her own abilities and capacities. When the other fails or refuses to provide the needed selfobject function, Kohut observed a response which he termed 'narcissistic rage' (1972) which arises out of the person's fear of imminent self fragmentation: the fear that without the appropriate mirroring support, the self is liable to fall apart. The idealising selfobject transference occurs when the other is related to as though she represents all that the person wishes and hopes to be. All goodness and worth, all personal ideals, are located in the other with which the person then merges so as to attain, or at least so as to share in, the perfection of the other.[21] The twinship selfobject transference occurs when the person attributes to the other features and attributes that correspond with those that he imagines himself to have, so supporting his own sense of kinship and belonging.

In all three transferences the other may be treated, not as a person in her own right, but as a means to support a fragile self. The need to soothe the self, to be made to feel strong, capable and complete by means of selfobject transferences, is not the way in which a person who is capable of character-friendship maintains a sense of self. As Aristotle's discussion shows, a person capable of character-friendship is not one with a fragile self. A self psychologist would say that such a person will have replaced many archaic selfobject needs with internal psychic structures so that the need for external selfobjects is greatly reduced, if not completely removed. In such cases, the selfobject function, in effect, has become part of the self function that the self is able to provide for itself. We saw above that, according to self psychology, the acquisition of virtue, and the living of a virtuous life, is the kind of thing that can provide such self function.

Friendship based on the recognition of good moral character is useful and pleasant (1156b13–15; 1157a1–3) in the way that advantage- and pleasure-friendships are, but the *kind* of concern for the other is different in nature from the latter kinds of friendships: 'men who are good, and alike in virtue... wish well alike to each other *qua* good' (1156b7–8). The object of concern here is what the other *essentially* is – the other person *qua* person of good character. This is why 'those who wish well to their friends for their sake... do this by reason of their own nature and not incidentally' (1156b10–11).[22] The friend is loved because he is a good human being. What he recognises as lovable is something that is good as such, i.e. good without qualification for a human being as such. This is not a mere contingent feature the friend happens to have, but, without his goodness, he would be an essentially different person. While the loves of advantage- and pleasure-friendships are transient because they depend on advantage, pleasure or support for the self, the love of character-friendship depends on nothing but itself: on the recognition of goodness in the other's character, and this goodness is something that does not easily change. So this kind of friendship is enduring because it will last as long as the friends are good, 'and goodness is an enduring thing' (1156b12): it proceeds 'from a firm and *unchangeable* character' (1105a34; my emphasis). This is why Aristotle says that character-friendship is 'self-dependent': it is not dependent on anything except what the self can provide for itself by way of goodness and psychic strength, and the self retains its capacity for character-friendship so long as it remains what it essentially is: a virtuous being that acts for the sake of its own understanding ('its reasoning part').

We have seen above that the relation to the self from which the best type of character-friendship flows is, like character-friendship itself, also self-dependent. And it is enduring because it does not depend on the continued possession of any particular qualities or attributes, on others' continuing recognition or esteem of these, or on others providing suitable selfobjects. Love of self depends rather on what the person essentially is: it depends on the person's own good character. The object of concern here (or the conception under which the self values itself) is, as in the case of character-friendship, the self *qua* good. A lover of self does not love himself for certain talents, qualities or possessions he happens to have, but he loves himself *qua* person who instantiates human goodness or excellence. Aristotle writes that 'no one chooses to possess the whole world if he has first to become some one else... he wishes for this only on condition of being whatever he is' (1166a20–2): a good person will not change his character or behaviour, or cut himself off from his own inner life, in order to achieve some desired satisfaction. This means that the development of a false self is precluded in a good person since he will not change his responses to fit with what others happen to want, value or expect.[23]

The development of a false self begins in childhood, where the child must comply with parental demands. These demands may concern emotional behaviour: for example, to appear happy since unhappiness, sadness or distress are not tolerated by the care-giver. In complying, the child disavows the capacity to express feeling fully. The life and vigour of the bodily accompaniments of an emotion are not experienced, so that what is expressed by the child lacks 'sensory-motor aliveness' (Winnicott 1965b: 149). The individual who suppresses emotion to conform to expectations often feels that she is 'not real':

> The words of emotional expression come from what the individual reads in the other's face... [he] ceaselessly scans the social environment in order to judge the expectations of others. One finds one's face being endlessly searched and small nuances of expression being responded to.
>
> (Meares 1992: 100)

The false self is based on compliance to the reality of the other; its function is to hide the true self in order to excite a suitable response from the other. A consequence is that areas of personal experience remain neglected, never having being responded to. A false self has little, if any, access to an inner life, since it must focus its attentions on the external world in order to ensure that it complies with its demands.

Aristotle's paradigm of virtue, the *megalopsychos*, does not invest his energies in complying to external demands. The *megalopsychos* is open in his hate and in his love, and he cares more for the truth than for what people think (1124b26–30): 'His words, passions and actions reflect the "inner man" '(Carver 1991: 145).

An Aristotelian virtuous person has no need to form a false self or to hide a true self, since he is at one with his own cohesive inner life. He will only pursue a satisfaction on condition that he can maintain this inner stability and retain a conception of himself as a person of good character. Accordingly, 'If his goal in life requires honesty at one time, cheating at another, kindliness now, and cruelty later, it does not secure happiness for him. For in order to secure such a goal he has to sacrifice some of himself' (Irwin 1988: 380). A good person will not change his character to ensure success: what counts for him is not merely the achievement of some external end (as is true of a vicious person), but also the kind of self that is being formed and maintained through the various acts that the self performs. Love of self depends, not on achievements in the world, but rather on the self's own goodness: on the conception of non-contingent human good that the self has, and on its 'straining every nerve' to act in accordance with this conception.

To have as the object of self-love the self *qua* good is for Aristotle to love one's practical reason (1168b33). It is to love one's understanding, and to want to be guided by a clear, true and just understanding of what is before one.[24] A virtuous agent cares for himself only through caring for justice and the truth. A self for which the object of self-concern is the self *qua* good is self-supporting and self-sustaining since this object can be promoted only by the self's own love of, and striving for, goodness.

It seems clear that if a self is to be able to relate to others without depending on them for pleasure, advantage or selfobject functions, without needing to develop strategies to avoid self fragmentation, or developing a false self, it must be a self that is self-supporting and self-sustaining. Such a self has the inner strength and certainty of what it is that confers a certain kind of psychic health. Aristotelian character-friendship requires that the person have the capacity to be attracted to and moved by what she recognises, both about herself and about another, to be unqualifiedly good as such. This means that the person must be committed to certain values that relate to a conception of human good, to a normative conception of what it is to be a good human being and lead a good human life, and must also have the inner strength to be able to act in accordance with such a conception. Self psychology refers to this inner strength as 'psychic cohesion'.

A cohesive self, as described by self psychology, is needed if a conception of human good is to guide a person's thoughts, deliberations, actions and relationships. This kind of commitment to, and guidance by, certain values is precluded in a person whose self is in a state of fragmentation. For a fragmenting self will need to invest all of its energies in those strategies and activities that might hold it together as a self, albeit precariously, precluding it from committing itself to, internalising, or investing its energies in enacting, a normative conception of human good. A fragmenting self is capable of neither virtue nor character-friendship.

Cooper has pointed out that it is not the case, on Aristotle's view, that only perfectly virtuous people can have character-friendships: the basis for character-friendship 'is the recognition of good qualities of character, without in any way implying that the parties are moral heroes' (1977: 629). A person does not have to be a paradigm of moral perfection in order to recognise the good moral character of another and love the other and wish her well *qua* person of good moral character. Nor does a person have to be a paradigm of moral perfection in order for another to recognise and love her for those aspects of her character that are morally good. Similarly, the relation in which a good person stands to her own self does not require that she be some kind of saint. Rather, love of self requires that the self relate to and love a self (be it one's own or that of another) in virtue of the self's own goodness.

There are modern theorists who find the Aristotelian view that the best kind of love is love for a person's moral character objectionable since they believe that love should be for the person herself.[25] While Aristotle assimilates a person's character with what the person essentially is, modern views separate these. Modern views hold that one can continue to love a beloved even when her character changes and she becomes selfish or wicked, since what is loved is the person herself, not simply her character. For Aristotle, virtue is something that is very difficult to lose (excellence proceeds from a firm and *unchangeable* character) (1105a34); what a person essentially is does not easily change. So the question of whether one continues to love a virtuous person who becomes wicked does not arise for him. In a similar way, self psychology holds that inner cohesion and self function is not something that belongs to a self merely precariously. The psychic strength and unity that result from the laying down of internal organising principles via transmuting internalisation are not easily reversed.

Though giving different accounts of the psychic unity that makes virtue possible, Plato and Aristotle agree that an ethical life without a certain kind of psychic health is not a real possibility. Conflict, instability and changeability within the self preclude the presence of the kind of psychic strength and harmony required for virtue. The nature of a person's inner life and the moral status of her actions are for both philosophers interdependent. Aristotle's account of the achievement of *eudaimonia*, and Plato's account of a person's coming to know and love the Forms, can be seen to reflect the presence of an harmonious psychic structure which excludes a dependence on the pleasure or advantage that others might provide, as well as the obsessional style of selfobject-hungry individuals, while at the same time being a structure into which the various elements of a virtuous person's life may fit in a stable, coherent and meaningful way.

My own account of the constitution of the moral self that is presented in the next four chapters shares with Aristotle and Kohut their converging perspectives regarding the self. I begin in the next chapter with an account of individual self-making and moral self-transformation.

CHAPTER V

Significant action and the self

the idea of goodness did attract me, for I did not regard it as the opposite of sin. I saw it as something bright and positive and sustaining, like the sunshine, something to be adored.

(Hartley 1953: 70)

INTRODUCTION

We will see in this chapter that my account of the moral self takes as basic a certain level of understanding and quality of reflection. Where for Hume a self is moral in virtue of a conversion from certain impressions to certain ideas, where for Rousseau a self is moral when it adheres to certain absolute moral limits (articulated in terms of the general will), where for Hegel a self's morality is a socio-cultural manifestation, on my account the moral self is constituted by its motivation to justly understand the particular circumstances before it, and by its understanding of the significance of certain values in these circumstances.

My account is consistent with, and builds on, an Aristotelian view of ethics. It was suggested in Chapter 4 that for Aristotle a self needs a certain psychic capacity to be able to take pleasure and pain in the appropriate things, and so to love the noble and hate the base. Similarly, on my account, not just any self will be motivated to achieve a just understanding of the circumstances before it: a certain kind of inner strength and resilience is required for the self to be attracted to the idea of goodness, and to ensure that its acts are guided by this idea. The self needs a certain kind of psychic life to engage in what I term 'significant action': I employ this as a technical term that refers, not to objective importance, but to importance for the agent. An agent who engages in significant action does so because the action matters to her in a particular way.

SIGNIFICANT ACTION AND RATIONALITY

The concept of significant action will be shown in this chapter to play a key role in our understanding of moral action. I will argue that significant action is not reducible to rational choice, that rational choice, while a necessary condition, is not a sufficient condition for significant action. Significance will be shown to be a differentia which separates the class of moral actions from the remainder of the class of rational actions. Understanding the reasonableness or rationality of a significant action can serve to justify why a person performed it, but it is not able to explain what lies behind its motivation. We may endorse a significant action as the rational one to have been taken in the circumstances without referring to what makes it a significant action: to understand the motivation of significant action we must look beyond its mere rationality to a quite different dimension.

I define significant action as action one of whose consequences is some transformation of the self. Significance is concerned with a deepened understanding of the nature of values which a person wants to conserve, while I take rationality, as it is commonly expounded in the literature, to be chiefly concerned with methods of conserving these values, and much less with their nature and real worth.

This demarcation of significant from non-significant action is made with the intention of focusing on those actions which are meaningful in a particular way for agents who perform them, actions whose importance does not lie merely in the achievement of some empirical end, ones which are not describable merely in terms of their instrumental rationality, but whose value and importance has a significance for the agent's own life. Significant action expresses a commitment which is at once ethical and ontological, and it is a commitment which, while rational,[1] is not reducible to a commitment to rationality. I take moral[2] action to express such a commitment.

There is considerable difficulty in expounding a simple or definitive account of rationality (MacIntyre 1988: 2). Some work with extremely broad conceptions where, for example, caring for, and the possession of a deepened understanding[3] of, reasons and values are included. Thus it is said that if a person does not care much about, or have a real understanding of, the significance of his beliefs, reasons and values, this is a reason for being dubious about whether he in fact holds them. A philosopher who makes such a claim takes 'caring for' and 'having a deepened understanding of' to be part of what it is to be rational.[4] Yet such a claim indicates the holding of a conception of rationality that is far more inclusive than those commonly found in the literature.[5] It is these latter conceptions with which I contrast significance.

One can agree that caring for, and having a deepened understanding of beliefs, reasons and values is not completely independent of intending, desiring and having certain reasons for action. Yet the former is not simply reducible to the latter. A philosopher who makes such a reduction makes a mistake that is similar to the mistake of reducing Aristotelian *phronesis* to the ability to construct consistent practical syllogisms. The mistake in the latter emerges when we consider that an agent may construct a consistent practical syllogism without the syllogism having any practical force *for her*. What she needs is 'right desire' (1139a25) to bear on the major premise. The *akrates*, for example, may construct a consistent practical syllogism, but since her desires are not ordered rightly, the syllogism has no practical force *for her*. Right perception and right motivation require a certain ethical maturity: the reasons there are to act in a certain way must be made by the agent into her own reasons. What is needed in addition to certain desires, intentions, values and reasons, is that the person care for, and have a deepened understanding of these.

We need to distinguish between holding a value and taking that value as one's reason for acting in a certain way. Philosophers who reduce 'having a deepened understanding of' and 'caring for' to intending, desiring and valuing, find it difficult to concede this distinction. For, they hold, unless one takes the value as one's reason to act in a certain way, doubt must be cast on the fact of one's holding that value: 'The less her evaluations are expressed in action the more suspect the claim that she values the relevant type of behaviour' (G. Taylor 1985: 118). It needs to be pointed out that one may hold a value because one recognises it to be important to one's country, neighbourhood or family: one still assents to (and so holds) the value.[6] But this value is only made into one's *own* reason to act in a particular way if one comes to *take the value in a certain way*. We have here a distinction between the reasons and motives a person might have for holding a value, on the one hand, and the kind of *attitude or quality of attachment* that a person might have to those reasons, motives, and to the value, on the other. We will see

90

below that essential to action being significant action is a certain kind of second-order attitude to reasons, values, motives and desires.

Some philosophers believe that not being moved by what one values indicates a cognitive dysfunction, such as a failure of inference. Implicit here is an action-guidingness principle: to hold a value *is* to be guided by it. Some close the gap, in the case of morality, between recognising that there is a reason and making it *one's own* reason (or between having a value and making it into *one's own* value) by giving an account of the function of morality in terms of a mutually acceptable mode of behaviour by all, and for all. Morality is viewed here as a means to establishing and preserving such a mode of behaviour, and so as *having a point*. Moral motivation is thus regarded as being reducible to the motivation involved in establishing and preserving such behaviour, and so our understanding of moral motivation is regarded as being reducible to our understanding of rational choice.

A conception of rationality such as that expounded by Richard Brandt (1979) concerns itself exclusively with beliefs, desires and values, but not at all with the attitude or quality of attachment that a person might have to them. Brandt's conception holds that a person is rational if he has undergone 'cognitive psychotherapy' (criticism and correction by facts and logic) to 'fumigate' desires and interests, so as to be able to take into account all the relevant information. Brandt must accept the conclusion that those desires and interests that survive cognitive psychotherapy must count as being rational. And a mark of rationality is the successful satisfaction of one's desires and the pursuit of one's interests. We have here a value-neutral account of 'rationality'. A person can be fully rational and be without benevolence altogether: Brandt gives as an example the operators of Hitler's concentration camps (1979: 145). So a complete lack of concern, of caring, and of awareness of the significance of what a person is engaged in doing does not count for Brandt as elements which should affect our judgements concerning the person's rationality.

Brandt's conception does not concern itself with the notion of an agent making a reason into a reason *for her* to act in a particular way because of the kind of attachment or affective attitude she has to it.[7] If a person takes into account all relevant information, and arrives at a reason for x-ing, nothing more is ever required in order that she x. Rational action is action whose causal factors have been 'fumigated' of all mistakes, and the 'mistakes' Brandt refers to are all cognitive mistakes (1979: 14–15). Rationality is for Brandt exhaustive of significance. It is with this kind of narrow conception of rationality that I contrast significance.

The Brandtian conception of rationality, and others like it, take rational deliberation to refer mainly to means–ends reasoning: rational deliberation is first and foremost instrumental. Rationality is concerned, for example, with the best way to conserve one's values, but not with an understanding of the nature and real worth of the values to be conserved (see Harsanyi 1982: 42).[8] Rationality is here, for all intents and purposes, value-neutral.

The conception of rationality with which Rawls (1972) works is also value-neutral: according to it, the actual content of a person's beliefs and desires escapes assessment (so long as these do not contradict each other). On Rawls' conception, rationality can be assessed according to how successfully the agent maximises the satisfaction of her desires, and consists in attaining the means that will achieve one's ends and in the policy of maximising the benefits of the worst possible outcome. There is for the parties to the original position neutrality with respect to conceptions of the good: the only criteria according to which a Rawlsian agent would change his desires or aims are criteria pertaining to long-term maximisation of satisfactions.

Where rationality is understood in Brandtian or Rawlsian ways, actions are regarded as purely instrumental and, as such, devoid of significance. The more the agent is aware of all the relevant facts, the better her action will be at achieving her aims and fulfilling her desires: the better her action is in this regard, the more rational it is.

One might want to say that such conceptions of rationality leave one cold, and that one does not need to accept them. Yet the literature abounds with conceptions of rationality along Brandtian and Rawlsian lines. In fact, utilitarian, and indeed most con-sequentialist theories, regard rationality to consist in maximising calculation where all value is reducible to happiness, welfare or pleasure.[9]

Such conceptions leave out a whole dimension of rational choice. The dimension in question is an affective dimension, but it is not one that is to be understood merely in terms of a *pro* or *contra* attitude to one's reasons, motives or values; the affective dimension is not one which merely contains approval or disapproval of these. The dimension is a far more fundamental one than that, and when we understand the implications of its existence, it becomes clear that to hold a value is far more than to be merely moved by it.[10]

Significant action is rational action, but not all rational action is significant action. We may know and understand all there is to know about the rationality of an action, but not have much understanding of its significance. We may know the agent's desires, beliefs, reasons and intentions, and so know why she did what she did and completely understand the reasonableness of what she did, but understand little, if anything, about the action's significance. We may look at the predecessors of action and find a perfectly cohesive and integrated rational pattern in what the agent did. But this formal rational consistency may not reveal a more substantive, and what I also want to call 'ethical' cohesion and integration that is required of significant action. And, most importantly, this ethical requirement is not reducible to a requirement of practical rationality.

By using an example, the next section discusses the ethical consistency that is a requirement of significant action. I begin by considering two different ways in which the same act can be described with respect to its significance or 'non-significance'.[11]

VALUING, ACTING AND SELF-CONSTITUTION

Putting a kettle on in order to make a cup of tea is, in itself, a 'non-significant' action, since the agent does not usually conceive of herself to be responding to any deeply held values, to be expressing some ideal, to be changing in a fundamental way, or to be doing something which represents part of what she stands for. Nor does performing such an action do anything with respect to the conception the agent has of her own self. She makes the tea because she is thirsty and wants it. There is no thought here given to whether she wants to be the kind of person who makes tea when she is thirsty. Indeed, any such thoughts would be extremely odd. In relation to the agent's most deeply held values, the action is devoid of significance. The kettle is put on in order to make a much needed cup of tea after a tiring day: the significance of the action is exhausted by its rationality.

It is not for reasons relating to the objective unimportance or triviality of this action that it is non-significant. It is non-significant because of the relation in which the action, in these circumstances, and at this particular time, stands to the particular agent and her values. An action may be objectively important but, in relation to the particular agent and her values, be non-significant. Conversely, an action may be quite trivial but, in relation to the particular agent and the circumstances, be a significant one. Significance and non-significance are always relativised to a particular agent in a particular circumstance and at a particular time.

Under another description, the same bodily movement involved in putting the kettle on may be an indication of significant action. Let us consider that the agent is making the cup of tea for another whom she perceives to have done her some injustice, and makes the tea with the intention of forgiving her so that the cup of tea is seen by her to be, in large part, an expression of forgiveness for the other. And if we imagine, further, that this is being done for no other reason or purpose than to relieve the other of the guilt feelings the agent anticipates her as likely to have, such that the tea is made in the hope that it will make her feel welcome rather than guilty, the same outward action takes on a significance that is not exhausted by its rationality.

Some might say that the person in this description is now simply utilising means to what is a larger end, and that this use is rationally appraisable. It might be said that this action is now simply being performed for more complex reasons than before, and that its motivation can be explained in terms of these reasons. The act can certainly be viewed and understood in this way, but to do so is to completely miss its moral dimension, as well as to fail to understand the kind of self that is engaged in the action.

Seeing the act as simply being a means to a larger end that is rationally appraisable is to understand the agent's motivation purely in terms of the act's goal-orientedness. If we do this, then we understand the self that acts as one whose energy is completely invested in the rationality of what it does. There is then nothing in addition to the rationality of what is done that needs to be considered in order to understand the action and the self's motivation to perform it. If this were right, then the difference between making tea in order to quench thirst and making tea as an expression of forgiveness could certainly be explained simply by pointing to a difference in goals. In what follows I will argue that to understand the act as being one that is an expression of forgiveness is to understand the self that acts as one whose energy is not completely invested in the rationality of what it does. For it is to understand the self as having developed a certain quality of attachment to the value of forgiveness such that the act is not 'chosen' in the traditional sense of deciding which means will be adopted to achieve a particular goal.

Of course, a person might choose to perform an act that expresses forgiveness for a number of different reasons, any one of which will render the act a mere goal-oriented one. In such cases, the act can be completely understood in terms of its rationality. Some examples: a nun wanting to impress the mother superior as being the very best nun in the convent strives to be as forgiving as possible; a person wanting to avoid the unpleasantness of her own guilty feelings does the forgiving thing with such avoidance being the end in view; a person makes a cup of tea to make another person feel welcome rather than guilty because it would be a nuisance having the other at the staff meeting feeling guilty (it will interfere with what needs to be achieved at the meeting). In each of these cases, the agent utilises certain means in order to achieve some end, and the use is, in each case, rationally appraisable. The motivation of each can be understood simply in terms of certain desires and reasons. If we understand the goal-oriented nature of these acts, we have all that is needed in order to understand them.

The act under consideration is also goal-oriented, being aimed at making the other person feel welcome rather than guilty. But the act is not *merely* goal-oriented, since it expresses a value that has become central to the agent's own self-understanding: the self that acts here, in instantiating the value of forgiveness in what it does, defines and constitutes itself as a self of a particular kind, one for which the value of forgiveness is, in these circumstances, and at this time, *inescapable*.

The nun who acts forgivingly in order to be the best nun in the convent, the person who acts forgivingly in order to avoid the unpleasantness of her own guilty feelings, and the person who wants the other to feel welcome rather than guilty because it would be a nuisance to have the other feeling guilty at the staff meeting – all find a certain value in forgiveness. But for our agent, for whom the value of forgiveness is central to her self-understanding, and so for whom it is inescapable, this value is meaningful in a way that is different from the other cases. For it is not a value which she merely finds in the circumstances before her and which she experiences as one which she can either take or leave in the way in which the other agents, if they could achieve their aims without bothering with forgiveness, could do.

What our agent might well have in common with these other agents is an understanding of the value of forgiveness as being important for her society or community. But even though she shares this with the others, she finds that it is also meaningful *for her* in such a way that, in these particular circumstances, she finds she cannot but be actively concerned with respect to it, no matter what story we tell about the goal she wants to achieve and how else it might be achieved by her (or by someone else).

The contrast with the other examples might best be understood in terms of the quality of attachment that our agent has to the value of forgiveness, or in terms of the way in which this value attracts her. This attachment and attraction cannot be accommodated by the mere rationality of what she does.

Despite the fact that she may be full of doubts concerning her relationship with the other, the meaning of forgiveness is something that now attracts her. It is as though she responds to a call, initiated by this value, to act in such-and-such a way, and she finds that, whether she likes it or not, she is, in these particular circumstances, actively concerned that she express forgiveness.[12] We can explain why the action of making the tea takes on a special meaning for her in terms of her having developed an affective attachment[13] to this value. Forgiveness is not for her merely a means to an end. It is rather a value which she finds has a congruence with her own conception of what is *good as such*: this is why we say that this value has become central to her self-understanding.

So we are not helped to understand the agent's motivation by simply seeing the act as one where certain (rationally appraisable) means are employed to the achievement of some goal. To explain and understand the agent's motivation we must look, not merely at what the agent values, but also to the agent's conception of what is good as such: we must look at the *kind* of worth that she attaches to certain values, at the way in which these values attract her, and at the quality of attachment she has to them.

Understanding the circumstances and the value as she does, a certain kind of action presents itself to her as being practically necessary, while certain other types of actions are for her now impossible.[14] Yet it is not the requirements of practical reason that are categorically binding for her, but rather *her own conception of what is good as such*, and her wanting to be consistent with this conception.[15]

Moreover, what is causally efficacious is not the desire to make welcome, but rather the fact that the desire to make welcome is expressive of forgiveness, and that this conforms with her conception of what it is to be a good person.

Thoughts concerning what kind of person it would be good to be may seem to some people too indulgently self-reflective to qualify as being part of moral deliberation, which they believe must concern itself exclusively with other-regardingness. However, I see no need to restrict the realm of the moral to other-regardingness. I take the Aristotelian position that there are certain standards and ways of being and of acting which make a person into a good example of what a person is and should be, and that achieving such goodness does not compete with, but is rather intrinsic to, being morally good in the strict other-regarding sense. In any case, the agent I describe comes to a conclusion about what sort of person it would be good to be as a result of focusing on the feelings and needs of another, and on the value of forgiveness and making welcome in such circumstances. One might say that her desire to be a certain sort of person is parasitic on a previous moral understanding. So her self-concern regarding what kind of person she would be making herself into were she to act (or refrain from acting) in a certain way, is not in any way narcissistic: without a prior concern regarding how the other should be treated, this self-concern would not arise.[16]

Thus, though the self of an agent performing a significant action is crucially involved in the action, the action itself is not in any way self-oriented, but entirely other-oriented.[17] The action is directed at the other, though the significance of the act has a bearing on the agent.

Our agent is attracted to the value of forgiveness on account of its perceived inherent goodness: its goodness does not depend on some other condition being fulfilled (e.g. it does not depend on the other recognising that she is being forgiven). Nor does it depend on what might be achieved by her enacting it (e.g. it does not depend on the achievement of a reconciliation between her and the other). She values forgiveness as an end and not merely as a means. Because of where she locates the value of forgiveness and because of the way in which she values it, we say that she values forgiveness non-contingently.[18]

An agent can be affectively attached to a non-contingent value but not find this particular value to be the appropriate one to enact in certain particular circumstances. Given the particular circumstances, she may find some other value to be more pressing, but this need not alter her attachment to the value that she finds she must here relinquish: this can remain valuable for her because of what it is, and the significance of the value still need not depend for her on any condition of the world being fulfilled. That is, it can remain for her a non-contingent value to which she retains an affective attachment, but her assessment of the circumstances might be such that some other value presents itself as more salient.

This is to say that circumstances may arise in which an agent of significant action will need to set aside what she takes to be a non-contingent value, in order to act in a way that her understanding of the particular circumstances requires. In such cases a sense of loss and/or regret will not be uncommon. For what is required of the agent is that she distance herself from the very value that accords with her conception of how it would be good to lead a life.[19] A capacity for such distancing enables an agent to choose and act coherently despite being confronted with moral dilemmas and 'impossible choices' where, no matter which option is chosen, there will be an inescapable loss of value.

Since a central concern of an agent of significant action is to properly understand what, in the circumstances, would be the good and right thing to do, she is an agent who has an ever-present readiness to distance or detach herself from non-contingent values to which she is affectively attached: in order to see, and be able to act in accordance with, the good and sufficient reasons before her for acting differently.[20]

This means that an agent of significant action is engaged in an ongoing process of growth and self-transformation. So the self of significant action is a dynamic rather than a static construction. The next section explores the self-transformation that is central to significant action.

SIGNIFICANT ACTION: MAKING A REASON INTO ONE'S OWN REASON

The motivation of significant human behaviour is grounded in an agent's focusing on and coming to a certain understanding of some reality external to her own self that is held to be of non-contingent value. In responding to her understanding by acting in a certain way, the agent makes a reason she recognises for action into a reason *for her* and, in so doing, transforms her own self.

Choices of significant human actions, for example the job one chooses, the person one marries, the commitments one has, the kinds of relationships one has with others, where and the manner in which one chooses to live, are choices which give direction to a person's life: they are choices of self-realisation and self-actualisation. They are choices through which a person expresses and manifests what he intrinsically is. These are choices which are made after having engaged in 'strong evaluation' (C. Taylor 1977).[21]

According to Charles Taylor (1977), a human agent can be concerned not only with mere preference but also with the non-contingent value of what is done. The agent Taylor describes does not flee from the enemy because of a contingent conflict with some other desire or goal, but because cowardice *consists* in this, and the mode of life he values necessarily includes courage. An agent capable of significant action incorporates into his actions what he holds to be of ultimate, non-contingent value.

Not fleeing from the enemy depends on the agent having first focused his attention on, and understood, just what it is he would be succumbing to by fleeing in these circumstances. It is, in the first instance, a focusing on something quite unconnected with his own self. This results in his understanding that fleeing from the enemy in these circumstances is cowardly, an understanding of what cowardice is, and an understanding that by fleeing here a person does what is cowardly. In understanding these things, he attributes a certain meaningfulness to 'coward' that this concept may have for him previously lacked. If there is a self-consciousness here, it is as yet minimal.

On understanding, in its (now full) meaningfulness, what he would be doing by fleeing – i.e. the cowardly thing – the agent then cannot do this. Reflective evaluation is followed by reflective self-evaluation, and this necessarily involves a certain self-consciousness. In doing the cowardly thing, one makes oneself into a coward. The concern is now with the quality of one's motivations and actions rather than merely with outcomes or quantities of satisfaction. It is this self-consciousness which facilitates but, I maintain, does not ground the transformation of the self which is definitive of significant action.

The self-transformation depends, as we have seen, on a prior attention having been paid to some reality external to the self. This attention motivates a particular kind of response to the world: the action of fleeing becomes an object of reflection, is understood in its full significance as an act of cowardice, and is responded to and acted on by the agent in the world with rejection.[22]

An animal flees from danger because it perceives the danger as a threat. We might say that not fleeing from the danger conflicts for it with some other desire it has. Unless the bird flies off on hearing the familiar sound of the bell tied around the cat's neck, it will not feel the comfortable safety of its nest again. Yet the bird's behaviour is not mediated by belief at all. And it acts rationally without being able to express in words the rationality of what it does. Despite the fact that the bird does not articulate its action, we are able to understand the act's rationality. We do this by externalising through verbalisation what the bird is doing. We can reconstruct a rational practical syllogism for the bird's action. Moreover, what the bird does is reducible to the rationality of what it does. Unless we think that its life can be meaningful for it, unless we think the bird can be self-interpreting and self-defining, its actions are not, and cannot be, significant ones.

It is when a human agent gives consideration to what she values and so to what she wants to constitute her will, and assents only to a will that she wants, that we have the possibility of significant action.[23] It is now that she experiences herself as one who is capable, by that initiation, of determining what kind of will she will have, and so of determining, defining and affirming what she, in her actions, is.

In making such a decision and determining what she will be, she experiences an integration, a harmony and a consistency of a kind that is not exhausted by the formal consistency of the instrumental rationality of her actions. She creates a consistency and harmony between the way in which her actions define her and the way in which she views herself. Having a concept of what is valuable and worthwhile, and so of the kind of self it would be good to have, she makes her self into what she wants it to be by acting as she does. Her actions then provide her with an experienced congruity with her own self-hood. This is the 'ethical consistency' to which I have referred above. I call it an 'ethical' consistency because it necessarily involves a valuation of great ethical importance: what kind of life it would be good to lead and, with this, what kind of person it would be good to be. This consistency is ethical in a second way: its achievement requires the exercise of a courage which is of fundamental ethical significance: the courage to authentically be one's own self.[24]

One way in which this ethical consistency differs from a formal rational consistency is that a person is to be held accountable for a lack of it in a way that is different from his accountability in the case of rational inconsistency. 'He could have done otherwise' can be true if he could have seen and transcended the irrationality of what he did. Anyone who has the capacity for rationality could, barring exceptional circumstances, have done the rational thing. But 'If only he had paid proper attention, he would have caught the right train' is a quite different criticism from 'If only he had properly thought through what he was actually doing, he would have treated his daughter like a daughter ought to be treated instead of like a household drudge'. In this latter case, 'he could have done otherwise' captures a quite different criticism and a quite different sense of 'could have' from the train-catching case. What he needed to do was quite different in each case in order to be able to do otherwise. Ethical consistency is more than rational consistency.

In the remainder of this chapter I will show that the intentionality of significant actions expresses one's moral aspirations in a way that the intentionality of merely rational actions does not. We will see that significant actions reveal more of what goes deep with a person.

Failing to catch the right train could have been avoided by being more rational: taking in and concentrating on all the information at the station would have ensured it. He had reason to catch the right train; no more work on his part was needed in order for him to take this reason as his reason. There being a reason for him to do it was reason enough for him to take it as his reason. Being more rational was all that was needed in order for him to have done otherwise.

In the father/daughter case I am envisaging, no amount of taking in and concentrating on information would have led him to treat his daughter any differently. The kind of 'focusing of attention' or the 'just and loving gaze' to which Iris Murdoch refers is, as will be seen below, motivated by something which would not enter into this man's deliberations, no matter how much information and facts he gathered. Even information regarding the proper relationship that should exist between father and daughter would have probably failed, by itself, to get him 'to have done otherwise'. For while such information might have communicated to him a reason to treat his daughter differently, what he would need, in order to treat her differently, would be to take this reason as a reason *for him*. Rationality alone is not enough to do the work that is needed here in order for him to have done otherwise.[25]

Now treating his daughter like a household drudge need not be, by itself, irrational, although there are some who would say it is irrational since, in doing it, he failed to pay proper attention to what he was doing – in the sense of failing to pay proper attention to its significance. Yet it remains the case that despite knowing and understanding all there was to know and understand regarding the circumstances of his daughter, and despite his fulfilling what has widely been taken in the philosophical literature to be the requirements of rationality, the man could quite rationally conclude that certain things needed to be done, and the most efficient way was to get his daughter to do them.

To those who want to say that an action is rational only if a person has reflected sufficiently on its significance, I reply that I have trouble here with 'sufficiently'. I believe we are entitled to call this man's action rational, but with the qualification that it could have been more rational had he reflected better, or more, or differently, and so we can say that his action would have been 'more rational' had he had a better understanding of, or deeper insight into, what he was doing.

While we can admit that his action is rational, we do not call it significant action unless we tell a special story about it. For if the man needs certain things to be done and sees his daughter's doing them to be the most efficient way of getting them done, and for this reason treats her as a household drudge, the rationality of his treatment of her exhausts its significance. There is nothing more to consider in an attempt to gain more understanding of what he is doing.

It is when we consider what goes into his changing the way in which he treats her, after having given consideration to 'what it is he is actually doing', that we can come to understand his changed action as being significant. Reflecting on what it is he is actually doing, and contrasting this with what he in fact values, can lead him to consider the nature of his own will, and what he can come to see is exactly what kind of will he then has, and so what he is making himself (and her) into by treating her that way. He will still need certain things to be done, and getting her to do them will still be the most efficient way of getting them done, but now there can be for him other considerations.

These other considerations pertain to a certain understanding he comes to have of his daughter and her needs, one that does not merely cause a change in his treatment of her (the motivation to treat her differently is not merely a causal consequence of his changed understanding), but rather the motivation to change his treatment of his daughter is *constituted* by this change in his understanding. And the significance of his changed treatment of her is grounded in considerations that are *other-concerned*. For his changed treatment of her can be seen to be grounded in his activity of focusing on, understanding, and then responding to, what he recognises to be a certain reality external to his own self: in this case, the reality of his daughter *as another person*.

There are two quite distinct descriptions that might be given of the father in explaining his changed behaviour. Only the second encompasses significance.

According to the first description, certain empirical features of the daughter that the man may or may not have noticed before now register with him as being important. For example, he comes to see that his daughter is very pretty, that she has a beautiful singing voice, that she is artistically talented, and that she deserves better treatment than he had been giving her. He comes to see that she really ought to have singing and painting teachers, and that time should be set aside for her to develop her talents to the fullest possible extent. According to this description, the father's focusing on the daughter's empirical aspects and his seeing them as important leads him to an understanding of his daughter which *causes* him to treat her differently. What he understands is that by treating her as a household drudge he was failing in his role as a father. His wanting to be a certain sort of father might be seen as motivating his changed treatment of his daughter.

According to the second description, the father comes to understand that there are certain implications of treating *anyone* as a drudge, that treating persons in that way means that one does not place any value on how they feel or on what they need as individuals. What he comes to understand when he changes his behaviour is that his daughter is not a mere functional being, but is a growing adult with her own feelings, needs, judgements and aspirations. What he understands is that his treatment of her entails that he does not see her in that way at all. Here, the motivation to treat her differently is not a mere causal consequence of his changed understanding, as it is in the first description, but his changed treatment of her is rather *constituted* by his changed understanding. So one says that his motivation to treat her differently is constituted by his coming to see her 'as a person' or 'as an individual'.

It is not the case, according to this second description, that he merely comes to have sympathy for her. Rather, he sees either that he must deny that there is a person there or, if he accepts she is a person, some change in his behaviour is required, otherwise he would not be honest in saying that he saw her differently. Without changing how he treated her he would be engaging in some kind of self-deception.

The first description is compatible with the father not coming to see his daughter 'as a person', and his changed treatment of her is only contingently connected with what he comes to understand. For what he may come to understand is something about society's expectations, or something about his 'sense of role-responsibility'[26] as a father. So here, if he changes his behaviour *vis-à-vis* his daughter, it is because of his coming to hold as valuable the kind of behaviour appropriate to the father/daughter relationship.[27] But the understanding he gains of his daughter here is compatible with his not changing his treatment of her. For he might decide that even though she needs teachers and time for herself, his needs are more pressing than hers. Only if he sees her talents and needs as being equally or more important than his own needs, will he change his behaviour. Moreover, his change in understanding here, and the reason he sees there is to treat her differently, is quite compatible with this reason not being made into a reason *for him*.

It is only when the change in understanding is *constitutive* of the changed behaviour that a reason there is to treat her differently becomes a reason for *him*. Only then do we have significant action. For it is only then that, in changing the way he treats his daughter, the father's self is reconstituted in such a way that it is in complete congruity with his own ideals. For he makes a commitment that is at once ethical and ontological and, in acting in accordance with this commitment, transforms his own self. This transformation involves his making the reason he saw to act differently into *his* reason.

He may still want his daughter to do certain things for him. But now he does not want this want to determine his will because, having a different understanding of values pertaining to his daughter and her needs, he also understands the significance of, and what is entailed by, allowing this want to determine his will. So he changes what will determine his will, and makes himself into a different sort of father.

It would be right to say that he now wants to be a certain sort of father more than he wants to get certain things done by getting his daughter to do them. (This would also be true of the first description.) But if someone asked why he now has this want, we would need to refer to his new understanding of the significance of wanting his daughter to do these things for him, and of what this entailed. We would also need to say that the motivation of his now significant action is not to be located, in the first instance, with his wanting to be a certain sort of father, but rather with a certain understanding he comes to have of this individual who is his daughter.

So we must say that the father does not change the way he treats his daughter in order to fulfil his desire to become a certain sort of father (here, were the desire absent, he would not change his behaviour), but that he does so because of the new understanding he has. In the case of the former possibility, were the costs too great, he might choose not to make himself into the kind of father he now wants to be. But in the case I am portraying, given his understanding, certain alternatives are no longer alternatives for him, no matter what the costs might be of his not choosing them: his new understanding rules out the possibility for him of performing certain types of actions. While his changed treatment of his daughter is still the product of means–ends reasoning (he does certain things in order to promote the satisfaction of his daughter's needs), the significance of his action is not at all grounded in means–ends reasoning, but is grounded instead in his new understanding of values and reasons that pertain *exclusively to her*. He has looked to the specific needs of this particular other person who is his daughter, and the result of his moral work is the gaining of a deepened understanding of her as a person.

But the main moral work he does does not consist in his changing the way he treats her. His changed behaviour can be seen instead to be a result of the moral work in which he engages: a work that culminates in an understanding that creates and determines the nature of his own will as well as of himself as a particular father and as a father of a certain kind. His changed treatment of her is significant action because it is a direct expression of what are now deeply held values of his which, by being expressed in action, are transforming of his own self.

One might here compare Murdoch's description of the moral activity engaged in by the mother-in-law who, through being moved by justice and love, comes to see her daughter-in-law in a new moral light. She gives 'careful and just attention to an object which confronts her' (Murdoch 1970: 17). It is not in her capacity of 'mother-in-law' or in virtue of her standing in any particular kind of relationship with her, or because she wants to be any particular type of person or mother-in-law, that she alters her vision of the daughter-in-law. Rather, 'M *looks* at D, she attends to D, she focuses her attention' (Murdoch 1970: 22). It is not to any aspect of her own self, or to her own self under any particular description, that M looks; she looks exclusively to D, and the moral progress that she makes is not dependent on her awareness of any moral category or relationship. Nor is it dependent on anything she outwardly does.

Murdoch does not have M doing anything outwardly as a result of this moral work of hers, but if she did, we should say that M's actions would be significant ones since they would be expressive of values pertaining to a reality external to her self: values that she came to understand due to this moral work of hers, while being at the same time transforming of her own self. In coming to understand and to see D in a new light, her actions with regard to D would express this new vision of her.

Murdoch says that at the moment of action all the moral work is already done. In the case of M, this consists in her focusing exclusively on the particularity of D and seeing her as an individual. The Good is sovereign for Murdoch because it guides one in such a way that one is able to focus unself-concernedly on the particularity of another.

Returning now to the man who changes the way he treats his daughter: what is ethically fundamental is his understanding and valuing of his daughter as an individual or 'as a person'. If he were to change his treatment of his daughter because he came to value the kind of behaviour that was appropriate in those circumstances, and this without first reaching an understanding of his daughter as an individual, we should complain that this man is concerned more with appropriate behaviour than with his daughter. And we should have a similar complaint if his changed treatment of her were grounded in his valuing being a certain sort of father.

When the other is seen as an individual, and the meeting of her needs is held to be in itself valuable, the change in behaviour that is grounded in these valuations expresses an existential commitment which transforms the self. It is an existential commitment because it asserts what is here and now and in itself of concrete importance. It transforms the self because the person's will becomes determined by the thought of what another individual needs, and by placing a value on the meeting of those needs. The father wants to have a self

106

that values certain things, but in order to want this, he must understand the significance of those values. The causal direction is from 'the understanding' to the 'wanting to value'.

This grounding in an understanding of another human being is different from other types of grounding: the desire to understand is not grounded in some other want. It is not like a desire to understand engineering in order to pursue one's desire to build better bridges. This desire to understand (ourselves, others, the universe) is not a desire we have in order to achieve anything at all in particular. It is instead a desire which is part of our ontological predicament: we are 'making sense of' beings such that having this desire to understand is for us to be motivated by it. It would perhaps be more accurate to refer to this 'desire' as an 'aspiration'.

The desire to understand another human being might be seen to have its motivation in two sources. The first is provided by values internal to understanding itself; understanding has its own drawing power in virtue of goods (truth, coherence) internal to it. So what might be seen to motivate Murdoch's mother-in-law to focus on the reality of her daughter-in-law is not some other want, but rather understanding (and goods internal to understanding) itself. The desire to understand arises from a sense of inadequacy, of a lack, or of ignorance; to want to understand is to want to overcome one's own inadequacy or ignorance, and so it is another way of wanting to be true to oneself: one wants one's actions to be guided, not by ignorance or inadequacies, but by one's values. The desire to be true to oneself is a categorical desire, and it presents one with an imperative. For it is not a desire with respect to which one could choose to be either active or inactive: it would be difficult to make sense of a person who understood the value and significance of being true to herself, and yet chose not to be.

The second kind of motivation to understand another person might be seen to have its source in the agent's own sense of justice or fairness. Accordingly, Murdoch's mother-in-law suspects that certain inadequacies in herself (being old-fashioned, conventional, narrow-minded, snobbish and jealous) (Murdoch 1970: 17) might be things which prevent her from understanding her daughter-in-law justly. Her attending to her daughter-in-law is an expression of her desire to understand her justly, and out of the new understanding she gains of her, she comes to value her. Here, the motivation to understand is not merely goods internal to understanding itself, but also her own sense of justice.

Of course, when the object of understanding is another human being, the distinction between these two sources of motivation to understand becomes rather blurred. For it is difficult to see why one would be concerned with knowing the truth about another person unless one was also concerned that the other be perceived and/or treated justly.

The mother-in-law's valuing of her daughter-in-law derives from her capacity to understand her. But while understanding causes the mother-in-law to value the daughter-in-law, it does not provide a rational basis for this valuing. She does not exercise her capacity to understand *in order to* come to value her; she does not engage in a means–ends activity. There is no rational foundation for her focusing on and understanding her daughter-in-law. For this understanding is a non-contingent value which does not depend on the desirability or goodness of anything else in order for one to choose it.[28]

In a similar way we have seen that what is fundamental for the father to come to value his daughter and the meeting of her needs, is a certain understanding of her and her needs. Having this understanding, what he then must do is an expression of his own character.[29] Williams writes that 'to be an expression of character is perhaps the most substantial way in which an action can be one's own' (1981d: 130). It is by performing actions that are 'one's own' that one builds integrity and finds significance.

There is no real argument in my sketch of the father and his daughter. In using the example I have aimed to convince the reader, not by taking her through a number of irrefutable logical steps, but by articulating the capacity that a self has to find value and meaning in a certain understanding of another human being and her needs, and, in directing its energy towards the other, to at the same time transform itself. This transformation of self, while being a consequence of significant action, is not separable from the activity of understanding and responding to another human being as a person. The transformation of self and the response to the other are interdependent.

We can now see why the making of a reason into one's own reason is so central to my account of significant action. For significant action involves the important choice of what one will be: in making this choice, an agent participates in the actualisation of what he considers to be valuable by incorporating it into what he is and does. This is to say, in effect, that the reason he sees there is to act in a certain way is made by him into *his* reason.

This choice concerning what kind of person one will be is, to be sure, a rational choice, but as we have seen, the significance of the choice is not reducible to its instrumental rationality. It is a choice which, when enacted, also encompasses ethical and ontological dimensions. For the constitution and transformation of the moral self is entailed by there being such a thing as significant action.

So being a moral agent, on my view, involves placing oneself in a situation of constant risk. For in actively being a moral agent, it would seem that one must constantly risk changing one's moral identity. Since certain values to which one is non-contingently committed may, according to one's understanding of the particular circumstances before one, need to be set aside in order to pursue some other value (also seen as non-contingently valuable) that the situation demands, being a moral agent may need to involve distancing oneself from those very values that are constitutive of one's self-identity.[30] This does not mean that one loosens one's identification with the value from which one detaches (one's self-identity is not threatened), but in effecting this detachment, and pursuing the new value, one transforms one's moral self since the new value becomes incorporated into the conception one has of what one morally is. What is at stake in being a moral agent, on my account, is any fixed conception of moral identity that a person might have. This feature of my account distinguishes it from both a Kantian or utilitarian theory and, indeed, from any moral theory that emphasises rationality as being of central importance.

My account is also to be distinguished from Bernard Williams' writings (1973; 1981a; 1981b; 1981c), which see the need to set aside deeply held values as a threat to selfhood. My account sees this need rather as a causal agent of the transformation and reconstitution of the moral self, and so as being of great moral importance.

We now need to consider why a person should engage in significant actions and be a moral agent. Someone might claim that she sees no compelling reason to bother with significant actions, and that if significant action is a mark of moral agency, then she is quite content not to be a moral agent. In other words, the question to be addressed is why one should not be content to not be a moral agent. In the next two chapters I will show that a person who is content not to be a moral agent misses out on a certain relation that she can have to her own self, a relation that is distinctive of living a human life. This is to say that a person who is content not to engage in significant actions is a person who, in living her life, misses out on an important constituent of what it is to be a human being.

CHAPTER VI

Valuing the self and moral life

a man should be a lover of self; but in the sense in which most men are so, he ought not.

(Aristotle 1941: 1169b1–2)

INTRODUCTION

If significant action is to be maintained, a relation to the self as a bearer of predicates of significant action is required. This relation is not captured by standard modern conceptions such as self-esteem and pride. The modern conceptions do not capture what is central to Aristotelian thought and, following Aristotle, I will call the relation that a good person has to his self 'love of self'.[1]

Being a lover of self is central to Aristotle's accounts of friendship and virtue. He saw this relation as extendible to others; according to him, one must relate to oneself in a certain way before one is able to relate to others in that same way: 'Friendly relations with one's neighbours, and the marks by which friendships are defined, seem to have *proceeded from* a man's relations to himself' (1166a1–3, my emphasis). I will present love of self as emerging from the connection between the performance of significant actions and self-transformation.

Modern conceptions of the various kinds of relations that a person may have to himself begin with the relation that he has to others, and they extrapolate from this relation to others and arrive at certain conclusions regarding the relation a person may have to himself.[2] Aristotle reverses this direction: his account of friendship grows out of his account of the relation in which a virtuous person stands to himself. This is the direction that my account will follow. In this respect my account of what makes a self moral overlaps with

111

that of Rousseau: we both go from what is true of an inner relation to the self to what is true of outer relations.[3]

My account contrasts with utilitarian and Kantian accounts. My complaint against utilitarian and Kantian theorists does not lie so much with any particular proposals they put forward regarding what it is that makes an action a 'moral' action, or with respect to what they take to be the criterion of moral goodness or moral agency, as much as with the fact that they systematically neglect a particular relation to the self that I believe needs to be emphasised. So it is not so much the content of their theories to which I take exception; I take exception to their mode of procedure: what I would most complain about regarding Kantian and utilitarian theorists is their manner of investigating the moral agent.

The following section continues my investigation of the moral agent.

LOOKING FOR A RELATIONSHIP TO THE SELF: WAYS OF VALUING THE SELF

An agent of significant action, being concerned with the quality of her own motivations, and with how these bear on the constitution she makes of her self, places a particular kind of value on her own self. Yet 'attributing a measure of value to oneself' may be covered by a number of concepts: it varies between meaning what Hume termed 'pride' and considering oneself to be a worthy and capable human being. Yet these ways of self-valuing do not exhaust the ways in which a person may value her own self. Nor do these fit the way in which certain cares and concerns about the self present themselves. We need another concept to cover the experience of self-caring and self-valuing not captured by the conventional terms, one that has different properties. Following Aristotle, I call this other kind of self-valuing 'love of self', but my account extends beyond what can be found in Aristotle.

I begin with a negative characterisation of love of self. Since the concept I am after is not easily captured by those found in much contemporary literature, I will differentiate it from these other conceptions.

Stephen Darwall writes: 'Whatever qualities ground our self-esteem are qualities of which we are proud' (1983: 153). Darwall refers here to a valuing of self that, if accurate, is in proportion to a person's objectively observable qualities and achievements or to her correct judgements of these. This self-valuing is closely connected to 'pride', and it serves to indicate how worthy and capable a person considers herself to be. It is caused, or perhaps even constituted, by the judgements a person makes of her own observable qualities and achievements.

This kind of self-valuing is modelled on the valuing of others: self-esteem and the esteem of others are quite symmetrical (Thomas 1978: 259). Just as we can find out how much esteem we have for another by examining our assessments of her, so we can find out how much esteem a person has for her own self via a scrutiny of *her* self-assessments.

Just as our esteem of others is grounded in judgement pertaining to their qualities and achievements, so the kind of self-valuing involved in self-esteem and pride is also grounded in an assessment of one's own qualities and achievements.[4] The way in which we value others is extended to the way in which the self values itself. By contrast, 'love of self' is not grounded in any assessment or judgement regarding qualities and achievements.[5]

When a person makes a mistake regarding how worthy and capable she is, we say that her self-esteem is 'mistaken', or that her pride is misplaced, the 'mistake' being located in the assessment she makes of the material evidence which provides the grounds for her feelings of worth. Her qualities and achievements stand in an evidence relation to her self-esteem and, if the evidence is mistaken, her self-esteem is the result of a mistaken inference.[6]

Just as our mistaken evaluations of another can result in our mistakenly esteeming the other, so mistaken self-evaluations can result in an elevated or lowered self-esteem, both of which might be shown to be unwarranted. The direction is from what is true of external relations to what is true of internal relations. By contrast, love of self, not being grounded in judgement regarding qualities and achievements, cannot be 'false', 'mistaken' or 'unwarranted' in the same way.

Moreover, according to conventional conceptions, the appropriateness of the value placed on the self is objectively verifiable. Its non-verifiability can be revealed by taking a standpoint divorced from any one particular perspective, since in the case of 'accurate' self-valuing, the qualities judged must not be qualities that a person merely thinks that it would be good for *herself* to have, but they must be qualities that are 'admirable or estimable in anyone' (Darwall 1983: 153). So self-valuing, on the conventional conception, is based on those aspects of the self conceived of as being, in principle, applicable to anyone else. It refers to features of the self which are impartially and impersonally discoverable, not to features of the self conceived of in its particularity. It does not deny that the object of self-valuing is the self, but it is believed to be so in an impersonal way. This connects with the fact that values which, on this conception, ground the attribution of value to oneself must also be impersonally baseable and intersubjective (Darwall 1983: 153).

Consistent with this outline is William James' belief that people can arrive at a sense of their own worth by employing communal standards: '[a man] may... truly *know* his own worth by measuring it by the outward standard he applies to other men' (1890: 328). The evaluative relation to the self involved here requires the belief that others would share one's evaluations.

Darwall's account shares this common ground with James: the person who has self-esteem must believe that the qualities being assessed are 'genuinely' admirable, and be reasonable in his belief that others would esteem him for these same qualities (Darwall 1983: 153). If qualities are genuinely admirable, they would be admired by anybody, not merely by the agent himself.

Again, the direction is from the external to the internal: what is true of our evaluations of others is extended to the evaluations we make of our own selves, and so to our self-esteem. Love of self is not like this since it is not modelled on the relation in which others stand to one. Rather, it is a relation to the self that is extendible to others. This is consistent with Aristotle's account: the love of a character-friend is dependent on the relation that a virtuous person has to himself, i.e. it is dependent on his love of self (Aristotle 1941: 1168b6–7).

A slightly different version of the conventional conception of self-valuing drops the epistemological requirement that in building self-esteem the agent must believe others would share her evaluations, but requires instead that she universalise the basis of her self-esteem. That is, one must be prepared to esteem others for the same traits and grant these traits to be grounds for *their* self-esteem (Hill Jr: 1986).

Both versions take the valuing of self that is involved to be grounded in self-assessments, the values of which are, if not impartial and impersonal, then at least intersubjective. For the verifiability of self-esteem can be judged by abstracting from the particularity of the self rather than by focusing on features that are characteristic only of it: if one focuses on one's unique features, one will likely arrive at an assessment according to which one is more or less worthy than one in fact is. So to verify the soundness of self-esteem and pride one must go beyond what is incomparable about the self. We will see below that this is not true of love of self.

Rawls' account of 'self-esteem' or 'self-respect' follows the conventional conceptions (1972).[7] His account seems to be derived from that of William James. High self-esteem was taken by James to be the result of achievement approaching or meeting aspirations, and low self-esteem to be the result of a wide divergence between these:

> our self-feeling . . . depends entirely on what we *back* ourselves to be and do. It is determined by the ratio of our actualities to our supposed potentialities; a fraction of which our pretensions are the denominator and the numerator our success. Such a fraction may be increased as well by diminishing the denominator as by increasing the numerator.
>
> (1890: 310–11)

Since the numerator here is subject to the person's own self-assessment and judgement regarding her 'actualities', the fraction which 'determines' the way in which we value ourselves is dependent on rational self-assessment.

Rawls takes it that the parties to the original position would concur with James in regarding an absolute level of achievement as irrelevant to the maintenance of self-esteem (Rawls 1972: 441–2). As a primary good, Rawls presents self-esteem as depending on certain distributive arrangements, as well as being sensitive to distributive adjustments. For both Rawls and James, self-esteem need not be something comparative, and a consequence of their accounts is that it is possible for all persons to possess self-esteem: so long as they do not aim too high or associate with those whose abilities and achievements are much greater than their own, they can feel good about themselves. We will see below that love of self is associated with something more integral to the person than merely this.

Another consequence of the Rawlsian position is that if my self-valuing is arrived at as a result of my having successfully pursued a plan of life chosen in full knowledge of all the relevant facts,[8] a plan of life where my natural capacities were called upon,[9] then anybody else who made the same choice under the same conditions and was just as successful as I was, would, if his judgement and choice were accurate, have exactly the same self-esteem. By contrast, one may be just as successful as another person in pursuing a plan of life, chosen within Rawls' parameters, but fail to have love of self, while another, whose self-esteem matches one's own, is very much a lover of self.[10]

I will now describe the kind of self-valuing involved in love of self. We will see that love of self captures the relation to the self that falls out of the connection between significant action and self-transformation.

AN ALTERNATIVE WAY OF VALUING THE SELF

no one chooses to possess the whole world if he has first to become someone else... he wishes for this only on condition of being whatever he is.

(Aristotle 1941: 1166a20–3)

If we regard the conventional conceptions of self-valuing to exhaust the ways in which a person can value herself, then an explanation is needed for certain commonplace observations. I refer to observations of persons who are proud of their considerable achievements, who are not lacking in those feelings of self-worth which accompany the recognition of their own talents and qualities, and who have a secure sense of their own capacity to succeed. But these same persons experience their lives and actions as missing some important element, the presence of which would be experienced by them as lending their lives and actions the kind of reality and wholeness that is regarded as being truly valuable. This missing element is central to love of self. I will illustrate what is missing in the conventional conceptions by making use of Tolstoy's portrayal of Ivan Illych (Tolstoy 1986).[11]

Tolstoy portrays Illych as possessing qualities and achievements that gave him feelings of self-worth, and as being aware of how very well he was faring regarding how his achievements stood to his own aspirations. Among his qualities was 'an exactness and incorruptible honesty of which he could not but feel proud' (237). It was typical of Illych to do things 'with clean hands, in clean linen, with French phrases... with the approval of people of rank', being 'by nature attracted to people of high station... assimilating their ways... and establishing friendly relations with them' (236). He became Assistant Public Prosecutor, married well, and his life was 'pleasant and proper'.

Illych had plenty of reason to be proud of himself, and he possessed those feelings of self-worth which accompany the satisfaction that one is succeeding in all aspects of life. He firmly believed himself to be a worthy and capable human being:

> The consciousness of his power... the importance, even the external dignity of his entry into court... his success with superiors and inferiors... his masterly handling of cases... all this gave him pleasure and filled his life, together with chats with his colleagues, dinners and bridge. So... Illych's life continued to flow as he considered it should do – pleasantly and properly.
>
> (242)

Yet something was missing. For on his deathbed Illych comes to realise that, despite the good feelings he has for, and the value he and others place on, his qualities and achievements, he does not in fact evaluate his own self in a positive way at all:

> it is as if I had been going downhill while I imagined I was going up... I was going up in public opinion, but to the same extent life was ebbing away from me.
>
> (273)

Material, professional and social success, and the reflected esteem of others provided Illych with secure grounds for a certain sense of his own value. This value was reflected back to him in the form of his own image as seen in others' eyes. But these grounds failed to provide him with what was necessary for him to value his own self in the way I want to draw attention to here: they failed to provide Illych with a sense of the reality and integrity of what he had been engaged in doing with his own life and self. They failed to provide him with what was needed for him to be a lover of self. For, on his deathbed

> It occurred to him that his scarcely perceptible attempts to struggle against what was considered good by the most highly placed people, those scarcely noticeable impulses which he had immediately suppressed, might have been the real thing, and all the rest false.
>
> (276)

For the sake of those feelings of self-worth that come with pride in success and achievement, Illych had forgone the experience of living an authentic (and so a worthy) life. In deriving his sense of who and what he was from an image of himself as an object of admiration, he could only value himself by seeing himself as others saw him.

So on his deathbed Illych has serious doubts about his own self, and he does not value it in the way in which one would expect of a man of his position: one would expect him to place considerable value on his own self if the conventional conceptions of self-valuing were exhaustive of the way in which a person could value his own self. If we were to assume self-valuing to be always in proportion to observable qualities and achievements, and if Illych has no doubts about his position, rank and success, we would need to ask exactly what it is that throws him into the agonising self-doubt and self-despair he experiences during his last days.

Tolstoy makes it clear that Illych's self-doubt does not revolve around a wish that he had possessed different talents, or that he had chosen a different career in which to exercise these talents. Nor does he come to a realisation that there are different and better ways in which he could have achieved good feelings for his own self: he does not believe that he would have a more positive regard for his own self if he had invested his energies in more worthwhile ways. So he does not think that, had he incorporated different values into his life and his actions, his life and actions would then have been more significant. For Tolstoy tells us that whenever the thought occurred to Illych that the horror of his life might be the result of his not having lived his life as he ought to have done, 'he at once recalled the correctness of his whole life and dismissed such a strange idea' (273). On thinking about the 'legality, correctitude and propriety of his life' (275) Illych firmly dismisses the possibility that he had not lived as he ought to have done.

Thus the failure to value his own self in the way in which I want to draw attention to here is not grounded in questions pertaining to some other choice of life-plan which might for him have been the basis for an increased or a better pride.

The kind of self-reflection in which he engages and which focuses his low self-regard concerns rather the way in which he had colluded with, and allowed himself to be carried along by, certain causes which had decided for him what he would be. He had tolerated being acted on by causes which had determined how he would conduct himself in his life. There is one sense in which we would want to say that he did not *choose* his own life, despite the fact that he made all sorts of important decisions regarding his life. For the values which he incorporated into his life were *derived* values (or values that had been dictated by others)[12] rather than values grounded in his own reflective evaluation and understanding. These derived values operated for him as causes which he did not ever recognise and take as good reasons to act in any particular way. The derived values were never taken as reasons *for him* to act in such-and-such a way. Accordingly, the actions that expressed these values could not be what I have termed 'significant' actions. So, in retrospect, Illych sees his marriage as 'a mere accident' (273): Illych married his wife because 'his social circle approved of the match ... it was considered ... right ... by the most highly placed people' (239–40). He married because of the valuations and opinions of others. Moreover, he advanced in his career, not because he placed any particular value on the type of life which he would then lead, but because he had the talents required when new judicial institutions were introduced (237). And he allowed his career to determine every other aspect of his life: from his friendships, to his attitudes towards the authorities, his political opinions, and even a new style of personal grooming (239).

By saying that Illych had allowed himself to be acted on by causes which determined his manner of living, one indicates that at no point did he himself actively take responsibility for his own self, its conduct or its achievements. What he allowed himself to become was determined by forces external to his own self.[13] In Aristotelian terms, he had allowed his own rational agency to be subordinated to the pursuit of certain desired ends.[14] Aristotle says we *are* our intellect (1169a1–2): for him, subordinating what we are to anything else is a mark of an absence of virtue.

Illych's self-reflection consists in surveying other possible scenarios of self-making and, in his imagination, he renders inoperative the causes which led him to make himself into what he now sees he is. So, in retrospect, were it not for his possession of certain qualities and talents, and were it not for certain pressures which led him to his career, he might have acknowledged the need to incorporate what he perceived as being overridingly valuable into his life and actions. Being overriding, he knows that this value which he recognised then (he immediately suppressed this recognition whenever it surfaced) (276), and which he still now recognises, is particularly applicable *to him*, since it was *he* who had neglected

119

it. He now knows that, not having incorporated this value into his life and actions, he did, and still does, what goes against the inner dictates of his own being. In Aristotle's words, in his striving to 'possess the whole world', he had 'become someone else'. Not having fashioned his own self according to what he himself saw to be of ultimate value, but instead according to what others valued and wanted, the affective experience he had of himself was not one from which he could derive good self feelings. So his self-doubt is connected with the moral problem he must face concerning whether or not he can now, on his deathbed, act in accordance with what he recognises to be of non-contingent value.

The self-reflection that conduces to the kind of self-worth he lacks is quite different from that which provides the basis of his pride or his self-esteem. The positive regard he would like to have for his own self is one which would accompany his creating an authentic relation between himself and the world, and his living an authentic life,[15] and this is quite different from the feelings of worth connected with the pride he has for his talents and achievements. For, not having fashioned his own self according to what he saw and now still sees to be inescapably valuable, he feels proud of, but alienated from, his own family, talents and achievements.

Tolstoy makes it clear that the positive valuing and love of self which Illych finds is missing during those days before his death is not based on any assessment he might make of his talents or achievements since it is the kind of self-valuing and love that refers to an inner reality: this is a self-valuing which comes with the experience one has of one's own capacity to shape one's own self according to what one finds in the circumstances before one to be of ultimate importance. This self-valuing falls out of the relation between significant action and self-transformation: since Illych had never been an agent of significant action, he could not be a lover of self.

Let us now consider a quite different example in order to further clarify the kind of valuing and love of self I wish to invoke.

It is not unusual to notice that an ugly person can have a more positive regard for his own self than the beautiful.[16] The ugly person who acknowledges his own ugliness but values himself highly is not thereby necessarily proud of his ugliness: it is not a feature which he thinks of as one which, if possessed by others, would be a ground for *their* pride. Nor is it a feature, the self-assessment of which could be viewed as grounds for love of self. The crucial difference between an ugly person who, while acknowledging his own ugliness, has a positive self-regard and experiences himself as being in a state of ease with himself, and an ugly person who, because of his ugliness, lacks this positive self-regard and does not experience the same well-being, is not a difference in self-assessment regarding their own physical appearances. Instead, the ugly man who, due to his ugliness, does not feel good about his own self, is one who allows his ugliness to determine the manner in which he conducts himself, whereas in the case of the ugly man who builds a positive self-regard, the description 'ugly' is not something he allows any causal efficacy. The picture I am presenting is one where the latter man builds a conception of himself where there is no space for the description 'ugly'. It is a picture where the man's own ugliness is something which he acknowledges, but where ugliness is not something which he deems appropriate for him to take as a reason to act in any particular way.[17] The latter man, but not the former, is a lover of self.

In understanding what it is about the latter man that explains his positive self-regard and love of self, we do not need to refer to any opinion, taste or whim of his: it would be a mistake to portray him as thinking, for example, that physical appearance is completely unimportant; nor would it be accurate to present him as fooling himself that he is not as ugly as he in fact is. In order to understand his positive self-regard and love of self we must refer rather to how what he is engaged in doing with his own self is inextricably accompanied in a relationship of mutual reinforcement with the sense he has of his own self-worth so that he experiences himself in the particular way he does. The rest of this section will attempt to explicate this.

While his ugliness may provide him with grounds for a negative assessment of his physical appearance, it does not lead him to a negative self-attitude since he experiences this ugliness *as a mere passive subject or onlooker* of this particular attribute. He values his own self despite his self-acknowledged ugliness because ugliness is not something which is for him part of what he, *as subject and object*, makes himself into: it is not something which he actively incorporates into the constitution of his self.

It is not merely the case that self-assessments regarding external or bodily goods are of the wrong kind to ground love of self, and that the right assessments pertain to goods of the soul, such as intelligence or the moral virtues. It is rather that love of self does not require self-assessments made on the basis of any qualities whatever.[18] There is no one or interesting set of properties of the kind that is necessary and sufficient for pride or self-esteem which is necessary and sufficient for love of self.[19] Something of a quite different kind is necessary: the acknowledgement made by a person that he must make his self into something that he believes to be good. While it would be correct to point out here that to make something of one's self one needs, after all, to make something of one's qualities or properties, so that a possession of qualities is still necessary for love of self, a self-assessment in terms of the qualities is not necessary. The qualities are only relevant as belonging to the object of the person's self-making: what is relevant to love of self are not the person's qualities *per se* but the fact that the exercise of his own understanding has resulted in his seeing that such-and-such qualities are worthwhile developing in virtue of the place these qualities have in his own conception of what is good as such.

Moreover, while the valuing of qualities and achievements involved in conventional conceptions of self-valuing may follow from a mere possession of them (I feel proud of my musical skills because they are *mine*), the valuing of qualities and achievements involved in love of self follows from a person's making himself into one with those qualities (I value my musical skills because their development is the result of my own evaluations and choosings).[20]

When a person is a lover of self, the activity in which she engages when she evaluates and chooses involves a dynamic interaction between the characteristics she develops in forming her own self (such formation being dependent on nurture and upbringing),[21] and what she makes of her experience of herself and the world. 'Experience' here is not something passive (one need not be passive in experience), but refers to the person's active constitution of herself in the world. So being a lover of self means that a person is involved in a continuous self-creative activity.

It is to the way in which our two ugly people are constituted in the world that we must look to locate the crucial difference between them: when we look here we find that only the one who is a lover of self has acknowledged an ethical and ontological commitment to make something of his self.

The man who is a lover of self is engaged in an inner-directed employment of reason. He considers, for example, what he would be making of his self if he did not complete a certain project due to a believed unlikelihood of success by one whose physical appearance renders him unworthy or incapable of completing such projects. Having acknowledged a need to make something worthwhile of his own self, he is then actively concerned with the quality of his own motivations and with the bearing these have on the constitution he makes of his self. This concern is an essential aspect of the active valuing of self which attends the building of his positive self-regard and, having the kind of understanding he secures as a result of his self-reflection, it is a concern which is for him a crucial one.

The man who builds a positive self-regard gives 'careful and just attention' (Murdoch)[22] to the circumstances before him, an attention which results in the kind of understanding whereby he comes to hold certain values: values to which he is attracted because of their perceived inherent goodness, ones which he converts into a reason to act in certain ways.[23] So a desire for understanding is fundamental to his being a lover of self,[24] and it is the kind of desire which, as argued in Chapter 5, is not based on any other want: this kind of understanding, I have claimed, has its own drawing power in virtue of goods which are internal to it.[25]

This desire for understanding is a desire for something quite unconditional, and any criticism we might make of our ugly man who gains the understanding he seeks would need to be directed at what he now values as a result of his understanding, and we may want to say that he is making some type of moral mistake,[26] since the mistake concerns not his judgement of the circumstances, but of how he ought to conduct himself in life.

If we consider the case of his not allowing his ugliness to determine his acts, we portray his decision as being taken after the act of allowing this has been for him an object of reflection, and understood in its full significance as, for example, being a defeatist act. For this is a man who, having attended to and having come to a certain understanding of the particular circumstances and of the possible courses of action, follows up his understanding in the world by responding to and acting on what he now understands by rejecting his own ugliness as a reason to act in any particular way. Reflection has resulted in an understanding that to allow his ugliness causal efficacy is to accept defeat too easily. And in understanding this, 'the acceptance of defeat' takes on a new meaning for him. He follows up this reflection with reflective self-evaluation: in accepting defeat in such circumstances, one makes oneself into a person who too easily feels and becomes defeated. It is by means of a capacity which he finds within his own inner resources that he comes to understand not merely what it is in these circumstances that constitutes a too easy acceptance of defeat, but also the significance of what it would be *for him* to do such a thing.

The exercise of this capacity reveals the value of optimism, of striving and of courage, and these values are not experienced as ones which he merely recognises to be important for his community, ones that he can choose to either take as being important or unimportant. Rather, they are values which are meaningful for *him* in such a way that he finds that he *must* take them seriously. That is, he finds they are values that *he* must take seriously. So he finds that, in understanding the significance of these values, he cannot but be actively concerned with them. In understanding their significance, there is no alternative but for him to incorporate them into what he makes of his own self (since were he not to, he knows he would be missing out on what he recognises to be of incomparable value: the self-determination of his own self), and in so doing he shapes his own experience according to what he finds to be worthwhile. He finds that the capacity he has to choose comes from within himself[27] and, while not being indifferent to others' opinions, he finds he has the courage to resist certain promptings and pressures from without. The perception he has of his own capacity to do this, the recognition he has of a capacity in himself to decide things solely in terms of his own inner resources, means that he experiences himself, in his actions, as one who sustains an authentic relation between himself and the world. This gives him the experience of 'being good with his self' or of 'being whole with his self', which characterises the inner integrity and sense of invulnerability that accompany this kind of self-valuing.[28]

The process of evaluation in which our ugly man engages does not merely play a justificatory role; it also has a causal efficacy since it leads him to make a fundamental ethical commitment that is crucial to his love of self: to be one whose actions will be guided by those causes in himself which are acknowledged and welcomed as operative for him as reasons.

We find that the ugly person who, because of his ugliness, lacks this positive self-regard is one whose actions are not expressive of this ethical undertaking. For he is a man who, not having acknowledged a need to make anything of any particular significance of his self, allows his ugliness to be causally efficacious, and in so doing demonstrates that he does not consider the capacity to make something of one's self to be important. Perhaps he simply allows his ugliness to 'get him down', or he allows what will become of his self to be dictated by others. In either case, he does not engage in any reflection that might reveal in what way it is truly good to behave.

When, due to his ugliness, he does not complete a certain project, his will is avoiding of his own self: it does not take account of the possibility that the self may want the will to be different from what it is (Frankfurt 1971). Such consideration might lead him to acknowledge a need to make something of his self, for it might reveal, for example, the self-destructiveness involved in allowing his ugliness to determine his will. He could then not allow himself to have that kind of will. For if causes are seen as self-destructive, they cannot be taken as reasons.

Unless this man engages in a self-reflection which takes account of the ethical and ontological context in which he acts, he merely copes with an external situation. Merely being able to do this successfully, while being sufficient for the establishment of a relation to the self such as that involved in pride and self-esteem, is not sufficient for love of self.

This man's incapacity to value his self in the required way is not grounded in negative self-assessments, but is associated with a methodical avoidance of any thoughts regarding what it would be good to make of his own self. So if he does have feelings of self-worth, they will not be tied to the way in which he is fashioning his self, but rather to the surrounding circumstances. He may demonstrate certain abilities and talents, but without making the required commitment and taking responsibility for his own engagements with the world, he will be alienated from his own self and its achievements.[29]

By contrast, a person who is a lover of self has the capacity to make an undistorted assertion concerning what he finds to be truly good, and this without the expectation of any gain in satisfactions for his own self. Unless a person has this capacity, and can act in accordance with what he finds to be valuable and worthwhile, rather than being in possession of the kind of positive self-regard I am highlighting here, his feelings of worth may merely be consistent with the relation to the self that Hume called pride.

The positive self-regard which accompanies the acknowledgement of the need to make something worthwhile of one's self can be seen to pertain more closely to the active valuing of oneself rather than, as is true of conventional conceptions of self-valuing, to the passive seeing that one has value. Love of self and the positive self-regard that attends it, do not require that one judge oneself to be, for example, a good rather than an evil person. It requires instead that one actively incorporate certain standards of what one takes to be good and right into what one is and does. What implies an absence of this relation to the self is, then, not a negative assessment, for example being ugly, criminal, disgraced, unintelligent *per se*, since a recognition of these attributes together with a negative assessment of them can be quite consistent with love of self. Rather, we must look to whether the person acknowledges, and is committed to, the need to make something worthwhile of his own self. We must look to whether the person considers the living of an authentic life to be important.

In the next chapter I will further explore the difference between feelings of self-worth derived from pride and self-esteem on the one hand, and those derived from love of self on the other. When we properly distinguish love of self from relations to the self such as pride and self-esteem, it can be seen as centrally important for the constitution of the moral self.

CHAPTER VII

The ethical significance of love of self

the virtuous person loves herself as she really is, as a rational agent with a stable character that accords primacy to practical reason in the choice of ends.

(Irwin 1988: 390)

PRIDE, SELF-ESTEEM AND LOVE OF SELF

The distinction between the kind of self-valuing involved in relations to the self, such as self-esteem and pride on the one hand, and love of self on the other, must be clearly drawn if we are to understand the importance of love of self for the constitution of the moral self. The character-structure of a person who depends completely on pride for self-worth parallels that of a narcissistic personality type:[1] just as the latter is incapable of what we would regard to be genuine benevolent giving, so a dependence on pride for self-worth precludes the possession of a proper moral capacity.

Hume noticed that we feel pride, not because the thing of which we are proud merely exists, but because it is connected in some close way with ourselves: the proper object of pride for Hume is the self. I would have preferred Hume to have said that the proper object of pride is not the self as such, but the self considered in some aspect or other. Of course, Hume could hardly have made such a distinction since by the end of Book 1 of the *Treatise*, 'the self as such' has been revealed as a mere fiction, disposed of and replaced by the self of thought, memory and imagination.

However good Hume's analysis of pride might be, he is metaphysically debarred from holding that 'love of self' might describe a way that a person values her own self. For there is for Hume no 'self as such' to relate to or love. Any talk of 'love of self' in which we might engage buys into a metaphysics that, on his view,

127

we cannot have. So Hume makes no reference to any relation that resembles love of self, but if we wish to distinguish this relation from pride, we ought to say to begin with that love of self, in contrast to what Hume understands as pride and self-esteem, takes in the self as such.

A lover of self feels at ease with herself as such; it is not merely one aspect, or even several aspects of herself with which she feels at ease. By contrast, pride takes as an object the self considered in some particular aspect. The pride felt by a person for winning the tennis tournament has as its objects, first, the particular achievement, and second, her own self considered as an accomplished tennis player. Yet such a person need not have a positive regard for her own self in the way that a lover of self does.

As we have seen in the case of Ivan Illych in Chapter 6, a person may engage in positive accurate self-assessments, but have serious doubts about the evaluation of his own self.

While pride requires a possession of estimable qualities, love of self requires that these be ones that the possessor has chosen as qualities it would be valuable and worthwhile to cultivate, since they fit what she conceives a good life to consist of. A lover of self does not experience herself as a mere possessor of certain qualities and achievements, as might a person who is merely proud of these, but rather as a self-originating author who is capable of creating what she is. It is this process of self-creation and self-determination,[2] and not the attributes and character traits that may be the result of the process, that is involved in the development of love of self.

Thus a person does not need to achieve anything in particular in order to be a lover of self, but if achievement is relevant, then love of self requires that the person must conceive of values associated with her achievement as being a constitutive part of her self-understanding. This means that these values must be experienced by her as belonging to her inherently, as representing what she is engaged in doing with respect to her own self, as something without which she would be essentially different, and as something which is part of what she stands for.

While pride is felt for achievements that we and others value and care about, the possession of which issues in the conviction that one is worthy and capable, these achievements cannot by themselves provide a source from which a person's love of self might be derived.

For Rawls (1972: 441) self-esteem depends on our goals and achievements being valued or admired by others. Such dependence parallels the way in which a person's pride is related to a monitoring of how aspects of the self appear to an audience. Hume, for whom the non-metaphysical self is predicated on a mirroring relation,[3] points out that how various aspects of the self appear must be reflected back to the person in order for pride to be sustained. So insofar as a person relies on pride for feelings of worth, she experiences herself as depending for a sense of who and what she is on a reflected impression of herself.[4] Rawls' account does not differentiate between a person who builds an authentic relation between herself and the world by incorporating perceived values into the constitution she makes of her self, and one who accommodates her self to others' valuations and expectations in order to gain their esteem, so deriving good feelings for aspects of her own self. The notion of feeling at ease with one's self as such is left out of the accounts of those who confine their writings to relations such as pride and self-esteem. Yet feeling at ease with one's self as such is central to love of self.

The feelings of self-worth that accompany love of self are derived from a different source from those that accompany pride or self-esteem. The source, in the case of love of self, is the core of the person's own being, this being constituted by a commitment to certain non-contingent values. In the case of pride and self-esteem, the source is the external environment comprised of the recognition and attentions of others.[5] Unless resorting to drugs, perversions or some such artificial source, a person with no love of self will be dependent on pride or self-esteem for self-worth.

Now a person whose feelings of worth are *completely dependent* for their continued existence on the attentions of or on comparisons with others, can be seen to be guided by values that have their source in narcissistic tendencies. Any person, to some extent and in some circumstances, may resort to pride for self-worth, but 'pride-dependency' is characteristic of the narcissistic self, i.e. the self that believes and feels itself to be worthless unless it is being constantly admired and reminded by others of how wonderful it is.[6] The reflected confirmation and validation by others provides the narcissistic self with a limited range within which it experiences itself as worthy.[7]

It is not being suggested that what differentiates love of self from pride is the latter's narcissism: a proud person, or one who has self-esteem, is not thereby a narcissist. And pride does not need to be narcissistic to make it different from love of self. Yet pride relates to the narcissist *par excellence*. He is addicted to pride, since he has no other source of self-worth. Such a person, deriving no self-worth from within but depending completely for self-worth on external sources, is what I term 'pride-dependent'.[8] While love of self (which is predicated on a commitment to non-contingent values and so built on a solid core) is constitutive of the moral self, the self of a narcissist is built on an empty shell: while the latter may be a complex and effective structure, it has no core. Any values held by a narcissist are not his own, but belong to others, since the values are held by him for a reason other than his recognition of them as being non-contingent. The values are rather held because they assure him of a means to achieving self-worth, that is, the values he holds are merely contingent ones.

The chief concern of a narcissistic self is to secure its own feelings of worth; what it wants more than anything is to be treated as unique: without specialness it feels worthless. Since it draws its feelings of worth from *anything at all* in the environment that will treat it as unique, narcissistic preoccupations carry with them the danger of a wantonness which is antithetical to the development of love of self. For a narcissistic self has one ever-present supreme concern – to derive self-worth from *any occasion whatever* that can provide specialness.[9] Quality here is unimportant; what is important is the mere fact of specialness. This so-called 'fact of specialness' provides a narcissistic self with its sense of who and what it is; it can still have strong and positive feelings of self-worth, so long as it is able to keep deprivation at bay by maintaining its grip on the security provided by a positive reflected self-impression. But this self-worth turns out to be extremely insecure, being predicated on merely transient reassurances.

So a narcissistic self must defend its boundaries of specialness by clinging defensively to its fictional product. This defensive clinging rules out the possibility of love of self, since without the 'unconditional availability of the approving mirroring function of an admiring selfobject' (Kohut 1972: 386) a narcissistic self will experience a loss of self (Kohut 1972: 383) – i.e. the transient and fictional will appear as transient and fictional.[10]

Any contingent psychic or bodily change, or a change in the surrounding circumstances, has the potential of presenting this fiction for what it is. Accordingly, Ivan Illych, on falling ill, is confronted by the so-called 'fact of his specialness'. Having derived self-worth exclusively from the contingency of his talents and achievements, and from the reflected esteem of others, when these fade he is left with nothing which can compensate for the fact that he is not a lover of self.[11]

Positive reflected esteem from others had given Illych a certain good feeling or mood, but it was completely the wrong sort of thing to provide him with what is needed for the development of love of self. The feelings of self-worth that accompany pride and self-esteem (as is also true of the feelings of worth of one who is guided by narcissistic preoccupations) are achieved primarily by means of social transaction, and so in effect, they represent a merely reflected impression of one's own reality.

While it may be true that social institutions and the opinions of others influence the way we view ourselves and the things we hold to be valuable and worth pursuing, love of self, as Tolstoy went to such pains to show, is not dependent for its existence on social institutions or on the opinions of others. On the contrary, one might argue that a critique of social and political institutions, and of the opinions of others, is rather dependent on a person's love of self. To depend on social institutions and the opinions of others in order to perceive oneself as capable of striving for and having the ability to achieve those things which one holds to be valuable and worthwhile, is to lack what goes hand-in-hand with being a lover of self: a confidence in the integrity of one's *own* judgements, decisions and actions.[12]

A person lacking confidence in her own integrity may bolster her self by deriving feelings of self-worth from pride, and pride may then compensate for the fact that she is not a lover of self.[13] Pride and love of self can comfortably coexist, but those who are not lovers of self and need to use pride to compensate become vulnerable in their complete dependence on a comparison with, or on the compliments of, others. For a pride-dependent person has intense selfobject needs: without a constant feeding of the esteem and recognition of others, she will become depressed, or angry and resentful, doing her utmost to become what she perceives the world wants her to be. While we all need selfobjects, the difference for a pride-dependent narcissistic personality is that the selfobject is *crucial*. For, due to the fact that such a person is not a lover of self, she *depends completely* on selfobjects for self-worth.[14]

While a pride-dependent person may need to bolster her self by finding new sources of pride, to the extent that a person is a lover of self, she does not need to bolster her own self by focusing on particular aspects of herself which, by comparison with others or by means of the regard of others, she comes out ahead. She does not need to use aspects of her own self in this way since it is not difficult for her to be humble and to admit her particular shortcomings. If humility consists in the capacity to resist temptations to over-estimate oneself and one's accomplishments (Richard 1988: 255), a person who depends completely on pride for feelings of worth is far less likely to have the virtue of humility, since she must conceive of as many aspects of her self as possible as being excellent. Yet rather than being able to resist the temptation to overestimate her own accomplishments, the temptation for a pride-dependent person is to over-invest some particular aspect of herself as being crucial to her worth.

If this temptation is succumbed to, pride is apt to be unwarranted, and it can be seen to rest on a disproportionate allocation of value and importance to certain aspects of the self: to feel that one is valuable or worthy merely on the basis of one or several particular qualities or things that one possesses or has done, and to depend on these completely for self-worth, is to reveal a specific vulnerability when those limited assets on which one bases one's worth are threatened.[15]

By contrast, an ideal model of a lover of self does not need material evidence to sustain her integrity and authenticity. She has the capacity to be genuinely assertive or comfortably submissive since, unlike a pride-dependent person, she has no need to convince us or herself that she is worthy. Freed of the constraints that bind a pride-dependent person to bolstering her sense of worth, and not needing to convince herself and others that she does in fact have securely held values, she can readily admit her uncertainties. Such admission is far more difficult for a pride-dependent person whose values are held tentatively, being related more to what others think and say than to the experienced reality she has of her self, i.e. to her experience of what she is engaged in doing with her self.

Since the qualities of our ideal person who is a lover of self include the positive and true holding of values, she does not need to pretend, and therefore has the possibility of *real* rather than false humility. Moreover, when she performs a benevolent action, it is truly benevolent, rather than self-centred: since her feelings of self-worth are derived from her own evaluations and judgements, she has no need to perform the action for extraneous considerations (e.g. in order to be, or to be thought, benevolent) in the way that a pride-dependent person who acts with an audience in mind does. In other words, a pride-dependent person is more likely than a lover of self to be motivated by what we think are the wrong sorts of reasons.

If the development of love of self ought to be viewed, not as an outcome or an adjunct of self-assessment and judgement, but as part of the very process of the active self-formation of the self, it can then be seen to be a capacity of agency whereby the constitution of a person's experience becomes fixed, certain and part of character, integrity and meaningfulness. For a person's love of self is then something that shapes her own experience, not merely her experience of the world, but also of herself: it can then be seen as one of the determinants of the way in which she approaches circumstances in the world, the kind of person she is, how she incorporates features she sees herself to have into her experience, the nature of the character she has, the strength of her own convictions, and so the very opinion she has of herself, and the feelings she has for herself. The way in which a person will experience the world may largely be set down early in life; but since her love of self does not crucially depend, as does her pride, on what she has and does in the world, but is associated instead with the experience she has of what she is engaged in making of her own self, this does not mean that a person is unable to change the way in which she experiences the world, and so unable to change both herself and the relation in which she stands to her own self.

When being a lover of self is understood as belonging to the realm of self-constitution as I have described, the ideal quantity of love of self must be the maximum possible. Persons can be conceived of as having a greater or lesser deficiency relative to this ideal. This means that there is no such thing as a person with excessive love of self.[16] Love of self sustains a person when, from a strictly evaluative standpoint, she should be demoralised. It is a developed quality of a person which enables her to feel good about herself so she can carry on without distortion or fleeing the truth, and this despite severe blows to her pride. Her self-concept can remain unchanged despite the fact that she is able to be severely self-critical regarding various particular aspects of herself.

Having an increase in pride can render one unreasonable in one's dealings with the world: one is apt to focus on features pertaining to one's own self instead of on the circumstances before one. Having an increase in love of self does not in any circumstances make one less reasonable. On the contrary, it is more likely to make one more reasonable, since love of self, being grounded in one's reflective evaluation and understanding of the particular circumstances before one, and in the significance and meaningfulness of certain values, allows one to function without being impeded by peripheral considerations, including considerations pertaining to aspects of one's own self. So rather than allowing the rigidity of certain beliefs, values or ends determine her acts, a lover of self has the capacity to distance herself from these, making it far easier to focus on the good and sufficient reasons provided by the circumstances and values before her, and so to see that there may be certain other values which must, *in these particular circumstances*, be embodied in her response. It is in this capacity to be guided by her own reflective evaluation and understanding (rather than by fixed beliefs, values and ends) that a lover of self experiences the meaningfulness of her acts and her life to be grounded.

While a person who is not a lover of self will need to strive to find meaningfulness in a series of impingements outside herself since she lacks a sense of meaningfulness from within, insofar as a person is a lover of self, she feels her core to be consistent with the meaning of her life:

> There then blazes forth the absurdity of a life which has sought outside of itself the justifications which it alone could give itself. Detached from the freedom which might have genuinely grounded them, all the ends that have been pursued appear arbitrary and useless.
>
> (de Beauvoir 1970: 25)

We are able to portray a lover of self as having the capacity to act and react directly and honestly in any arena, including the social, according to the contingencies of the circumstances, undistracted by fixed beliefs and values, or by the pressure to act and react so as to compensate for insecure feelings of worth associated with pride. This capacity to stand alone does not imply isolation or arrogance. It implies, rather, that one's engagement in society is more meaningful because it is done in a state of freedom rather than in an imprisonment in pride-determined roles which preclude a genuine receptivity to others. As we saw in Chapter 4, this freedom enables the agent to respond to the whole breadth of another person instead of merely to that aspect of another which reflects positive aspects of her own self. Having this freedom, she then has the capacity for active and genuine concern for others rather than being confined by concerns relating to her own self-worth. We may turn here to the poetic words of Martin Buber: 'Not before a man can say *I* in perfect reality...can he in perfect reality say *Thou*' (1973: 145).

This capacity to 'say Thou' represents an ability to surrender one's own egocentricity in such a way that one can focus exclusively on the needs or plight of another and respond to those needs without thought being given to how one's action might relate to, or reflect on, some aspect of one's own self. It represents an ability to engage in what Murdoch calls 'a just and loving gaze' where another's good can be seen as in itself valuable and worth promoting. This contrasts with a pride-dependent person who, seeking good self feelings, is more likely to promote another's good in order to receive reinforcing confirmations of what she is doing.

In the next section I will illustrate the difference between love of self and pride-dependency by discussing two characters from Tolstoy's *Anna Karenina*. I do this to demonstrate the moral importance of love of self.

PRIDE, SELF-ESTEEM AND LOVE OF SELF: AN ILLUSTRATION

the virtuous man 'will bear the chances of life most nobly and altogether decorously, if he is "truly good" and "foursquare beyond reproach" '.

(Aristotle 1941: 1100b20–2)

It is part of the human condition to seek feelings of self-worth and meaningfulness in life. These may be derived from various sources. I have argued that a person who is able to locate self-worth and meaningfulness within the core of her own being by being true to values which she expresses in her actions, rather than depending for these on a series of impingements from outside herself, is one who has the capacity to relate and respond to the world in an authentic, receptive and truly benevolent way. I have argued that if a person has securely held values[17] and, with this, a secure sense of her own worth, she is more likely to be able to respond in a genuine and unmediated way to the plight of others than is a person who is lacking in this regard. A pride-dependent person, needing constant confirmation and validation of her own self and of what she is doing, has been presented as one whose values are tentatively and insecurely held (depending on the changeable opinions of others) and less able to focus sufficient attention on a reality outside her own self so as to find value and meaning in that reality. In drawing a parallel between pride-dependency and narcissism, I have shown that for the pride-dependent person there is in effect no tangible reality outside her own self to which she can relate and where she might find value and meaning.

A pride-dependent person does not value and love herself too much to be able to give benevolently to others; rather, she values and loves herself too little. In examining the characters of Kitty and Varenka in Tolstoy's *Anna Karenina*,[18] I will illustrate my contention that to be able to give benevolently to another it is required that one be able to attend in an unmediated way to the reality and value of another self, and that this capacity requires not that one merely 'feel' good about various aspects of one's self, but that one be actively engaged in genuinely valuing the being one recognises one is. Love of self, so conceived, will be shown to be a requirement of benevolent giving.

The two women, Kitty and Varenka, are contrastingly portrayed by Tolstoy. The different ways in which they derive feelings of self-worth can be seen to have an important bearing on their moral capacities.

Kitty is presented in Parts One and Two of the novel as an individual whose aim is to appear as a 'good' person in order to overcome her feelings of guilt, shame and humiliation, and to instead possess peace of mind. Her shame and humiliation are the result of being treated by Vronsky, a man whom she had been sure would ask for her hand in marriage, with what she sees to have been contempt. This leaves her so devastated and miserable that she is completely unable to function, succumbing instead to a mysterious 'illness'. Vronsky's jilting her results in everything now seeming

> hateful, loathsome, coarse...and I myself most of all...as though everything that was good in me was all hidden away, and nothing was left but the most loathsome.... In old days to go anywhere in a ball-dress was a simple joy to me, I admired myself; now I feel ashamed and awkward.... That's my illness
>
> (140–1)

Any positive feelings Kitty had for her own self were entirely derived from how she believed others perceived her, or from how she, as an imagined audience, perceived herself. For example, we are presented with a picture of what Kitty takes to be one of her 'best days':

> her lace berthe did not droop anywhere; her rosettes were not crushed nor torn off... the thick rolls of fair chignon kept up on her head as if they were her own hair.... The black velvet of her locket nestled with special softness round her neck.... Kitty smiled... at the ball, when she glanced at it in the glass.... Her eyes sparkled, and her rosy lips could not keep from smiling from the consciousness of her own attractiveness.
>
> (86)

Kitty certainly felt good about herself: she was proud of her appearance and of the effect it had on others.

Yet when Vronsky does not reciprocate her love, she is not merely sad or disappointed, but feels terribly ashamed:

> long afterwards, *for several years after* – that look, full of love, to which he made no response, cut her to the heart with an agony of shame.
>
> (89, my emphasis)

Shame (rather than disappointment, sadness or anger) appears to be a strange reaction to being jilted, yet we can explain Kitty's shame by the fact that what she wanted and needed from Vronsky was not merely his love but, through that love, a positive impression of her own self. For her feelings of worth depended on Vronsky's opinion of, and love for, her: her feelings of shame indicate that she does not merely think that Vronsky feels less warmly disposed towards her, but that her own worth is thereby vanishing. Vronsky, in jilting her, had done great injury to her vanity and, with this, to her self-worth.

Kitty had interpreted his apparent fondness and love for her as a response to particular aspects of herself: especially to her attractiveness. On the withdrawal of his affection, she felt loathsome, hateful, unattractive, and so humiliated and ashamed that she was unable to face the world.[19] Her feelings of worth depended entirely on another's regard for various features of hers, features which can be seen to have been over-valued by her as being crucial to her worth. Thus her pride rested on a disproportionate value that she had allocated to various aspects of herself. When her pride is destroyed by Vronsky, she has no other source from which to derive feelings of worth to sustain her, and lapses instead into a mysterious illness.

But her not being a lover of self, and her accompanying low self-regard, were not caused by Vronsky's jilting her. These were not caused by something which, if present for someone else, could be understood as causing *them* to have a low self-regard.[20] Instead, Kitty's low self-regard determined her interpretation of Vronsky's behaviour as reflecting badly on her own worth.

If we consider the time Kitty spends 'recuperating' at the German springs, we see that in focusing on those aspects of her self pertaining to her own moral character, and so imitating what she saw as Varenka's 'goodness', she in effect prevented herself from attaining what she most wanted: a secure self-regard which she believed would follow from a devotion to others.

The fact that she was not a lover of self is revealed in her own view of herself, which causes her to engage in a constant comparison of aspects of herself with those of others. 'How good you are! How good you are!' she says to Varenka. 'If I could only be a little like you!' (250). The 'goodness' she perceived was Varenka's busyness in looking after the needs of the invalids: 'Either she was taking the children... home from the springs, or fetching a shawl for a sick lady... or trying to interest an irritable invalid, or selecting and buying cakes for tea for someone' (244).

In Varenka Kitty realised that 'one has but to forget oneself and love others, and one will be calm, happy, and noble. And that was what Kitty longed to be'. Kitty then planned to 'seek out those who were in trouble... help them as far as she could, give them the Gospel, read the Gospel to the sick, to criminals, to the dying' (253). Unfortunately, what was of real value to her was a view of herself as good and worthy. Others' needs were perceived by her as providing a potential means to achieving her own peace of mind: in being kind, selfless and giving to others, in Varenka's manner of life, 'Kitty felt... she would find... what she was now so painfully seeking: interest in life, a dignity in life' (243). Since what she most valued was her own peace of mind, helping others could not be experienced by her as immediately or directly expressed in what she was actually engaged in doing. The good of others was not taken by her as a reason which she embodied in her motives: it was not for her a value which she made into *her reason* for helping them.[21] She did not help others for their own sake, but it was a means to her own ends.

Kitty notices Varenka's lack of pride in both her 'goodness' and her considerable musical talent, very aware that if she had Varenka's qualities and talents, 'how proud I should have been' (249). To gain self-worth, Kitty needs to compare herself with others and perceive herself to come out ahead. We will see below that because of this she is unable to be committed, as is Varenka, in a genuine way to the circumstances of others. Because she is not a lover of self, she is precluded from virtue.

Kitty wonders about Varenka 'What is it that gives her the power...to be calm independently of everything?' (249). Kitty wonders here about Varenka's self-possession and love of self, about why she does not have the same need for pride that Kitty herself has, and why she is able to devote herself selflessly to others. Kitty notices these things about Varenka despite the fact that Varenka had been jilted by a suitor in a similar way in which Kitty had been 'cast aside' by Vronsky.

Kitty notices that 'Varenka, alone in the world, without friends or relations, with a melancholy disappointment in the past, desiring nothing, regretting nothing, was just that perfection of which Kitty dared hardly dream' (253). Varenka had suffered the same blows to her pride that Kitty had, but was sustained by a secure unified centre and a confident knowledge of who and what she was. So her acknowledged disappointments and past failures had not affected her self-worth, and she could devote herself to others without needing to shore up her own self-concept.

Kitty and Varenka each found quite different types of things to be 'important'. Varenka is unable to convey to Kitty what she finds important when Kitty begs to be told: 'What is...of such importance that gives you such tranquillity? You know, tell me!'. Kitty wants to know what gave Varenka the 'calm and dignity so much to be envied' in order that she achieve that same calm and dignity. But Varenka, not being one to have put much effort into thinking about aspects of her own self, 'did not even know what Kitty's eyes were asking her'. What she did know was what she had to do right away for Madame Berthe and mamma (251–2).

Without being able to explicitly verbalise the nature of what she found important, it was instead her actions which revealed this. What was of importance to Varenka was the good of those for whom she cared. She thought of and treated others as persons: the moral relationship in which Varenka stood to others was such that persons were never seen or treated by her as mere means.

Varenka knew where value lay, and she fashioned her own self in accordance with it. We see this when Kitty tells Varenka about her humiliation, that she will never be able to forget what Vronsky did to her, 'even if I live a hundred years'. Varenka's response is to ask: 'Where is the humiliation? Why, you did nothing wrong' (251). We should here compare Aristotle's comments that we ought not to fear 'the things that do not proceed from vice and are not due to the man himself' (1115a17–18), and that 'no happy man can become miserable; for he will never do the acts that are hateful and mean. For the man who is truly good and wise... always makes the best of circumstances' (1100b35–1101a2). Kitty was not a lover of self, so she could not be 'truly good and wise'.

Being 'truly wise', Varenka knew that becoming humiliated and losing dignity were not appropriate responses. The circumstances in which these would be appropriate were ones where she, for example, would perceive that she had violated certain standards of good and bad, right and wrong, these representing values which were integral to the view she had of her self. Such values were of the greatest importance to Varenka, while the kind of experience with Vronsky that Kitty had experienced, and which she had herself experienced, was 'all so unimportant' (251). We might say that Varenka knew, while Kitty did not know, 'what was what'.

Varenka's past failures and disappointments had not affected her self-concept because her awareness of who and what she was was conditioned by a relation of authenticity to the world, one which she was continuously engaged in renewing. Although her helping actions served to also actively fashion her own self, considerations pertaining to aspects of her own self or to her own self-satisfaction did not enter as motives into her will as they did for Kitty. This self-fashioning activity in which Varenka was engaged conditioned her own love of self, and no failure of hers or disappointment in life could undermine the feelings of self-worth that she was accumulating through the experience of herself as a being capable of making herself into what she was. For her, the value of helping others was located exclusively in the promotion of their good: in instantiating this value in what she did, she actively identified her own self with it, as well as created and determined what she was. She had no need to define herself in terms of how others regarded her or in terms of her own 'successes', 'failures' or 'disappointments'. Her love of self gave her the courage, in which Kitty was sorely lacking, to act for reasons unconnected with how her actions would affect or reflect aspects of her own self.

Varenka experienced a congruity between what she took to be valuable and important and what she made of her own self. Her actions did not express, as did Kitty's, what she perceived the world valued or expected, nor were her feelings of worth derived from successfully accommodating her self to others' definitions. Instead, she had the courage to be her own self.

By contrast, Kitty had a certain blindness to her own self: she was not aware of what she truly valued, what she held to be important, or what she really wanted. Despite feeling more at ease with Levin than with Vronsky, despite believing herself to be in love with Levin, and despite Levin's proposal of marriage causing 'Her soul [to be] flooded with happiness' (54), she turns down his offer. Moreover, she then does not know 'Whether she felt remorse at having won Levin's love, or at having refused him...her happiness was poisoned by doubts' (61). This was because while marriage to Vronsky promised to present her with a more highly regarded impression of herself than marriage to Levin, this was not something that she was herself certain that she wanted. So she allowed her mother to sway her. Not being a lover of self, she could not trust her own judgements or valuations.

Kitty is portrayed as lacking a secure centre from which to think, speak and act with integrity. Her need to focus on particular aspects of herself can be seen rather to blind her to her own self and to what was valuable and important. Instead of experiencing herself as one who had the capacity to be actively engaged in determining what she was, she had to strive to define herself in a narcissistic way: by looking to her own image as reflected in others' eyes.[22]

Yet what she cared about was not her own self, for she did not have much acquaintance with a self that was truly her own. Instead, Kitty cared about a merely reflected impression of her own reality: she cared for a fictive self. When Levin made her an offer of marriage she had the opportunity to decide for herself who and what she really valued and wanted, but she surrendered this opportunity in face of the valuations and desires of her mother and, indeed, of society in general.

The experience Kitty had of herself was of a passive possessor of certain attributes which could be admired or disdained: by herself and others. Her experience of herself was not of one for whom feelings of worth and meaningfulness in life could be derived from what she herself had come to understand as being non-contingently valuable. She did not conceive of herself as a being who was capable of fashioning her own self according to deeply held values with which she identified. She thus lacked what is a condition for love of self.

By contrast, Varenka's self-concept had grown out of an identification with those things which she held to be valuable and important, and which had found direct expression in her actions. One might say, first, that she was able to be something of immense value for those whom she helped, and second, that those whom she helped had a place in the conception she had of her own self and so also in the significance and meaning of her own life. The whole of reality was not exhausted by, nor did it converge for her on, various aspects of her own self: she was able to incorporate the reality and needs of others into her own experienced reality.

Lacking the capacity for understanding what Varenka was doing, Kitty was unable to accept and be committed to the same things as Varenka: she was unable to properly involve her own self in helping others. What she really pursued (her own self-worth and peace of mind) was disengaged from what was immediately and concretely before her (the plight of those in need). She did not conceive of the value of her helping actions as being located in what she was directly and concretely bringing about (the good of others). Since she was unable to stand in a relation of genuine benevolence to others, she was unable to be for others what Varenka was for them.

It was not merely the case that Kitty was not acquainted with her own self; she was also not aware of what her real motives were: so neither could she have been aware of what her motives *ought to have been*. So she was not aware of how it would be possible for her to become morally better; there was no awareness on her part of an ethical reality towards which she saw herself to be striving. One is reminded here of Socrates' claim that self-knowledge has ethical consequences, and that it is a prerequisite of virtue that one know oneself.

Since Kitty neither valued nor knew her own self, she sought to achieve self-worth and self-knowledge by helping others. She was, precisely for this reason, while not morally indifferent to others, precluded from the possibility of genuine benevolence. Because of her preoccupation with her own self, she was precluded from holding benevolence, charity and love as being non-contingently valuable. These could be valued by Kitty only insofar as they could be used to increase good feelings for herself. A value that Varenka saw as being internal to her own helping actions (the good of others) was for Kitty of merely subservient importance. Where Varenka's serenity, peace of mind, calmness and humility were not things which Varenka had set out to achieve for herself, but were internal to the moral perspective which she had, Kitty, in aiming to use a perceived goodness to gain what Varenka had, was precluded from taking that moral perspective from which the good of others could be understood and taken as a reason for helping others.

Varenka's love of self was not a matter of discovering which aspects of herself were worthy and good and then making sure that they were 'really good' by viewing them from a perspective others would have: her love of self did not follow the external-to-internal direction. Her love of self was engaged rather than contemplative and detached. What she valued and strived for was taken by her to be so much herself[23] that the value she placed on her own self did not depend on how others regarded her. Her love of self was instead inextricably bound up with her own striving to actualise those things which were for her of ultimate value.

When she acted morally well, she did not experience what she did as a sacrifice of her own interests. It did not involve self-negation or self-sacrifice since the experienced reality of what she was engaged in making of her own self was expressed in her actions. When she acted morally well she was actively interested in so acting, and her own tranquility and happiness, so envied by Kitty, were internal to this interest of hers, to the way in which she valued and loved her own self, and so internal to her own morally good helping actions. Tolstoy portrays her love of self and her morally good actions as parts of the same character-structure.

Varenka's love of self facilitated her paying genuine, unmediated attention to the needs of others. Having a secure self-concept that did not depend on a reflected impression of herself is presented by Tolstoy as a prerequisite for the capacity to engage in genuine benevolent giving: where the motive, and what is taken to be of primary value and importance, is the good of another.

The moral importance of the difference between pride and self-esteem, on the one hand, and love of self, on the other, will now be further exposed by considering their connection with another relation to the self: that of self-respect.

SELF-RESPECT AND LOVE OF SELF

Another area where philosophers have been operating without the notion of 'love of self' is in dealing with the concept of 'self-respect'. In neglecting love of self, they miss out on an important possible source and sustainer of self-respect: a consequence is a loss in our understanding of 'self-respect'. In this section I will show that self-respect has a sustaining source which is of great moral significance, but one that has been neglected in the philosophical literature.[24]

Self-respect is a relation to the self which is acknowledged in the literature as a fundamentally moral one. It is understood as being manifested in one's being averse to having one's wishes disregarded without good reason, to taking exception to the flouting of one's rights, and being resentful of, or finding shameful, being used or degraded, manipulated or exploited (Sachs 1981). It pertains to a sense of one's inner worth as a person. By contrast, neither pride nor self-esteem has been regarded to be of comparable moral significance.

One difference that the literature points to between self-respect and self-esteem is that self-esteem can be unwarranted whereas self-respect cannot. Since self-respect pertains to a sense of one's inner worth as a person, there is no clear sense in which one could be mistaken about this such that one thought one was more worthy than one in fact was. When it is said that a person has an unduly high estimate of himself, it is commonly meant that he is mistaken, not regarding his self-respect, but regarding his 'self-esteem'.

In differentiating self-respect from self-esteem, Sachs (1981) has argued that while the possession of self-respect is in every case a ground for self-esteem, a lowering of self-esteem does not provide grounds for a lessening of self-respect. While Sachs' arguments are persuasive, a problem with his account centres on his neglect of love of self. For while a lowering of self-esteem does not provide grounds for a lessening in self-respect, a loss in love of self *does* provide such grounds. Since Sachs neglects love of self, he naturally works from what is true of external relations (our esteem of others) to what is true of an internal relation (self-esteem). Accordingly, self-esteem and esteem of others are presented by Sachs as quite symmetrical: whatever is appropriate in causing us to esteem or disesteem others (e.g. fluctuations in their self-respect) is similarly an appropriate cause of self-esteem or self-disesteem.

This is right. Our observation of a loss or absence of self-respect in another is likely to cause us to hold him in low esteem. If a person does not appear to think he is of much worth as a person such that he does not mind being used, exploited and treated in a degrading way, it is difficult to hold him in high esteem. His having the best backhand in the country becomes somehow blurred by what he is. What he can do seems of only minor importance when compared with what he is or has become. Similarly, our self-esteem will fluctuate according to the respect we have for our own selves. Our continuing to submit ourselves to avoidable degradations will affect how good we feel about the backhand of which we were once so proud. To continue to glow with pride in our magnificent backhand in face of our continuing to submit to degradations could only be accomplished by resorting to some kind of self-deception which is itself, in turn, a kind of self-degradation. So what is true here of our relation to another (our respect and esteem for him) can be extended to the relation we have to ourselves (our respect and esteem for ourselves). But things do not remain exactly the same when we consider love of self.

While the direction from external to internal accurately depicts esteem of others and self-esteem, in order to fully understand the concept of self-respect (and those elements that can sustain it) we need the notion 'love of self', which does not follow this direction. When we acknowledge the presence and importance of love of self, we see that the direction from external to internal will not do for understanding self-respect.

For example, when a person loosens his identification with things which are for him important and worthwhile so that he no longer strives for those things which have made his life meaningful, and he perceives his capacity to actively fashion his own self to be undermined, he will find it far easier to submit himself to avoidable degradations than previously. In other words, when a person's love of self substantially weakens, a weakening of self-respect is likely to follow. A loss in love of self (unlike a weakening of self-esteem) provides grounds for a loss of self-respect. Yet this is not explicable in terms of some relation in which we stand to others.

A loss of self-respect will follow from a loss in love of self because the latter lowers one's confidence in oneself and in what one is by loosening the identification of one's own self with those things which have been for one important, valuable and worthwhile. Hamlet's tragedy illustrates this. What was important and non-contingently valuable for Hamlet was revenge for his father's murder. His perceived loss in self-respect manifested in the realisation of what he had become through his persistent failure to take revenge ('O, what a rogue and peasant slave am I!') does not result in his ceasing to hold revenge as centrally important. No other value presents as more important or pressing. Nor does the loss in his love of self consist in ceasing to value what has been for him of greatest importance. What his inaction and its accompanying loss of self-respect reveals him to be does not overwhelm his perception of the importance of revenge.

We should contrast this with a case where a person loses pride or self-esteem on perceiving a loss in his own self-respect. This can occur because knowing oneself to have submitted to degradations can make appear unimportant and trivial those qualities and achievements on which one would normally have prided oneself. These no longer appear as grounds for pride, but as unimportant, given the kind of person one has become. Since pride is grounded in perceptions, assessments and judgements of aspects of oneself which may belong merely contingently to one, while self-respect pertains to one's 'inner worth', it is not difficult to see how what one, as a moral being, has become can overwhelm the importance presented by these other perceptions, assessments and judgements.

But what altered for Hamlet was not his perception or judgement of what was important; rather, the way in which he identified his own self radically changed. This is because what caused his loss in self-respect was not a lowered pride or self-esteem, but a loss in his love of self.[25] When one loses love of self, one perceives that one's own actions (or in the case of Hamlet, inactions) are no longer expressive of one's own valued self: one no longer experiences a congruity with one's selfhood. Those capacities which enable one to express deeply held values in one's actions are perceived to be impaired. What is important and valuable remains the same, but what has now altered, on losing love of self, is the identification and constitution of one's self. One's own self can no longer be conceived of as being able to identify with these things on which one has placed such high valuations. So Hamlet wonders, not about the real importance and value of revenge, but about his own capacity to identify with that on which he has placed such value and importance:

> Am I a coward?
> Who calls me villain, breaks my pate across,
> Plucks off my beard and blows it in my face,

146

Tweaks me by the nose, gives me the lie i' th' throat
As deep as to the lungs? Who does me this?
Ha!
'Swounds, I should take it; for it cannot be
But I am pigeon-liver'd and lack gall
To make oppression bitter

(Shakespeare, *Hamlet*, Act II, Scene ii)

The conception Hamlet has of his own self is here becoming detached from the conception he has of those things which are for him of utmost importance and value. He is losing love of self and, with this, the sense he has of his own worth. His sense of unworthiness is not grounded in a negative assessment of his own inaction (as would be the case in a loss of pride or self-esteem) but is associated with his inability to identify the experience he now has of himself with what he holds to be of utmost importance. He experiences himself as one who is incapable of engaging in a self-fashioning activity which could express this importance and serve to maintain his love of self and, with this, his self-respect. What is losing value, in his own eyes, is not merely his own abilities with respect to taking revenge for his father's murder. So what he suffers is not a mere loss of pride or self-esteem. Instead, his self-identification and the very constitution of his self in the world are in question. He thus compares himself, in what follows the quoted passage above, with a whore, a drab and a scullion. A person who values what Hamlet values does not behave in the way in which he has been behaving. A person who behaves as he now does must be a coward, a villain or a drab, and such a person is incapable of maintaining an identification between his own self and what he considers to be of utmost importance and value: respect, and so revenge, for the memory of his father. What is being questioned by Hamlet is the very constitution he is making of his own self, not merely some particular attribute of it. It seems clear that what causes his loss in self-respect is not a loss of pride or self-esteem, but rather a loss in what I have termed 'love of self'.

Love of self and self-respect both have as their objects the self as such,[26] not merely, as do pride and self-esteem, the self considered in some aspect or other. Love of self and self-respect both involve a certain evaluation of the self considered as a unity. By contrast, pride and self-esteem involve evaluations of some aspect or aspects of the self, and they are consistent with inner conflict and disunity (e.g. pride is not denied to the self-deceived). Moreover, losses in both love of self and self-respect can be seen to be informed by, and to inform, each other: the maintenance of both depends on the continued existence of a certain amount of inner unity and harmony. They are evaluative relations to the self which are closely interrelated since they both involve ways of self-identification. Thus on perceiving that one has submitted to degradations, the disruption to inner harmony, the damaged self-identification and the accompanying loss in self-respect cannot easily be disentangled from the diminished confidence that one then has in one's own self, in one's own evaluations, judgements, decisions and actions. And these diminutions in confidence are constitutive of a loss in love of self.

The loss in self-respect is manifested in a realisation of what one has now become,[27] whereas the loss in love of self manifests in an inability to actively engage in self-fashioning activities that are expressive of deeply held values, and so in an incapacity to actively incorporate these values into one's self-identification. Both pertain to the way in which the self is being constituted in the world. In the case of Hamlet, the loss in self-respect appears as a consequence of the loss in love of self, although each of these losses is not easily distinguished from the other.

Love of self centrally involves a confidence in those values in which one has invested one's own self. Yet despite this confidence, it also involves a capacity to effect a certain distancing from them in order to be able to reassess whether, given the presence of other pressing values, they are the values one should here pursue. Those values which constitute the self as a psychological unity[28] may be re-ordered and re-assessed by the moral self according to its own understanding of what must and must not (in the particular situation) be done. The moral self is thus confronted with certain limits on action. These limits arise from the self's own under-standing of what is before it, and in effect they constitute what it, as a moral self, is.

Similarly, a person with self-respect has certain limits pertaining to his own behaviour and his treatment by others beyond which he cannot go without conceiving of himself as changing in some basic way, since the limits beyond which he will not customarily go are conceived of by him as integral to what he is. To transgress these limits is for him to change in a way that is fundamental to the conception he has of his own self. One's rights, if experienced by a person as part of what is constitutive of his selfhood, form a basis for his self-respect. Such a person will feel that a failure to oppose a denial of his rights represents a loss of his self-respect. The conception of his own self as a being worthy of respect becomes dissociated from what he now sees himself to be.

Losses in self-respect and losses in love of self both involve a dislocation of those elements in which the self has been invested and with which it identifies. They cannot be easily disentangled from each other since both relate to aspects of a person which are experienced by her as essential parts of what she is. The self-identifications involved in both pertain to the capacity a person has developed to fashion her own self according to values which, by incorporating them into what she strives for and does, she actualises.[29]

A moral being who gives benevolently can be seen to have developed just this capacity: the other's good is a value which is incorporated into what she aims for and does, and so into what she is. Understanding the value and the circumstances as she does, and understanding the kind of being that she herself is, this value is experienced by her as inescapable: 'What characterises a moral being is his or her realisation that a certain "gaze" on people and life is not an option among others, that it is one which is inescapable for anyone who fully realises the sort of being he or she is' (Lycos 1978: 9). In actualising the value in accordance with her under-standing of the particular circumstances, she identifies with, and constitutes her self in the world in a way that is consistent with, the value. The good of another is a value which she takes as *her reason for acting*: she then experiences herself as one who has the capacity to both create and express her own self in what she does.

Since the feelings of worth of such a person are grounded in her own self-defining and self-affirming agency, rather than in the way particular aspects of herself appear to others, she is able to devote herself in a genuine, unmediated way to values which are integral to what she is. Her morally good actions are thus affirmations of what she significantly is. She may then suffer a loss of pride without this affecting her love of self or her moral capacity, since such a loss leaves untouched the sense she has of what she is engaged in doing with her own self by acting the way she does.[30]

In the following section I will sum up this chapter by reviewing the moral significance of love of self.

LOVE OF SELF AND MORAL GOODNESS

I have wished to show that love of self is inextricably connected to a person's capacity to be committed to another's good in such a way that she is able to take the goodness of a helping action as being very much an expression of herself. In reviewing the moral significance of love of self, I will suggest that love of self is not merely a condition for a person's being able to be committed to another's good, but that love of self and the capacity to act morally well are parts of the same character-structure.

We have seen that by focusing on features of herself and immersing herself in self-pity, Kitty rendered herself unable to develop a positive conception of her own self according to which it would be *she* who determined what she would become. Being preoccupied with the regard of others, she was unable to engage herself in a genuine, unmediated way with others, and unable to be committed to their good.

She turned to Varenka in an effort to bolster her feelings of worth, but even if Varenka had been able to convey to her what was 'important', this would have done little, if anything, to enable Kitty to gain the love for herself that she lacked. For we have seen that love of self is a profound inherent quality of a person that is conditioned by what the person is engaged in making of herself. It is essentially tied to an agent's understanding of what it is good to be. Such understanding is little affected by the kind of rational self-evaluation involved in pride and self-esteem. So Kitty's love of self would not have been affected by her being brought to a realisation that the various particular aspects of herself were in fact not as 'bad' as she thought.

Furthermore, love of self is needed in order to be able to accept, and so deal with, those features of ourselves which we judge to be unpleasant or disagreeable. We have seen that Illych failed in this regard, not being able to cope with the fact of his illness. Similarly, Kitty could not cope with being jilted by Vronsky. In both their cases, a consciousness of their own shortcomings destroyed any feelings of self-worth they had. Yet the nature of love of self is such that it may be possessed by us despite our being completely aware of our shortcomings. Having a secure knowledge of what we are means that we have a strong core of values with which we identify: strong, because it is something we have ourselves shaped through our own reflections, understanding, valuations and actions. It is this strong

150

centre on which we can fall back in facing up to those aspects of ourselves which we consider to be less than ideal. It is in fact something we can fall back on in facing up to any issue whatever.

Love of self enables a person to act morally well, since she can focus exclusively on what is before her, self-centred needs being far less likely to dominate or take over consciousness and life. This is not to say that being a lover of self *leads one* to be able to act morally well. The former is not a means to the latter. Instead, they are both aspects of the same (virtuous) state of character.

A person in possession of such a state of character is able to clearly see the good and sufficient reasons before him to act in certain ways. His self-possession enables him to be much less distracted by considerations which are peripheral to those concretely present than is the attention of one who is concerned with how he appears. Without such self-possession, he will be unable to commit himself properly to anything unless it relates in some way to his own needs and satisfactions. Without love of self, a person is far less likely to achieve the quality of attention Murdochian morality requires: where the agent is able 'To silence and expel self, to contemplate and delineate... with a clear eye...[which is]...the checking of self-ishness' (Murdoch 1970: 64–5).

A person who is not a lover of self might do the benevolent thing from a morally good motive, and be deserving of moral praise. But she will only be a benevolent person if she has the perspective and motivational character-structure of one who gains a just under-standing of the particular circumstances, persons and values before her. For actions to be morally good, 'The agent must... be in a certain condition when he does them... he must have knowl-edge... he must choose the acts... for their own sakes and... his action must proceed from a firm and unchangeable character' (Aristotle 1941: 1105a29–35). I have wished to show that constitutive of 'a firm and unchangeable character' is a commit-ment to gaining a just understanding of the particular circum-stances confronting one, as well as of the appropriateness (in *those* circumstances) of enacting non-contingent values to which one is committed.

I have presented the achievement of moral character as an individual achievement requiring what is in effect the exercise of an important constituent of a person's humanness – a certain kind of understanding and valuing, together with an active engagement in the world on the part of the agent.

In light of my account, it seems that the moral aim should not merely be to perform good and right actions. The aim should be that we intend and will the good and right thing because our motives are what they are, and this because we have made ourselves into the kinds of persons we are.

I complained in the previous chapter about the way in which utilitarian and Kantian theorists go about investigating the moral agent. Their mode of procedure is such that their agents will often experience giving to another as self-deprivation or self-denial, if not as self-sacrifice. Morality is experienced by the utilitarian as a demand from the multitudes, each of whom is just as worthy of moral respect as he himself is. For the Kantian, morality is a demand of pure practical Reason. Yet this Reason is an abstraction: it is by abstracting from everything empirical (including the agent's own desires) that the Kantian arrives at the categorical moral command. The seeds of benevolent giving are not presented by either utilitarian or Kantian theorists as lying within what moral agents are themselves engaged in making of themselves: giving to others cannot be experienced by their agents as something which flows in an unimpeded way from their own desires, and which fits what they 'want' to do. The utilitarian is never able to 'put his feet up', so to speak, since he must always be alert to the possibility that something morally better could be done, while the Kantian experiences morality as a struggle between the demands of inclination and desire on the one hand, and his proper rational self on the other. The character-structure of these agents is such that morality is experienced by them as an imposition that interferes with what they would rather be doing, rather than as flowing from what they are engaged in actively doing with respect to what they most value, and so from the core of their own beings.

Moreover, the ultimate determinant of action for Kantian and utilitarian agents is a fixed belief regarding the content of the ethical (i.e. duty, utility). What is missing is the motivation to distance themselves from their beliefs and values (in light of an understanding of the prevailing circumstances) so as to reassess and reorder these.[31]

Rather than self-negation and self-sacrifice being seen as necessities of moral consciousness and response, I have wished to present the moral self in a quite different light. Rather than morally good action being seen as action which disregards or neglects what we most care about and which (it is thought) we ought morally to care less about (our own selves), it can be seen instead to be something to which the self can be completely committed when the self is cared for and valued in the right way.

Rather than seeing morally good action on the model of replacing my interests with everybody's interests, I have wished to suggest that we see it instead on a model where every person (in virtue of their ability to make a value into *their reason for acting* in a certain way) can be seen as potentially having morally good action as one of their interests.

Neither Hume, Rousseau nor Hegel have room in their ethics for the notion of an agent making a reason into *his* reason. So I do not attribute to any of them the notion of 'love of self'. None of these philosophers focus, in their accounts of the moral self, on the various practices that are involved in critically reflecting on and re-evaluating beliefs, values and ends.[32] For Hume, what is approved is good, and the constitution of the Humean moral self depends on its being an object of others' approval: there is no room here for the self's own re-assessment of what, given the particular circumstances, would be just. Similarly, for Rousseau there is nothing to ensure that the general will will conform to an individual's own assessment of what in the particular circumstances would be the just thing to do. We cannot in any way understand willing in conformity with the general will as a form of love of self. And we saw that an Hegelian agent may, especially during time of war, need to perform acts which he regards to be morally abhorrent. My charge against Hegel was that the Hegelian moral self may need to be an unjust self. In the next chapter we will see that this charge cannot successfully be directed at the account of the moral self that I have presented.

CHAPTER VIII

Love of self and morality
The search for good and evil

Therefore the bad man does not seem to be amicably disposed
even to himself, because there is nothing in him to love.
(Aristotle 1941: 1166b25–6)

INTRODUCTION

We saw in Chapter 3 that on Hegel's account a person might
become a moral being while acting unjustly. To deny Hegel's belief
that the 'ethical substance' should have complete priority such that
any acts which further it are justified, it is necessary to reject his
thesis regarding the socio-political constitution of the self. This is
one of the concerns of this chapter.

The major concern of the chapter is to show that the objection
directed at Hegel regarding injustice is not justified when directed at
my account of love of self. The imagined objection claims that a
person who develops love of self might not see or realise what is
quite obvious to more enlightened observers: that what she does is
in fact evil.[1] My account could not be charged with the possibility
of a person developing love of self while responding to the world
unjustly, for it has been shown that a lover of self is motivated by a
sense of justice. A lover of self cannot be an unjust self in the way
that it seems an Hegelian moral self can. The imagined objector
therefore substitutes 'evil' for 'injustice'. She holds that a person
might be well-meaning, but ignorant or misguided about what she is
conscientiously doing, and so develop love of self while engaging in
evil.

My response to this objection will not be to reply directly to it,
but rather to resist certain assumptions that underlie it. By the end
of the chapter the reader will understand why there is, in effect, no
need to reply to this objection.

154

The objector may have in mind the possibility of a person holding evil to be of non-contingent value and, in actualising this value, developing love of self. This possibility has a certain incoherence. For to understand the nature of evil *is* to turn away from or be repelled by it.

> The idea that evil could be clear-sightedly desired for its own
> sake and that its enactment could be clear-sightedly celebrated
> is based upon a confused conception of the nature of its
> reality... evil can be understood only in the light of goodness.
>
> (Gaita: 1991: 191)

When one recognises something to be evil, one recoils from it because one recognises it as destructive of a cherished good.

When a person holds something to be of non-contingent value, she apprehends it as being good, and is on that account attracted to it. Now one might be simultaneously repelled by and attracted to something in virtue of its different aspects. One might be attracted to a person because of her breathtaking beauty while simultaneously repelled by her unkindness. But to value evil non-contingently a person would need to be simultaneously attracted to and repelled by it in virtue, not of different aspects of evil, but of the very same quality: the evilness of evil. I doubt that much sense can be made of this.

The objector might have in mind the possibility of a person holding something to be of non-contingent value which turns out to be in fact evil. Here, the thing is evil in virtue of some objective content. This version of the objection does not contain any incoherence, but contains an assumption I cannot share: that the criteria for good and evil are objective. Since I am unable to share this assumption, my reply will not be in terms that this version of the objection lays down.

My denial that the criteria for good and evil are objective should not be taken as tantamount to a denial of the objectivity of value in favour of the subjectivity of valuing. Quite the contrary, I hold that some valuing may need to be criticised on the grounds that it does not take due account of value. We saw in Chapter 5 that significant action requires a certain kind of civilised sensitivity to human values, i.e. values that everyone, in virtue of their human nature, is capable of seeing. Human values, on my account, are discussable and shareable, ones that everyone can approach, and about whose existence agreement can be reached (even though there may not be agreement with respect to their ultimate nature). The values are not merely a matter of taste or preference. So my account does entail a certain moral objectivity. But this objectivity does not involve complete independence from a subject's understanding. My account does not entail a moral realism according to which values exist in the world whether or not there are subjects to apprehend them. On my account, the content of a value essentially refers to, and values depend for their goodness on, some agent's understanding.

We can agree with the moral objectivist that an understanding of good and evil requires one to be sensitive to certain objective facts, for example, one must (among other things) be aware that acting in a certain way will result in a person's death. But one can hold this without also holding that acting in that way is evil simply in virtue of the person's death. For this leaves out the subject's own moral understanding of what she is doing. This is consistent with thinking, for example, that the evil of the Holocaust can be comprehended simply in terms of the number of dead bodies. To think this is to ignore the important distinction between natural and moral evil.[2]

I begin with the possibility of the objector holding that there is one true and correct moral theory or system, and pointing out that a whole society might be mistaken regarding its moral practices. The objection is that a whole society might hold certain non-contingent values, and its members, in virtue of (mistakenly) holding these (evil) values, might engage in evil practices while developing love of self.

A PRESUPPOSITION OF MORAL ABSOLUTISM

If the objector holds that there is one true and correct moral theory, and that this theory presents objective criteria for good and evil, then the problem seen with my account is that a person might develop love of self while performing acts that turn out to be evil because of a failure to be cognisant of or adhere to this theory. In other words, a lover of self might be a complete failure so far as moral virtue is concerned.

Michael Slote (1987) might present this objection, which could equally be directed to the accounts of Aristotle, Hume, Rousseau and Hegel. Slote's argument is based on absolutist foundations. He argues that if slavery offends the rights of slaves, then slave-keeping 'not only is but was wrong', and 'those engaged in such practices were not morally virtuous individuals' (1987: 101). Slote questions the assumption that virtue is a possibility for any of us, given that the practices of every society are superseded by new moral knowledge that reveals them to have been morally wrong. Accordingly, our objector's point may be that any practice might, with new moral knowledge, be shown at a future time to be evil. Such an objector holds that virtue is to be explained in terms of moral knowledge.

The objector asks: If a person can make the kinds of moral mistakes that result from living in a particular cultural epoch, and develop love of self by performing acts which we know in retrospect are evil, how can I claim that there is an internal relationship between the development of love of self and moral growth?[3] Societal and cultural factors can interfere with a person's apprehension of the true and correct morality, leaving her morally incapacitated. An agent following Aristotle, Hume, Rousseau or Hegel would, according to this objection, be subject to the same incapacity.

Such an objection insists that *moral knowledge or understanding has a certain determinate content* which an entire society may have failed to grasp, leaving it unable to see the moral wrongness of certain practices. Virtue is for Slote explicable in terms of moral knowledge: it will elude a society that does not grasp the specific objective content that constitutes moral knowledge.

Slote objects to Iris Murdoch's account which sees the self-centredness of particular individuals as a barrier to virtue, and he would object to my account which sees an excessive dependence on pride for self-worth to be such a barrier. Murdoch and I look at personal impediments to virtue; Slote thinks this is too narrow: 'If somebody has been trained from earliest childhood to believe that cannibalism is morally acceptable, can she come to see that stewing people is bad, just by bringing herself to take a less self-centred outlook?' (1987: 99). Slote thinks self-centredness is only one impediment to virtue, but that there are also cultural barriers. Thus an excessive dependence on pride for self-worth would be regarded by him to also be *just one* such impediment: he would claim that my account has overlooked cultural and societal factors that preclude a person from getting things morally right, allowing for the possibility of evil acts to ground love of self.

Slote's scepticism is focused on the possibility of anyone being able to disentangle themselves from their own cultural prejudices.

His is an epistemological, not an ontological scepticism: there is 'moral truth'; the problem is that we cannot easily reach it. So he charges Murdoch and McDowell with ignoring 'the historical dimension of our attempts to understand "moral reality" '(1987: 100). Some sort of moral realism is implied: some things can turn out to be objectively evil even though at the time we could not have recognised this. So the Slotian version of the objection to my account asks whether it can be shown that a person who develops love of self could recognise (in advance) what would turn out to be evil. An inability to do this allows for the possibility of evil responses.

Thomas Nagel shares with Slote the belief that there is an objective content of which a person must be cognisant if she is to morally understand what is good and evil. Both believe that moral conclusions must be 'correct in virtue of something independent of our arriving at them' (Nagel 1970: 149). While Slote does not explicitly spell out this belief, his argument would not make much sense unless we assume that he holds it. For according to him, the influences of being bound within the confines of a particular culture and historical epoch, and their determining the way in which we arrive at our moral beliefs, preclude our apprehending moral truth. What is morally good and bad, right and wrong, is independent of our culturally conditioned responses and conventions. Some day 'increased moral knowledge will enable people to look back on us and see how vicious we were' (1987: 99). Ideally, we would take a completely objective standpoint and extricate ourselves from our culturally bound condition, enabling us to be cognisant of moral truth. The objection to my account declares that it cannot be shown that a lover of self can be cognisant of moral truth in this way, and so such a person may be in no position to achieve virtue.

My response to this objection is to deny that in order to morally understand what is good and evil a person needs to have knowledge comprised by a certain objective determinate content. In the rest of the chapter it will be argued that *moral understanding is not to be located in any kind of content*. This argument will also claim that the result of the efforts of many modern moral theories to make ethics into a secular concern and to locate the ethical in a fixed objective content has been an inability to give a clear account of what it is to morally understand, of what it is to be an ethical subject.[4]

The denial that the locus of ethics is in an objective content, or the denial that there is one right and true moral theory, is not tantamount to an endorsement of an ethical relativism which is accompanied by scepticism with regard to judgements of, or to the existence of, good and evil, right and wrong. Nor should such a denial be linked with an emotivism which regards moral approval and disapproval as a matter of personal or group taste: where moral truth is relative to the individual (Hare and Stevenson) or to the group (Gilbert Harman). I do not endorse the kind of normative relativism where what is right and wrong, good and bad, is understood to merely indicate what is and is not the approved practice.

I want, rather, to endorse the kind of ethical relativism which allows tolerance of the practices and standards of other cultures, as well as an allowance that foreign moral judgements may be accurate judgements. To allow this is not to commit oneself to foreign moralities, or to have a reason to act in accordance with foreign moral judgements that one (from the outside) endorses. This ethical relativism also leaves open the possibility that members of a foreign culture may come to use concepts and adopt certain attitudes belonging to one's own, and to see that they had been morally mistaken.[5]

But when people revise their ethical attitudes and practices it does not mean that they come to recognise a certain particular objective content (beliefs, propositions, values) that they previously had failed to recognise. When, for example, a slave-keeper changes his views regarding the morality of slavery, it does not mean that he comes to have knowledge of the content of a true morality to which he previously did not have access. It means rather that the concept of an inferior human being is no longer one he can morally avail himself of,[6] and so the belief that inferior beings should be treated in such-and-such a way is no longer one he can embrace. Now, concepts which were previously not taken seriously by him (such as universal equal respect) are seen to have crucial moral importance. This is not to say that he has now grasped a particular content (beliefs, propositions, values) enabling him to get things morally right whereas he previously had them morally wrong since he failed to grasp this content. It means, rather, that he now sees things in a new moral light, and this in virtue of what he is now able to take seriously.

The claim is that such a person's virtue is not to be understood in terms of his moral knowledge of, or commitment to, particular beliefs, propositions or values. The claim in the rest of this chapter will be that such a person's moral understanding is rather to be explained in terms of his virtue.

This is also to claim that we are not entitled to say that a person or his acts are evil because he believes practices such as slavery, cannibalism or human sacrifice are right. Rather, his acts are evil if he, within the framework of the practices of his own society and culture, makes choices that involve him in being unjust, cruel, unkind, etc. This is to say that a slave-owner living in a slave-owning society performs evil acts when he is, for example, brutal in his handling of his slaves, but not in virtue of his owning slaves or his beliefs about their status. Our assessment depends, within the framework of his own culture, on how he conducts himself.

To deny the existence of a single true morality, or that moral understanding is given by a certain content, is not to claim that one chooses a morality in the way that one chooses a breakfast cereal (Wong 1984: 75), or that since morality is mere convention, there is no moral truth. Rather, my claim is that a person's moral understanding is explicable in terms of her virtue, and that moral truth is available[7] to the person who has the capacity and the will to exercise her own reason and reflective understanding: so as to build the kind of integrity which is an expression of her virtue. And, as argued in previous chapters, it is only through virtue that a person can develop love of self. But this is not to claim that a lover of self will never perform a bad act.

LOVE OF SELF, MORAL THEORY AND MORAL UNDERSTANDING: SOME QUALIFICATIONS

We should not take the objection regarding evil to be simply making the point that a person who develops love of self might perform a bad act, for it has not been claimed that love of self will guarantee morally correct behaviour. Indeed, it would be presumptuous to pretend that *any* state of a person could provide that kind of guarantee. The claim has been the lesser one that it is only through virtue that a person can develop love of self. If this is right, a person who develops love of self will not respond to others with evil intentions. We saw in Chapters 6 and 7 that such a person is unlikely to have any rancour or resentment in her dealings with others, that she is not dependent on others for feelings of self-worth, and that she does not depend on oppressing others in order to feel good about herself. So she is not one who will treat another unfairly or unjustly in order to bolster her own self-worth. Moreover, we have seen that such a person does not need to engage in narcissistic manoeuvres in order to gain self-worth. Thus much of the motivation for responding to others with evil intentions is removed.

It might be objected that while I have shown that a lover of self will not treat others cruelly or unjustly to gain feelings of self-worth, I have not shown that such a person would be ready to engage in activities such as feeding the starving of Ethiopia, and that a person who is not ready to do these sorts of things can hardly be described as virtuous.

A response to this objection must point out that catastrophic problems such as the various starving populations in the world are political problems, that they require political solutions, and that my account of love of self does not pretend to have any answer to them. My account confines itself to the claim that the motivation for responding to others with unkindness, oppression or injustice is removed in the case of a person who develops love of self. While such a person might do, or refrain from doing, something that results in a bad state of affairs or in others being harmed, the possibility of a lover of self responding to others with evil intentions is removed.

So rather than claiming that the development of love of self can guarantee morally correct action (correct in virtue of objective criteria), the claim is that there is a relation between love of self and ethical nobility which is far closer than a merely contingent one.

There is of course a way of understanding love of self which sees it as not at all closely connected to ethical nobility. There are numerous examples of self-satisfied people whose identities are constitutively related to a commitment to certain values, to others, and to particular communities, but we would deny that their lives were expressions of ethical nobility. Hitler and those Nazis who enacted his genocidal policies might be cited, but their actions could hardly be viewed as representing ethically noble responses to the world.

Yet there is a way of understanding love of self according to which its very development makes the self into an ethical subject, and this way of understanding it does tie it very closely to ethical nobility. This does not mean that a self that develops love of self, according to this conception, will never find itself having to do something it knows will have terrible consequences. It means rather that the development of love of self can be seen to be a sufficient condition for ethical nobility.[8]

The rest of this chapter will elaborate on the connection between love of self and ethical nobility. The moral understanding of a lover of self, while crucially important here, will be shown to not be given by any particular moral theory.

No matter how good moral theory[9] might be at assessing motives and acts, it will be shown to be unable to capture the nature of ethical reflection, and so unable to provide agents with what is needed in order to be in possession of moral understanding. Where theories such as Kantianism and utilitarianism might be taken to be telling us what it is to morally understand[10] what we ought and ought not do, I will argue that to point to a person's commitment to a particular moral theory to explain her moral understanding is to point in the wrong direction.

Moral theories would respond with the claim that they did not ever set out to give an account of moral understanding, but rather an account of moral goodness and rightness. The claim made by moral theory is that if a particular theory is true, it is true irrespective of the moral understanding of agents. An analogue might be drawn here with science: just as scientists aim to establish scientific truths (truths that hold independently of any particular person's understanding), so moral theorists aim to establish moral truths, and the moral understanding of agents plays no essential role here. If agents follow moral theory, they can behave morally well irrespective of the nature of their moral understanding.

By contrast, a claim of this chapter is that moral understanding is prior to moral behaviour.[11] While strict adherence to a moral theory might guarantee morally right behaviour, it is no guarantee of an agent's justice or goodness. In my discussion of this claim below I will suggest that there is a fault in moral theory's ignoring the central importance of the ethical subject (the subject of moral understanding), and focusing instead on the object of under-standing (i.e. the right kind of conduct).[12] The ethical is conceived of by many modern moral theories as being given by some determinate content, and the neglect of the self as the locus of morality accompanies such a conception.

One aim of many moral theories has been to make morality into a secular concern: the problem with this project is that this secularisation of the ethical has resulted in our not being able to give a clear account of moral understanding. Murdoch has reacted to the view that moral understanding is exhaustible in terms of some content or other, and she has seen this secularising movement as resulting in the neglect of the ethical subject, whose moral understanding she takes to be the primary locus of ethics. Her writings express a disenchantment with the modern search for an objective content for the ethical.

This notion that the ethical is given by an objective content underlies the objection regarding evil to my account, and in responding to this objection I will now use an illustration of a person's search for an objective content for the ethical that is presented by Dostoevsky in *Crime and Punishment*.[13] I also use Dostoevsky's work to show that the Hegelian conception of the moral self as being a socio-politically constituted entity is a mistaken conception.

RASKOLNIKOV AND THE SEARCH FOR AN OBJECTIVE CONTENT FOR THE ETHICAL

The protagonist of Dostoevsky's novel, Raskolnikov, might be cited by the objector regarding evil as an example of a person who is committed to the greatest overall good and to relieving the deserving poor of their suffering, but who, in responding with evil and killing the pawnbroker, appears as ignorant or misguided about what he is conscientiously doing. Raskolnikov is portrayed as a well-meaning person who, had he not given himself up to the authorities, might have built up the feelings of self-worth that accompany love of self while (the objector points out) responding to others with evil.

Yet what we have illustrated in Raskolnikov is precisely what we should find worrying about many modern ethical theories: a person's belief in or commitment to a secular conception of the ethical as given by some particular content, with an accompanying neglect of the self (the subject of moral understanding). Raskolnikov looks to theory to find out how to behave, and engages in a complete neglect of his own self as a possible locus of the ethical. Through this characterisation, Dostoevsky signals what he saw as a danger inherent in many ethical theories: the preoccupation with objective content. The objector to my account, assuming that good and evil are given by an objective content, regards Raskolnikov's killing the pawnbroker as the objective content on which a theorist's ethical attention should focus. The killing is seen as evil, and she questions whether my account of love of self is able to exclude evil: evil being understood in terms of some objective content such as harming, stealing or killing.

Were we to share this supposition regarding objective content, and were we to transpose it to an account of moral understanding, we would have moral subjects who would indeed be open to evil in a way that no moral subjects can afford to be. Furthermore, were we to engage in such a transposition, we would not be able to understand Dostoevsky's portrayal of Sonia in *Crime and Punishment*, or what it was about the murder of the pawnbroker that bothered her so. While Sonia was bothered by the injustice of the murder, the focus of her attention was not on this fact: the killing, as objective content, was not her fundamental worry. Her fundamental worry was, rather, what Raskolnikov had become, this being displayed in his failure to properly understand what he had done.[14]

While Sonia was bothered by Raskolnikov's looking to utilitarian theory for an answer to his moral worries, she was perhaps even more bothered by the very structure of his thinking. He thought he was 'ordinary', and that he could make himself 'extraordinary' by rejecting the values and morality of 'ordinary' people:

> men are *in general* divided...into two categories, inferior (ordinary)...material that serves only to reproduce its kind, and men who have the...talent to utter *a new word*...if one (of the latter category) is forced for the sake of his idea to step over a corpse or wade through blood, he can...find...in his conscience, a sanction for wading through blood....The first...preserve the world and people it, the second move the world and lead it to its goal. (230–1)[15]

Raskolnikov set out to 'overstep certain obstacles' by killing the pawnbroker, the justification being that he would then be a good member of humanity. We might compare the Hegelian-like thought that to be morally worried is to be a bad member of the rational state. We can imagine this thought to consist of something like: 'If only I could identify with the state I would be fine and not have these moral worries. Since I have moral worries, I must still be in the grip of some primitive kind of orientation: I have not yet transcended *Moralität*'. In Raskolnikov's terminology, 'To *be someone*, I must transcend the ordinary'. Sonia's answer to Raskolnikov is that if one transcends *that*, one transcends selfhood itself. Selfhood, on her view, is not a social or political construction, but something for which each person is solely responsible.[16]

Dostoevsky shows that in transcending the ordinary (or in leaving *Moralität* behind) Raskolnikov loses his own self. 'I murdered myself, not her! I crushed myself once for all!' (369).

We have illustrated in Sonia the moral self's preoccupation with itself and with the moral selves of others. The concerns of modern moral theory, in aiming to establish an objective content for the ethical, do not at any point connect with the kind of moral concern in which a person like Sonia finds herself to be immersed on being confronted by a Raskolnikov.

RASKOLNIKOV, MORAL THEORY AND MORAL UNDERSTANDING

Many modern moral theories would likely hold that Raskolnikov's moral mistake was caused by his not following a particular theory properly. A rule utilitarian would claim that Raskolnikov failed to engage in a utilitarian calculation that would have revealed that a world containing murders is far worse than one in which murders are absent. Had he properly weighed the relevant benefits and burdens, he would have realised that when a person is murdered, other people are put into fear of being killed, the family and friends of the deceased suffer pain and grief, and the killer is himself brutalised (Devine 1978: 22). Moreover, Raskolnikov applied a utilitarian calculation to his motives as well as to his actions and policies, and this, a sophisticated utilitarian would say, is also a mistake. Had he been aware of the good utilitarian reasons for acting justly and honestly, he would not have killed. He did not realise that utilitarianism does not need to be a decision procedure, but need only be a criterion of rightness (Brink 1986). A Kantian would say that Raskolnikov did not respect rational nature in the pawnbroker, and failed to test for the universalisability of his subjective maxim. Had he done so, he would have seen the murder as impermissible.

Dostoevsky does not locate Raskolnikov's moral mistake where many theories would want to locate it, but rather in his looking to theory for moral knowledge and guidance. A reader would be right to conclude that Raskolnikov was guided by his own understanding (given by utilitarian theory) of what he ought to do. Yet Dostoevsky shows that, as a follower of moral theory who sought the ethical in an objective content, Raskolnikov could only be in possession of what have been called 'blackboard conclusions': the inescapable conclusions of rational arguments (Gaita 1991: 328–9). This meant that he lacked an understanding of the significance of a human life, and of what it would be to take a human life. This lack is tied by Dostoevsky to the fact that a self that looks to theory for an objective content for the ethical is a self that lacks the motivation to engage in the kind of reflective evaluation that might have revealed the pawnbroker to be 'a human being',[17] and so have presented her as a limit to Raskolnikov's will. Through the character of Sonia the reader is shown that a good person's moral understanding is not given by theory. One might well take Dostoevsky to be raising a worry in *Crime and Punishment* about the very *need* for moral theory, and the reliance on it in the modern West.

Raskolnikov arrived at the conclusion, regarding the pawnbroker, that 'a louse is better off dead', and he embraced this thought as a result of what might be seen to be a wilful deprivation. For it is not merely the case that he arrived at a false thought; that his thought was false does not tell us what went wrong with his moral thinking. We need to see that he lacked the quality of character or mind to focus on the *meaning* or *significance* of such a judgement, and on the meaning of an action that might flow from such a judgement. He arrived at a false thought as a result of not allowing himself to retain any understanding of the significance, or the ultimate value, of a human life. This wilful deprivation can be seen to not be unconnected to his commitment to moral theory.

For the commitment that a self that follows moral theory has to the conclusions that theory propounds is a commitment to intellectually constructed conclusions.[18] Since such a self must be primarily concerned with the ultimate grounds of justification, it must not carry too many presuppositions regarding what is of ultimate value. To commit itself to the conclusions of moral theory, a self must believe that, and behave as though, its reason can overcome the most deeply rooted human emotions.

Accordingly, Raskolnikov is shown, via a dream he has of an old mare being cruelly whipped to death by its owner, to be horrified at the taking of innocent life. When he wakes from this awful dream, 'He felt utterly broken: darkness and confusion were in his soul' (54). When he thinks again about murdering the pawnbroker, he says: 'the very thought of it made me feel sick and filled me with horror. No, I couldn't do it' (54–5). Yet Raskolnikov sets aside the special moral understanding conveyed by his own emotions, effecting a dissociation between his intellectual and emotional-affective life so as to enact the conclusions that utilitarianism demanded. On restricting his commitment to intellectually compelling beliefs and values, he changed his mind about his ability to murder.

Raskolnikov overhears a conversation that repeats his own utilitarian ideas regarding the greater good to be achieved by killing the pawnbroker:

> Hundreds, thousands...might be...saved from destitution.... Kill her, take her money and with the help of it devote oneself to the service of humanity and the good of all... would not one tiny crime be wiped out by thousands of good deeds?... One death, and a hundred lives in exchange – it's simple arithmetic!
>
> (60)

On overhearing this conversation, he focuses again on the specific content that utilitarianism presents as the locus of the ethical. Despite his horror at the spilling of blood, he allows the irrefutability of a 'blackboard conclusion' to move him to murder: 'This trivial talk in a tavern had an immense influence on him in his later action' (61).

Dostoevsky's Underground Man said that man's intellect was merely one-twentieth of his make-up (Dostoevsky 1948), and Raskolnikov might be seen in *Crime and Punishment* to be taking this part as the whole. A central issue raised in the novel concerns the question of how a human being ought to respond to suffering and injustice, and Dostoevsky can be understood as wanting to convey the idea that a rationalistic humanism is unable to come to terms with the evil in human life, and that moral commitment is far more than merely intellectual commitment to certain beliefs, values, propositions, etc.

We have seen that what a person who develops love of self understands about certain values is conveyed by her emotional-affective life as well as her intellect. Love of self has been shown to involve an affective attachment to certain values. But Raskolnikov had to shut out his emotional-affective life and the moral understanding that this conveyed in order to be able to enact a utilitarian calculation and proceed with his plans to murder the pawnbroker. In looking to moral theory for moral guidance, he had to restrict his commitment to the particular content (certain intellectually compelling beliefs, values, propositions) that the theory propounded as being the locus of the ethical.

If we were to regard values and beliefs concerning the bringing about of maximum utility to represent the objective content that comprises the ethical, and if we were to transpose this content to an account of moral understanding, we would say that to morally understand is to know that maximum utility is the criterion of rightness of actions and policies. If we do this, then Raskolnikov's acting badly is seen to result from a serious miscalculation. If he had calculated accurately in accordance with his moral knowledge, he would have seen that murdering the pawnbroker was not the right way to proceed.

If we were to engage in the same transposition using a Kantian content as the locus of the ethical, we would say that an agent who has moral understanding is one who is concerned that her motives be pure so that her sole moral incentive is the thought of what duty requires. To morally understand is to know that one must never act on a maxim that one cannot will all rational beings to act on: it is to know that the criterion of rightness of actions is that they be performed for the sake of duty. A murder is an act that can never be right for it cannot fulfil the conditions laid down by the specific content that, according to Kant, comprises the ethical.

Modern moral theories such as Kantianism and utilitarianism can rightly claim to be able to exclude evil from the responses of agents who follow their theories properly, for such theories present agents with a limit on action so that they know what they must and must not do. There is for moral theory a theoretical, articulable conception of what a moral self is, from which the limits of moral action arise. A moral self is a self that passes thought through a kind of grid or filter that is constituted by a specific content. The filter acts as a constraint that serves to condition the self's responses so that its responses reflect its moral understanding of what it must and must not do. For utilitarians, the principle of the maximisation of utility filters moral good from evil; for Kantians, the filter is constituted by a universalisability test, conformity to whose results ensures the submission of the will to universally valid rules. The objector who asks whether *I* can also guarantee that an agent who develops love of self will not engage in evil has in mind something like the guarantee that moral theory can provide.

Moral theory can also guarantee that evil will be excluded in virtue of agents of moral theory (if they follow the theory properly) being related to their beliefs and values in such a way that these operate as the ultimate criteria of how they will behave. For example, when friendship conflicts with duty, a Kantian will be related to her beliefs regarding duty in such a way that duty will always determine her behaviour (Stocker 1976; 1990). A utilitarian will be related to the value of maximising utility in such a way that no other value would be permitted by her to override it. Since the specific content that comprises the ethical must determine action, moral theory can guarantee what kinds of acts agents following theory will perform in any given circumstance.[19]

Now a person who develops love of self will not be related to her own values and moral beliefs, *no matter how strongly these are held*, such that they will be the ultimate criteria of how she should act. For such a person there is always a measure of self-awareness that will not allow the content of a particular belief or value to determine her behaviour. This is a self-awareness of what kind of person she would be if, *in these particular circumstances*, she acted in such-and-such a way.[20] We have seen that for a lover of self there is an ever-present possibility of adjustment and revision of beliefs and values in light of the prevailing circumstances and conditions.[21]

So my account provides no guarantee regarding what kind of action will or will not be performed by a moral agent. For on my account, part of what it is to be an ethical subject is precisely that there will be no guarantees regarding action. Moreover, there is for an ethical subject no content that will determine action, since the ethical is not given by any content.

Furthermore, it must be pointed out that the ethical subject might come into severe conflict with the content of what is taken by moral theories to be the ethical: with the values, habits and modes of living of a culture or group.[22] The decision made by an ethical subject in certain particular circumstances might be that he should go to his death (e.g. the case of Socrates).

Rather than being able to guarantee that a certain kind of action will be performed by a good moral agent, my claim is that from the fact that an individual is a good moral agent, no decision regarding action directly follows. For example, in the case of being called on by her country to behave patriotically, a lover of self who believes that a person ought to be a patriotic member of her country will not, in virtue of this belief, do whatever her country asks of her, no matter what the particular circumstances are. Depending on the circumstances, and on what her country demands, the value of patriotism might be re-assessed by her as (in these particular circumstances) not being worthy of her commitment. Or she might judge that patriotism demands that she *not* do what her country asks of her. Even if her country requires something that 'the party of humanity' would regard as being good, a lover of self must first see it for herself as good in order to assent to the requirements presented to her.

While my account cannot guarantee that any particular type of action will (or will not) be performed by a lover of self, it can guarantee that we will have a world of ethical subjects, i.e. a world of beings prepared and able to exercise their own reflective evaluation in order to arrive at a decision concerning what they *must* do. Were a lover of self to act in accordance with some fixed, objective content, she would lose what it is that makes her a lover of self and a moral being: the ability to engage in a critical distancing from her own beliefs and values. While a lover of self is confronted with certain limits on action, these limits are not anything remotely like the limits which confront a self following moral theory. For a lover of self is confronted with certain 'internal' or 'built-in' limits on action:[23] she is confronted with the experience of what is known as 'moral impossibility'.

MORAL IMPOSSIBILITY AND 'ACTING WITH UNDERSTANDING'

The objection to my account regarding evil can be responded to by pointing to a certain conception of the moral self and its moral understanding. According to this conception, the moral self arises in the context of a certain kind of critical reflection which displays a moral understanding that it *cannot*, or that it *must*, do certain things. A lover of self engages in this kind of critical reflection because she wants to understand the truth about the nature of certain values, about her own self, and about other selves. We saw (Chapter 5) that the motivation to understand derives from a sense of fairness or justice. The moral self, on this view, is engaged in an infinitely refinable and endless task (Murdoch), but it is not a task that any *theory* imposes on the self. It is rather imposed by the self's understanding of the various situations in which it finds itself. Moral understanding, on this view, is not an understanding of a determinate set of things: how a person morally understands will show itself in different ways in different circumstances and at different times. On this view, a person's moral understanding might wax and wane. For example, a person's understanding of what it would be to kill a human being might weaken. But, in such a case, we would have a corresponding diminishment in the moral self.

On the account presented here, the constraints on action that confront the moral self are internal or built-in constraints because the moral understanding that it cannot do certain things is *constitutive* of what it, as a moral self, is, and not the result of an activity that passes thought through a filter so as to yield moral knowledge. For many moral theories, moral knowledge is like any other type of knowledge: there is a determinate set of things to be known, and when these are known the agent has the moral understanding needed to act morally well. Just as there is no clear sense in which a person's knowledge regarding the composition of water could wax and wane (she might simply forget that hydrogen and oxygen comprise water), so a person's moral knowledge is not regarded as being susceptible to waxing and waning. If a person has the requisite pieces of knowledge, she has what is needed to act well. Her forgetfulness or weakness of will might explain her acting badly, but her moral understanding of how to act well is derived from certain pieces of knowledge that theory can provide.

By contrast, on my account, the moral self's 'I *cannot* do this' is not derived from any particular piece of knowledge. If knowledge is understood in the traditional sense of something teachable, there is, according to my account, no such thing as moral knowledge. This is not to say that the moral self does not act with understanding, but rather to acknowledge that there is not a univocal meaning for 'acting with understanding'.

A reader of *Crime and Punishment* need not have misread anything in the novel to conclude that Raskolnikov acted with understanding. For Raskolnikov was committed to certain rational values, and one may well find no fault with his understanding of these. But rational values are not the kind of values by means of which a person can build *internal* barriers to performing certain kinds of acts. They are not the kind of values a commitment to which might yield moral understanding or give a person epistemic control over how he behaves.

Raskolnikov lacked epistemic control over his acts, even though he understood in advance of killing the pawnbroker that there was something wrong with murder. He certainly knew that 'ordinary people' saw it as wrong, and he did not think they were mistaken about this. He wanted to cross the moral barrier to show himself as an 'extraordinary' person whose vision did not need to be reduced by ordinary considerations. But while Raskolnikov saw the presence of a moral barrier, all he saw was a barrier consisting of public opinion. He did not understand the nature of the barrier that confronts a moral self. In looking to moral theory for moral knowledge, and in thinking in a utilitarian fashion about moral options, he could only arrive at 'blackboard conclusions', and so failed to gain any understanding of the barrier that confronted 'ordinary' people. Had he had an understanding of the nature of this barrier, he would have been unable to even *set out* to cross it:[24] in enacting the conclusions of moral theory he needed to be lacking a particular positive content of the mind, one that presents a person who develops love of self with certain *internal* constraints on thought and action.[25]

Raskolnikov saw the moral barrier as something which ordinary people were too cowardly or squeamish to challenge, but as something which an extraordinary person, if he tried, could cross. In effect, he managed to misconstrue what is a moral barrier as being a mere psychological barrier. The positive content of the mind that makes certain things appear as impossible for one to do (so that nothing could count as 'trying' to do them) (Gaita 1991: 109–14) was suppressed in him. So he was able to think that if only he could muster the courage to kill the pawnbroker, he would show himself to be (or make himself) extraordinary, as well as a good member of humanity. The corresponding Hegelian thought might be: 'If only I could identify with the state, I would transcend *Moralität* (the ordinary), be rid of my moral worries, and partake in leading the world to its goal'. Dostoevsky shows how dangerous and wrong-headed this kind of thinking is, and how it becomes Raskolnikov's personal and moral undoing. The self that successfully transcends *Moralität* may possibly be free of moral worries,[26] but it is no longer, in any intelligible sense, a self. In transcending the ordinary, Raskolnikov destroys himself as a human being. 'I'm a louse', he tells Sonia.

It is partly because we cannot coherently envisage ourselves as constituted in the Hegelian way that we are left, as moral beings, with our moral worries and dilemmas. To completely transcend these is to leave behind selfhood itself. In showing that what was (psychologically) impossible for others to do (the murders) was not at all (psychologically) impossible for himself, Raskolnikov does precisely that.

For a lover of self, the constraints on action are not merely *psychological*, but there are for it built-in *moral* constraints to performing certain kinds of acts. These constraints mean that, so far as action is concerned, there are for it no choices: 'If I attend properly I will have no choices and this is the ultimate condition to be aimed at' (Murdoch 1970: 40). This is consistent with denying that the moral self is constituted in the Hegelian way: rather, each moral self must go through its own dialectic and arrive at what it cannot choose.

This notion of there being certain things that the moral self cannot choose emerges from the findings of an empirical study of rescuers of Jews in Nazi-occupied Germany. The authors write of the rescuers that theoretically the choice of not saving Jews was available to them, but there was in actuality 'no conscious choice for rescuers to make; rather it was a recognition that they were a certain kind of person and that this meant they *had* to behave in a certain way' (Monroe *et al.* 1990: 118–21).

This 'having to' behave in a certain way pertains to the particular understanding a person has of the circumstances before her. On the account presented in *The Moral Self*, this is an understanding that arises in the context of a certain kind of self-reflection, and it is motivated by the self's own sense of justice. What is the nature of this sense of justice?

In 'The idea of perfection' Murdoch tells us that the mother-in-law who comes to see her daughter-in-law in a different light is 'a well-intentioned person, capable of self-criticism, capable of giving careful and just *attention* to an object which confronts her'. Murdoch describes her self-reflection: 'I am old-fashioned and conventional, I may be prejudiced and narrow-minded. I may be snobbish. I am certainly jealous. Let me look again' (1970: 17). While various interpretations are possible, Murdoch says that the case she is picturing is one where the woman is moved by justice or love. She wants to see the daughter-in-law 'as she really is', i.e. she wants to see her justly: 'When M is just and loving she sees D as she really is' (1970: 37). This does not mean that she wants to see her as any other good moral agent would see her. For Murdoch, justice in an agent's personal life is not something absolute; nor need it incorporate the ideals of universality and impartiality. Rather, a concern for justice shows itself in a concern to be guided unselfishly so that one has a clear and truthful understanding of the situation, values and persons before one. Murdoch believes it is a concern motivated by a certain kind of love.

Following Murdoch, my account does not require that a just life be one lived in accordance with a set of rules or principles. Many theorists believe that, just as a judge in a courtroom needs a knowledge of the facts, a good working knowledge of certain points of law, and a good discursive intelligence in order to reach a just judgement, so justice in an agent's personal life also requires a knowledge of the facts, a set of just principles and a good discursive intelligence. By contrast, my account holds that justice in an agent's personal life requires, above all, the capacity to set aside certain aspects of her own self in order to clearly understand the situation and persons before her.

This is not to say that a just person never acts in accordance with certain principles. Yet it is not in virtue of applying the principles that she acts justly. Rather, she acts in accordance with the principles because she has arrived at her own clear understanding of the particularities of the situation, and she sees that the just thing here is, for example, to act impartially (i.e. to act in accordance with the principle of impartiality). The moral necessity or moral impossibility derives from her own moral understanding, not from what the principle prescribes. A set of moral principles may provide a good summary of the main ethical considerations at work in the moral thinking of a just person, and so these principles may guide the deliberations of other agents. But an agent's justice is not the result of her living in accordance with a set of principles, but is rather an expression of her moral understanding. This is not to say that a just agent does not have moral principles, but that the way she is related to her principles is different from the way an agent of moral theory is related to her theory's principles. The former's principles may always be trumped by her own assessment and clear understanding of what is before her.[27]

The facts of the matter, a set of just principles that are consistently and impartially applied, and a good discursive intelligence are not enough to lead one to justice. Were a racist to consistently apply the principles of equality and impartiality, and give equal treatment to all racial groups, his acts would not be an expression of justice. To be just, his acts need to be done in the same way and for the same reasons that a just person would do them (Aristotle 1941: 1105b5–10). A just person's acts flow from a certain psychic state: one that takes pleasure in the doing of just acts. The racist is unjust, not because he does not have the facts of the matter, a set of just principles that he consistently and impartially applies, or a good discursive intelligence, but because he is not concerned (or he is not able) to rid himself of aspects of his own self (e.g. his fears, hatred, narrow-mindedness, envy)[28] so as to see other racial groups 'as they are'.

When a just person makes a judgement regarding action, there is a sense of impersonal validity to the judgement: a sense that this is in fact the right way to judge. But this does not preclude the acknowledgement that there might be other, just as good and just, ways to see the situation, and to act. This contrasts with a widely held view that if two just people have all the facts, they will, if they are being objective, come to a very similar conclusion about action. For according to this view, just people make objective judgements. To say that their moral judgements are objective is to say that if two just people disagree over a particular evaluative matter, at least one of them must be mistaken. On the account presented here, a just judgement is neither absolute, objective, nor merely based on subjective preference. This view of justice speaks in favour of a different account being needed in moral philosophy of the relation between the personal and impersonal, and between the subjective and objective.

A lover of self has concerns that cannot be accurately described as either personal or impersonal, subjective or objective, as these are currently understood by moral philosophers. Such a self's sense of justice manifests itself in the desire to understand the true nature of certain values, the truth about itself, and about other selves. Yet it does not want to see things from a completely objective standpoint, one that would be reached by any other good moral agent; nor does it want a merely subjective understanding of the world (where 'subjective' refers to what is a matter of taste, preference or whim).

In Murdoch's example of the mother-in-law, the relevant sense of 'seeing her as she is' or (in my account) 'understanding her' is neither personal nor impersonal, subjective nor objective. More-over, it is not something that could be given by any theory, but is given by the mother-in-law's sense of fairness or justice. One might say that her justice is a causal agent of her understanding.

The question that arises here asks where her justice comes from and whether it is teachable. If one follows Socrates and claims that virtue is not teachable (the *Meno* and the *Protagoras*) since there are no criteria for it, the reply with which one must deal claims that if describing something is evidence of knowledge of it, then surely it must be teachable: if justice or virtue can be described, then one must have knowledge of what it is, and it must therefore be teachable.

A person who describes the chemical composition of water as consisting of hydrogen and oxygen may or may not speak with knowledge. We have criteria according to which it can be judged whether she speaks with knowledge, and if she does not, the relevant knowledge can be taught. But in the case of a person who says that x ought to be done, it can remain unclear whether the person speaks with knowledge because we do not have criteria according to which this can be judged. To the extent to which we have no criteria by which to judge whether a person who speaks on moral matters speaks with or without knowledge, we are entitled to doubt the very existence of such a thing as moral knowledge, and this despite the fact that we speak of some things as being good and some evil, and despite the fact that we are prepared to sacrifice our lives for the sake of certain highly valued things.

Although the surface grammar is the same in the case of having knowledge when citing the chemical composition of water and in the case of having knowledge when saying x ought to be done, the former is in crucial respects different from the latter. For judging that someone speaks with knowledge in the moral case is radically different from so judging in the case of her citing the chemical composition of water.

In the water case, what is primary is the *object* of knowledge: what is primary is the fact that hydrogen and oxygen comprise water and that the subject of knowledge should understand what it is for this to be the case. The moral case reverses the order so that what becomes primary is not the object but the *subject* of understanding.

It is *as if* one said 'Were water to be the sort of thing that spoke or acted with knowledge, it would do so with knowledge when it spoke or acted in accordance with its nature'. Here the objectivity is reversed so that what becomes primary is the subject of knowledge, and it allows the possibility that saying that x acts in accordance with its nature does not entail knowing what its nature is. This means that the knowledge it has is not teachable. So while we speak of a person being morally wise, and of moral wisdom, the understanding of a morally wise person is not derivable from what the person *knows* about, for example, human nature or human conditions of existence.

This does not mean that there cannot be a theory of moral subjectivity, but that any such theory would need to be radically different in nature from a theory of moral objects, i.e. radically different from a theory concerning what one ought and ought not to do. The objection regarding evil to my account of love of self, in wanting to locate the locus of the ethical in a certain objective content, overlooks the centrality of moral subjectivity for the ethical, and its difference from moral objectivity.

According to my account, the moral self is the self that emerges in the context of a certain kind of critical reflection that is involved in the search for understanding. This self is not constructed in the way that the empirical substantive self[29] is constructed: in the next section I will refer to an illustration of the way in which the moral self in fact involves a certain critical distancing from whatever has been constructed.

THE MORAL SELF, CRITICAL DISTANCING AND LOVE OF SELF

It is in virtue of her own sense of justice, rather than following a moral theory, that a lover of self seeks an understanding of the nature of certain values, of her own self, and of other selves. In this section we will see that a self that follows moral theory could not be a lover of self because the requirements of moral theory, in focusing on a certain objective content, impose certain non-contingent moral limitations on agents. These limitations are imposed in virtue of the kind of thinking to which agents who follow moral theory are confined. While moral theory can guarantee the performance of right acts, it cannot guarantee the emergence of a self that has a proper understanding of good and evil: it cannot guarantee a world of moral selves.

A sophisticated utilitarian might argue that the moral limitations I claim are imposed on agents who follow moral theory are merely contingent ones. She might argue that Raskolnikov acted badly because he misunderstood what following utilitarianism entailed, not because of anything that it imposes on agents. A Kantian would say that Raskolnikov went wrong because his actions were not motivated by duty: not understanding the importance of universalisability, he was led to an act that violated rational nature. Many theories would agree that Raskolnikov went wrong because he failed to attend properly to the particular content that constitutes the ultimate justification of action.

What Raskolnikov misunderstood, according to a sophisticated utilitarian, was exactly *where* he should apply the utilitarian criterion of assessment. He was wrong in thinking that the achievement of maximum utility required utilitarian thinking to go all the way down, and so applied the utilitarian criterion to his motives as well as to his actions and policies. His moral mistake had nothing to do with what a moral theory such as utilitarianism requires of its agents, and everything to do with his failure to grasp the good utilitarian reasons for being just and honest. The sophisticated utilitarian claim is that the moral limitations displayed by Raskolnikov's thinking and behaviour are *the limitations of Raskolnikov himself*, not the limitations of any moral theory. A Kantian could concur: moral theories provide agents with strict guidelines for motivation and action so they are able to resist responding with evil.

The sophisticated utilitarian claim is that persons should develop a certain kind of character, and act from non-utilitarian motives such as justice, benevolence and friendship (Railton 1984) because if they apply a utilitarian calculus to their motives we would have a world of Raskolnikovs, and *what a terrible world this would be*: we would have a world where people performed acts that reduced rather than maximised utility. We would have a world with more rather than less evil in it. Had Raskolnikov realised that a world where there were no murders is a far better world than one which contains murders, he may have still *wanted* to kill the pawnbroker, but as a good utilitarian he would have been unable to carry out the deed. Similarly, a Kantian can rule out the murder because, as a good Kantian agent, Raskolnikov would have realised that his subjective maxim could not be universalised without contradiction. These moral theories confront their agents with limits on action that rule out evil responses.

The limit that these theories impose on action, though, does not confront the self that follows them with what the experience of moral impossibility confronts an agent who finds that she *must* or that she *cannot* act in a certain way. For where a utilitarian will not do a certain thing because the world will be a far better place if people do not do that kind of thing, and where a Kantian will not do a certain thing because she cannot consistently will that everyone act on her subjective maxim, a lover of self cannot do a certain thing because, in the particular circumstances confronting her, the thing is *not do-able* by her. This does not mean that she knows what evil is (where evil is given by an objective content) and she will not do it. It means rather that, because of her particular understanding of the situation and of the possibilities before her, certain courses of action are simply not available to her.

Where a sophisticated utilitarian wants to avoid a world of Raskolnikovs because such a world could not be a world where utility was maximised, and where a Kantian wants to avoid a world of Raskolnikovs because such a world would not be one of rational beings sharing in the making of universal law, and so fitted to be members of a kingdom of ends, *we* should not want a world of Raskolnikovs because such a world would not be a world of beings in possession of moral understanding. Where a utilitarian does not want a world of Raskolnikovs because such a world would be a world rife with murders and thefts, and where a Kantian does not want a world of Raskolnikovs because such a world would not be a world of beings who respect rational nature, *we* should not want a world of Raskolnikovs because such a world would consist of people completely unequipped to morally understand the various situations in which they find themselves. In other words, a sophisticated utilitarian can rule out a world of Raskolnikovs on utilitarian grounds, and a Kantian can rule out a world of Raskolnikovs on grounds of inconsistency of the will, but neither theorist is able to rule out such a world on grounds that relate essentially to the ethical subject's own moral understanding.[30] The grounds that each theorist has for assenting to the terrible nature of a world of Raskolnikovs are grounds that are fundamentally related to a certain objective content, but these grounds depend *for their moral import* on a subject's understanding.

These theorists might claim that the grounds they have are the best moral grounds that anybody could possibly have, and that they do not depend on a subject's understanding for their moral import. A sophisticated utilitarian might claim that if people are brought up in the right way so that they develop certain kinds of characters and act from good motives, they will be morally committed to right acts so that suffering will be reduced and happiness maximised. What better moral grounds could one possibly want? And what kind of special moral understanding is required in order to see that this is a most desirable state of affairs? A Kantian might say that if people only acted on subjective maxims that could be consistently universalised, we would have a world where people only acted toward others in a way that they could consistently will that everybody should act. The Kantian claim is that there are no better moral grounds than these, and that these grounds do not depend for their moral import on any particular agent's moral understanding.[31] According to these theorists, what we need is a world of selves like Sonia who did not apply a utilitarian calculus to her motives nor act in a way that violated the categorical imperative, but instead helped others when she saw they needed help.[32]

A utilitarian theorist might point out that Sonia had a good Christian upbringing and that her self-sacrifice and benevolence alleviated Raskolnikov's suffering and saved him from the moral anguish which might otherwise have completely destroyed him. If we had more people like Sonia who help others when they are in need, the utilitarian says, we would have far less anxiety and suffering in the world. So the conclusion of utilitarian policy is to have a world of selves like Sonia: selves committed to the alleviation of anxiety and suffering. Such a world provides both a barrier against evil and a guarantee of good acts. In a similar way, Kantianism can provide such a barrier and such a guarantee: so long as we have a world of people committed to consistency of the will and respect for rational nature.

The barriers against evil acts that sophisticated utilitarianism and Kantians can provide may well be *the very best barriers that there could possibly be.* But what these theorists are unable to admit is that a self committed to justice is a *precondition* of moral thinking and not the result of some general policy regarding what kinds of people it would be best to have in the world (utilitarianism) or the result of engaging in a process of deliberation that tests for consistency of the will (Kantians). An inescapable outcome for a self of thinking in a utilitarian or Kantian fashion about moral options is a limiting of the self's capacity to *morally* understand the situation before it. This might best be demonstrated by considering exactly why Sonia helped Raskolnikov and what it was she responded to through that helping. This will also further show why the Hegelian conception of the self is fundamentally flawed.

A sophisticated utilitarian will describe Sonia as an embodiment of everything a good moral agent should be: benevolent, kind, helpful, self-sacrificing. A Kantian might well join the utilitarian theorist in pointing out that Sonia saw that Raskolnikov needed help and that she gave this help, and while it is not clear that she acted from duty, she did nothing that violated duty. But such a portrayal is quite untrue to what Dostoevsky wants to convey through his characterisation. Sonia does not respond to Raskolnikov simply because she sees he needs help. Raskolnikov in fact persists in *not* asking her for help. What she perceives is that he is in *mortal moral danger*, and that he is not at all aware of this. The moral danger does not consist in the fact that he has killed a human being (it does not consist in any objective content at all), but rather in the way in which he *thinks* about what he has done. He thinks he has killed a louse, and that this is no crime. Sonia perceives that he is suffering anxiety over having morally transgressed, but that he has no understanding whatsoever of what he has done and is suffering because he thinks he has killed his own utilitarian principles. A sophisticated utilitarian is only able to talk about the kind benevolent person who alleviates suffering, and a Kantian is only able to talk about respecting rational nature and acting from duty. Neither theorist is able to give due recognition to the response of a person who responds to another's moral anguish. This is because both theorists must treat moral anguish as being like any other type of anguish. A utilitarian will say that moral anguish (like all other anguish) is anguish that it is better not to have, and a Kantian will say that just as it is a duty to help others where one can, so it is a duty to relieve another's moral anguish where one can. Neither theorist is able to attribute a positive moral value to moral uncertainty and anguish.

That an erosion in moral understanding is an inescapable consequence of thinking in a utilitarian or Kantian way is revealed in these theories needing to rule out moral anguish as a relevant moral category. The moral barrier I have described has a crucial place for moral anguish, because a person who experiences this anguish questions whether, in the circumstances, the values to which she is committed are in fact worthy of being pursued by her. A sophisticated utilitarian who then replies that we had better have people who go through this kind of moral anguish because such people will make a better world, again reveals the thinness of the thinking and understanding that results from locating the ethical in an objective content, since he completely misses the point. The point is not that it is better to have moral anguish because we will then have a better world, or because we will have a world of rational beings committed to acting from duty,[33] but rather because we will then have a world of selves who engage in the kind of reflective evaluation according to which they may then be able to revise their values, commitments and ends. That is, it is better to have moral anguish because we will then have a world of moral selves.

An Hegelian is at loggerheads with this view; for him the constitution of the moral self requires the stage of moral anguish to be transcended. Given that a mark of being a moral self is the experience of moral anguish, the Hegelian conception must be rejected.

When Raskolnikov confesses the murder to Sonia and tells her that he had merely killed a louse, she says to him in horror 'What have you done to yourself?' (362). She is concerned about the self for whose well-being he is solely responsible, the self which for Hegel merely represents a primitive stage to be transcended. (This is the self which, while missing in Hume, is very much at the forefront of Rousseau's thinking. If we accept the Hegelian story about the self's constitutive relation with the state, we lose what is of central value in Rousseau's thought.)

When Sonia asks Raskolnikov 'What have you done to yourself?' she expresses her horror at Raskolnikov's lack of moral understanding and lack of remorse.[34] For a utilitarian, good and evil are reflections of decreases and increases in suffering, and a better world is a world in which there is less rather than more suffering. Since the presence of remorse spells the presence of suffering, one expects the utilitarian claim to be that the less remorse that is being felt in the world, the better that world will be. A utilitarian might say that there are useful sufferings, remorse being one of these. Yet a utilitarian can only point to the possible *consequential* advantages of remorse: any other emotion that yielded the same consequences would be just as good. Utilitarians cannot regard remorse as being internal to an agent's moral understanding of the terribleness of what she has done.

It is difficult to know exactly what a Kantian might say here, but it would seem to follow from Kant's great admiration of the person who is overcome by his own personal sorrows, or who is cold in temperament and indifferent to the sufferings of others, but who still has the strength of will to obey the moral law (Kant 1969: 64), that were Raskolnikov a Kantian agent who had transgressed, he could understand the magnitude of what he had done *without caring* about the pawnbroker being dead.

A lack of caring, a coldness, an indifference and an incapacity for experiencing any emotion, including remorse, feature in the inner life of Maria von Herbert, who wrote to Kant in 1791 and 1793[35] telling him that she had no trouble at all in obeying the moral law. She is, as Langton (1992) points out, a Kantian saint, well on the way to achieving 'bliss': the state which includes 'complete independence from inclinations and desires'. Inclinations are 'always burdensome to a rational being...they...elicit from him the wish to be free of them...[and be] subject only to law-giving reason' (Kant 1956: 118, 122–3). Von Herbert's inner life represents the paradigm of Kantian moral perfection: she needs no longer resist, struggle with, or overcome inclination. In her letter she writes that she would eagerly do twice as much as morality commands. Yet morality does not spring here from an integrated, substantial, whole self, for there is for von Herbert no self she can truly call her own:

> I feel that a vast emptiness extends inside me... *I almost find myself to be superfluous, unnecessary. Nothing attracts me. I'm tormented by a boredom* that makes life intolerable.... I beg you to give me something that will get this *intolerable emptiness* out of my soul.
>
> (Langton 1992: 493–4, my emphasis)

Langton comments: 'It takes no expert to wonder if she is in danger' (1992: 498). Anyone with such a constricted, miserable, deficient and malfunctioning emotional life is of course in danger. No one should be surprised that von Herbert committed suicide. She no longer felt the pull of inclinations because she was completely out of touch with her own emotions, and so out of touch with herself. Von Herbert's inner life seems consistent with a borderline personality disorder[36] whose cardinal features are feelings of deadness, emptiness, boredom and low self-esteem. At the heart of this disturbance is the fear that 'there is no real me' (von Herbert writes that she feels 'superfluous', 'unnecessary'). Individuals suffering this disorder feel their lives to be futile, since their experience lacks a feeling of reality: being in a state of self-fragmentation, they have formed 'false selves' as defences. By reacting to impingements from the external environment, and conforming to its demands, a false self is maintained in order to achieve momentary satisfaction and fragile good feelings.[37] Such individuals, having a contracted inner life, are unable to genuinely respond to the world because they lack internal cohesiveness and a sense of personal agency. Morality for them can only be experienced as impingement from outside,[38] rather than as emanating from their own selves, since they are not attuned to their selves or to their own inner realities.[39]

The presentation of Kant's man in the *Groundwork* who is

overcome by his own sorrows and is cold and indifferent to the sufferings of others, but still manages to tear himself from his 'deadly insensibility' and obey the moral law, is consistent with von Herbert's self-presentation. It may appear that moral constraints for such a person are imposed from within rather than from without. For such an individual, in legislating the moral law for himself, ensures that his will is good, his motives pure, and his choice of maxims may be revealing of his freedom and autonomy. Yet moral constraints cannot be internal in the sense required on the account I have presented: von Herbert's case demonstrates that a Kantian self can be an insubstantial self which is unable to experience morality as emanating from within because it is out of touch with whatever is within, or there may in fact not be anything within with which it might be in touch and from which morality might spring. For moral constraints to be internal in the required sense, they must present themselves to a self whose self-description is only *partly* constituted by rationality.[40] This is a cohesive self whose emotional-affective life provides crucially important aspects of its moral understanding.[41]

Its moral understanding does not at any point connect with a Kantian agent's understanding. For the way in which Kantian understanding presents another human being as a limit to the will leaves out what is central to the moral response of a moral self: the Kantian concern with rational nature means that the particularity of the other is completely lost.

This has significance for Raskolnikov's relationship with remorse, had he been a Kantian agent. Since the object of remorse is the particular person one has wronged, as a Kantian agent Raskolnikov would not be one for whom remorse could have moral significance or who could regard remorse as internal to a proper moral response to what he had done.[42]

A sophisticated utilitarian might claim that Raskolnikov should indeed have felt remorse because we would have a better world if people who transgressed felt remorse. But the utilitarian justification for such a claim could only be made in terms of how this would affect future actions (and so in terms of how it would affect the content of the ethical: utility). Yet Sonia was not at all concerned with Raskolnikov's future actions or with utility. She wanted him to feel remorse only because of how this would affect himself: because of how feeling remorse would inform his own moral understanding of what he had done. She responds to Raskolnikov, not as one of the many suffering people in the world (and not as a rational being), but she responds to him in his particularity. This means that she is not concerned that it become true that he be saved (nor is she concerned to respect rational nature in him); she is rather concerned with helping him to acquire the capacity to save himself. She is concerned that he take responsibility for the self for which only he can be responsible. She does not simply respond to Raskolnikov, as a utilitarian would claim, out of benevolence; she does not respond to him as a result of considering what her duty is; nor does she overcome any obstacles of sensibility. Her concern is, nevertheless, of a deeply moral nature.[43] An inescapable feature of a thinking which locates good and evil in an objective content is an inability to recognise the moral nature of a personal concern with the moral self, whether that self be one's own or that of another.[44]

Moreover, in order to enact the conclusions of deliberation that assumes good and evil to be given by a certain content, the self must effect a certain distancing from its own values: one that relies on theory. To maximise utility, utilitarians must be prepared to distance themselves from what they may see as being of ultimate value. Kantians must do so for the sake of duty. But if we look at the distancing in which Sonia engaged, we find a critical distancing that does not at any point fall back on theory.

Sonia turned to prostitution to save her family from starvation. She was a person for whom self-respect was an ultimate value, but this value did not represent for her a particular content that, no matter what the circumstances were, would determine how she would act. Instead, she was able to re-assess the goodness of pursuing this value in light of the demands which her family's destitution made on her. To do this, she had to distance herself from the value of self-respect. Her distancing was a critical distancing, but the understanding she gained of what she had to do was not facilitated by turning to any theory.[45] Rather, it was as a result of her own sense of justice that she was concerned to understand what, in these circumstances, she should do, and whether *in these circumstances* self-respect was a value that should be pursued. She did not act merely in virtue of her beliefs or values, but, as an ethical subject, she had the capacity to distance herself from these, and to redraw the boundaries of what was and was not acceptable behaviour according to the particular circumstances. As an ethical subject, Sonia was not related (even) to her own beliefs and values in such a way that these would determine her actions. There was nothing apart from her own understanding of the particular

185

circumstances before her that could determine this. In other words, her virtue was not explicable in terms of her moral values, beliefs or knowledge (e.g. about self-respect or loyalty) but her moral understanding was rather explicable in terms of her virtue or justice: her moral understanding was explicable in terms of her own goodness.[46]

We should note that this claim concerning Sonia says nothing about the question that our imagined objector might ask: whether Sonia was a person who might become involved in evil. I remain silent on this question because it supposes that evil is given by some objective content, and I have made it clear that I do not take the ethical to be given by any particular content. I restrict the claim about Sonia to the observation that a person like her (whom I take to be a lover of self) will always retain that measure of self-awareness and self-concern that will not permit *the content* of any belief or value to take over and determine her acts.

It is precisely this – allowing the content of beliefs and values to determine action – that can be seen to characterise the mentality of those Nazis who enacted Hitler's genocidal policies. Hannah Arendt, who was present at Eichmann's trial and execution, writes that there was in Eichmann no sign of firm ideological commitment or specific evil motives. 'the only notable characteristic one could detect... was something entirely negative: it was not stupidity but *thoughtlessness*' (Arendt 1978: 4). She found this thoughtlessness terrifying because it was the same kind of thoughtlessness which explained Eichmann's conscientious service to Hitler's genocidal policies.[47]

Eichmann valued the 'Aryan race' and firmly believed that its welfare required him to do certain things. The objection under consideration might point out that Eichmann was loyal, conscientious and brave. He was committed to certain values and to a community. In virtue of the strength of his values and commitments, he appears to be the type of person who could develop love of self, but is a person who responded to the situation in Nazi Germany with the most horrendous evil.

Although the Nazis might have been kind, generous, reliable, committed to a community and beneficent to other German 'Aryans', *qua* Nazis they lacked epistemic control over their evaluations and acts because for them good and evil were given by an objective content, quashing any possible reassessment of their beliefs and values. *Qua* Nazis, their self-identifications, values, relationships, loyalties and loves had to be filtered through certain important considerations that employed a determinate objective content: they identified themselves in complete otherness to the Jews who were defined as sub-human. *Qua* Nazis, they defined themselves as existing in a totally different realm of being from the Jews. What was good, worthy, valuable, a conceivable object of their love or loyalty was definitionally 'other than Jewish'. The Jews, Gypsies and communists represented for them a fixed objective content that was definitive of evil, this being the ultimate determinant of action. One does not need to wait and see what acts might follow from, or what the consequences might be of this kind of thinking to know that we have here the paradigm of moral evil. Without wishing to trivialise the unfathomable evil of the reality of the Holocaust, the claim is that moral evil resides already in the structure of thought and valuing: it does not need to await action or action's consequences.

It is not merely the case that vicious values are not the kind of values that can serve to build love of self, but that values also have to be held in a certain way. It is not enough that a person be committed to kindness, loyalty, courage, conscientiousness, etc. A person needs to be committed to these as a result of her own justice: when motivated by her own sense of justice, a person has the capacity to decide for herself what the just thing to do in these particular circumstances would be, whether, for example, loyalty to the SS or conscientiousness in carrying out its requirements are worthy of her concern and commitment. The experience of moral impossibility marks the limits drawn by a lover of self of her own moral boundaries, and these might change from situation to situation.[48]

For example, while prostitution might normally have been out of the question as a possible way of going about things for Sonia, in light of her family's destitution it became the only possible alternative. Understanding the situation as she did, she had the capacity to redraw the boundaries of what was for her morally possible and impossible, and this in virtue of her own justice or goodness.

By contrast, Raskolnikov's beliefs concerning inferiority and superiority represented a fixed content that took over his consciousness and determined how he would act. Since the pawnbroker was 'ordinary', she could not be a conceivable object of his respect. It is already in the structure of his thinking and

187

evaluating that evil resides: we do not have to await the murder of the pawnbroker (the objective content) to find the evil. While some things are evil in virtue of their effects on recipients, we should recognise that some things are evil because of the mentality that is expressed.

Modern moral theory generally requires the thoughts, values and proposed acts of agents to pass through a set of considerations concerning an objective content before they can be regarded as the thoughts and acts of a moral being, and so as 'really good'. Utilitarians say they value friendship, justice, community and benevolence, but as values these are conditional on their maximising utility. For a Kantian, acts of friendship and benevolent acts motivated by sympathy can be valuable so long as they are informed by, and do not violate, duty. While nothing can guarantee an absence of action that might result in others being harmed, it seems that what makes evaluations and acts over which a person has minimal epistemic control possible, is that thinking which must first pass through a filter given by a fixed objective content. For with this kind of thinking present, what is given by the objective content, rather than the self's own understanding of the particular circumstances, and of what, in these circumstances, it *must* do, is the ultimate determinant of action. A fixed objective content through which thought must pass serves as a constraint to condition the self's evaluations, attachments and responses: for example, the object of attachment or love must not be Jewish; it must fit the category 'superior'; it must not conflict with duty; it must be a utility maximiser.[49] It is already in the structure of this kind of thinking, where theory is looked for as the ultimate justification, that we should be alerted to a lack of epistemic control over the self's responses. It is in this lack of epistemic control on the part of Raskolnikov that Dostoevsky locates his moral deficiency. By contrast, Sonia is presented as a person who does not need any theory or ultimate justification to know how to act.

Dostoevsky shows that the self that looks to theory for moral knowledge, being confined in its thinking by the particular content which describes the ethical, is not a self that will understand what a person like Sonia is about. So he has Raskolnikov tell Sonia that she too, through her prostitution (to which she resorted to save her family), had transgressed in exactly the same way in which he had himself transgressed in committing the murders (292). Having in mind a concept of the ethical as being given by a certain fixed content, he could not possibly understand Sonia's decision to prostitute herself. He thought in a utilitarian way about Sonia's situation, and concluded that the murders he committed were morally on a par with her prostitution. In seeking good and evil in an objective content, he could not see that while Sonia, because of her prostitution, might not have been a respected member of the community, she still preserved her constitutive ties to her immediate community (her family) through an act of self-sacrifice,[50] and her ties to her wider community (represented by Raskolnikov) by providing him with an opportunity for regeneration. While Raskolnikov, through the murders, destroys himself as a human being, Sonia, in spite of her prostitution, preserves what makes her a good moral agent: the quality of character or mind that enables her to reassess her own values and beliefs. The crucial difference between Raskolnikov's and Sonia's 'transgressions' is that Sonia, despite being a prostitute, retains a secure inner core that enables her to remain related to an immediate and a broader community: she remains, till the end, a self that is able to retain a clear understanding of right and wrong, good and evil, and does not need a moral theory to tell her why she should act in such-and-such a way. We might want to say that she, but not Raskolnikov, retains what is needed in order to know what it is to be a human being.[51]

It is not merely that Sonia had a clear understanding of good and evil without needing to turn to theory or any objective content that theory could offer; the nature of her understanding was such that it *could not have been given* by any theory. For her thinking contained no notion that any other person similarly placed would be obliged, forbidden or permitted to act in the way she found she had to act. Her decision to prostitute herself contained no judgement about what any other person in her circumstances should do.[52] For Sonia did not act merely in virtue of some *belief* that she held, one transferable to how others in the same situation should behave.[53]

We may surmise that Sonia held certain beliefs about love, loyalty, and perhaps debt. But the *beliefs* that are held concerning the content of the ethical do not separate the good from the bad people: the distinction between good and bad people cuts across the beliefs that people hold. Perhaps love, loyalty and debt were singled out in Sonia's thinking in a special way, but this says nothing about how another (good or bad) person might see the particulars if placed in the same circumstances (Walker 1987). The variety and richness of moral thinking and understanding cannot possibly be captured by those categories which describe the thinking and understanding available to the self that locates the ethical in an objective content: the categories of universalisability, reciprocity, impartiality and universal principle.

The portrayal of Raskolnikov as a person who seeks moral knowledge and guidance in an objective content is not intended to suggest that such a person will necessarily be a bad person. It is intended to suggest rather that certain requirements on thinking (and so on understanding) that are imposed when one locates the ethical in a fixed objective content can be shown to have non-contingent moral limitations. These pertain to a lack of epistemic control over evaluation and action. So, for example, Raskolnikov says 'No, I couldn't do it, I couldn't do it' (55). But two pages later he concludes he will perform the murder. His emotions continue to provide him with the moral understanding of the foulness of taking a human life, while his intellect focuses on a certain objective content: the greatest overall good that will be achieved by using the pawnbroker's money. We have illustrated in Raskolnikov's location of the ethical in an objective content the inevitable schism for the self between two levels of value. The ensuing portrayal of Raskolnikov's inner life illustrates how horrifying such a schism is for the self that experiences it. We have illustrated the schizophrenia between living the life of a self that locates the ethical in an objective content, on the one hand, and a moral self's ethical life, on the other (see Stocker 1976).

Dostoevsky's portrayal of Sonia is aimed at showing that there is a very close connection between the kind of thinking that expresses a concern with re-assessing and revising of values and commitments (a concern that I claim is constitutive of the moral self) and certain non-contingent limitations that this kind of thinking presents. I have aimed to show that the kind of thinking to which a moral theory which seeks to locate the ethical in some objective content confines its agents is the kind that is not able to deal with the moral transgressions of those limitations. We should consider, for example, the utilitarian possibility of taking seriously the perilous thought that if the world would be a better place with less justice and benevolence and with more of Raskolnikov's superior people, then this is what we should be motivated to bring about. A sophisticated utilitarian might be able to block this thought from being seriously entertained on the good utilitarian grounds that if it were seriously entertained the consequences of action would be less good. But the utilitarian is only able to address the *consequential* peril of this thought. He is completely powerless to address its moral peril. A Kantian could address the peril of this thought in terms of inconsistency of the will, but is also powerless to address its moral peril. The thinness of the thinking of a moral theory that locates good and evil in an objective content is unable to come to terms with the evil with which this thought is imbued. It is unable to come to terms with the recognition had by a lover of self that certain thoughts are evil because they are destructive of what is of ultimate worth.[54]

The objection that I have been considering – that a person might develop love of self while engaging in evil – shares with many moral theories the view that good and evil are given by a determinate objective content, and so suffers from the same moral limitations on thinking as do these theories. While I have no direct reply to this objection because I am unable to share the presupposition on which it is based, I believe that the account of love of self presented here, in avoiding the kind of theoreticism which Dostoevsky shows to be Raskolnikov's moral undoing, can ensure that a world of moral selves, as envisaged by this account, will be a world of selves who will 'strain every nerve' (Aristotle) to be good, because it will be a world of selves with a truthful concern for justice and for the significance of what they do.

Conclusion

The account presented in *The Moral Self* leans heavily on Aristotelian thought, and shares with Aristotle a commitment to not making some determinate objective content the locus of ethics. The general trend in much modern moral theory has been to take certain fixed beliefs and values to be prior to moral behaviour, and to conceive of these as being the particular content on which our ethical attention should focus. I have singled out Aristotle, Hume, Rousseau and Hegel as examples of four philosophers who, I believe, made an attempt to make the same point that I have tried to bring out in this work: that the development of the moral self is prior to any ethical content and so should be the focal point of ethical inquiry. What is most striking about the writings of these philosophers are their attempts, not to present a moral theory *per se*, but rather to present a theory about the moral self. These differences mark off their ethics from both Kantian and utilitarian theories.

For Aristotle, the relation that a person has to her own self has a very close connection to her moral capacity. The self must first be in a certain state if it is to be able to relate to others in the way in which a virtuous person is able. Rather than focusing on a theory of right action, or on any objective content that might describe the ethical, we saw that Aristotle focuses instead on what is involved in a self's self-realisation as a moral being: for him this centrally involves the self in developing a certain kind of self-love rather than acquiring a certain set of values or beliefs.

For Hume the perspective of the party of humanity does not represent any particular fixed set of beliefs which might be taken to be the content of the ethical. Adjusting one's outlook to this perspective is rather for him an adjustment which aligns one's view so that it fits with what is civilised. This adjustment involves a continuous adaptation of thought and behaviour in order to comply with trusted voices. Doing so enables one to be on guard against allowing a mere fixed belief to determine action. There is of course quite some secularisation in Hume's philosophy, but the trusted voices of the party of humanity cannot in any way be regarded as representing a fixed determinate content that is taken to be the ethical: these voices are not supposed to take the place of divine commandments, as do the tenets of Kantianism and utilitarianism.

Similarly, Rousseau's general will cannot be taken to represent a fixed content that marks the boundaries of the ethical. Society's interests are always liable to be revised and changed. So in Rousseau we also find an implicit denial that some fixed belief or value should be the ultimate determinant of action.

Rousseau's contrast between *amour de soi* and *amour-propre* distinguishes two distinct kinds of self-valuing, and it might appear that the distinction between pride and love of self that is central to *The Moral Self* is akin to Rousseau's distinction. Yet where pride in my account simply represents a way in which a person who is not a lover of self may gain self-worth, we have seen that *amour-propre* is for Rousseau far more than this. And while *amour de soi* is an innate possession of the self in the state of nature (what there is to love about the self is, from the beginning, already in its possession), according to the account of love of self presented in *The Moral Self*, what there is to love about the self must be achieved.[1]

Moreover, the distinction between pride and love of self in my account is grounded in quite different considerations from those that underlie Rousseau's distinction. While it might seem that Rousseau's *amour de soi* is akin to what I have termed 'love of self', particularly in view of the contrast he draws between it and *amour-propre*, my account does not contain any notion of a return to the goodness of some former state: it does not make any paranoiac references to the self being deprived of its inner goodness and unity; and nor does my account depend on a social or political structure for the development of love of self and the emergence of the moral self. Love of self centrally involves a desire to have a just understanding of the persons before one, of the particular circumstances in which one finds oneself, of the significance of certain human values and of what it is to be committed to such values, together with a capacity and willingness to distance from these. By contrast, as we saw in Chapter 2, what is central to

193

Rousseau's account is the three-tiered structure of advance, deterioration and return. Where my account is concerned to present an answer to the question of what a moral self is, Rousseau runs this question together with the question of how to alleviate a widespread catastrophic psychological malaise. And in answering this question he arrives at the concept of *amour de soi*.

We have seen that what makes the crucial distinction between *amour de soi* and *amour-propre* possible for Rousseau is his taking civilisation seriously as a self creating force. My account of the distinction between love of self and a dependence on pride for self-worth has nothing of the advance, deterioration and return that we find in Rousseau. There is in my account nothing that is lost that needs to be regained. The distinction rests for me instead on the level of understanding and quality of reflection had by a person who is a lover of self and a moral being. The making of this distinction in my account is motivated by a need to distinguish different levels of epistemic understanding; on my account, a self's understanding of the particular circumstances, of the significance of certain values, and its understanding of when and why it must distance itself from these, is constitutive of the moral self. For Rousseau, a self is moral only when it adheres to certain absolute moral limits. These limits are articulated by him in terms of the general will (his three-tiered structure having led him to the concept of the general will). So while it might seem that the distinction between love of self and a dependence on pride for self-worth in my account is close to Rousseau's distinction between *amour de soi* and *amour-propre*, the role that the former distinction plays in my account is quite unlike the role that the latter distinction plays in his.

We saw that Rousseau's account of what makes a will a moral will is given in terms of it conforming to the general will. There is in this account no commitment to a range of human values as there is in my account. Rousseau saw that people in society held *amour-propre* to be the only ultimate value, and his solution to the catastrophic consequences of this problem was to impose an idealised kind of filter (the general will) through which people needed to see themselves and others in order to be moral.

As both a psycho-social moralist and a political thinker, Rousseau failed to see that it is one thing to reduce the impact of the artificiality of *amour-propre*, and quite another thing to make explicit what sort of values must accompany the right kind of self-valuing. He had nothing to say about what kind of values a moral being should be committed to, or the consequences for a person of being committed to certain values. If a person were to be committed to certain values (as in the account of love of self presented in this book), the person would not, on Rousseau's account, be free. Rousseau failed to separate the question of what concrete values the right kind of self-valuing involves one in, from the question of how to alleviate the psychological malaise caused by civilisation. We saw that he ran together the question of the alleviation of this malaise with the question of what a moral self is, in such a way that the answer to both questions was the undistortion of the self. The result is that while the absolute moral limits (given by the general will) that Rousseau derives from his conception of what constitutes a substantive moral self ensure that no fixed beliefs regarding good and evil will determine the actions of a moral self (since the general will is not given by a determinate objective content),[2] there is nothing to ensure that the general will will conform to an individual's own assessment of what, in the particular circumstances, would be the just thing to do.

Rousseau's writings share with those of Hume a focusing on the moral self. Although quite different accounts of the moral self are given by these philosophers, both are centrally concerned with the question of what makes a self moral (rather than with presenting a theory of right action).

We saw that this concern was shared by Hegel, for whom the moral self was conceived of in universal terms. Hegel also shares with Hume and Rousseau the view that the ethical is not given by any determinate objective content. The ultimate moral aim for Hegel was that the individual should identify his own will with universal will, and universal will was conceived of as being based on rational principles. But what was rational could appear in different ways in different historical settings.

Of course Hegel (like both Hume and Rousseau) has no room in his ethics for the notion of an agent making a reason into *his* reason. So I do not attribute to him the notion of what I term 'love of self', but I have referred to Hegelian 'ethical self-valuing'. One might say that although Hegel does not refer to the moral importance of what I have termed 'love of self', implicit in his account is the view that since entrance into the moral domain involves a form of self-consciousness (consciousness of the self as a vehicle of *Geist*), and since the self becomes constituted via a reflection of this self-consciousness in the eyes of others, it is thus mutual recognition of this self-consciousness that takes the Hegelian agent beyond Hume's 'How I appear in others' eyes' to the importance of the state. So we can say that Hume's pride would be regarded by Hegel as a less advanced form of ethical self-valuing, a form that is superseded in Hegel's account by the importance of the state. Ethical self-valuing for Hegel derives from an individual's coming to a self-consciousness of itself as an integral part of, and from its participation in, the state and its ethical life. In addition, Hegel's holism would preclude him from allowing my account of individual self-transformation and self-making according to deeply held values to be a source of ethical self-valuing, meaningfulness or morality: for Hegel, it can only be with reference to the whole political community that morality and meaningfulness can be attained.

Neither Aristotle, Hume, Rousseau nor Hegel conceived of the moral limits that confront a moral self in the way in which these are conceived of by many modern moral theorists: as external, intellectually or socially constructed guards on action given by a determinate content. They all share with the account presented in *The Moral Self* a concern with the subject rather than the object of moral understanding.

On the whole, my account is probably more sympathetic to the Hegelian account than to Hume or Rousseau. Hegel and I both go beyond the Kantian account of autonomous achievement, and there are elements in Hegel's approach that I find preferable to the accounts that Hegel sets out to go beyond (i.e. those of Rousseau and Kant). Of course, the terms in which my account is developed are not Hegelian, and what motivates my inquiry is not what motivates Hegel's philosophy. Furthermore, Hegel regards the individual to be an abstraction, and the aim of the self to be that of recognising itself as absolute and universal. By contrast, the aim of the self is presented by me as the achievement of its own empirical expression in the world through embodying non-contingent values in what it does.

Moreover, I do not think that one needs to agree with Hegel that self-knowledge is something completable. While we can agree with him that the development of morality requires a community (whether it be an immediate or wider community), the account of *The Moral Self* denies the Hegelian thesis that a minimal condition for being an ethical being is a full political community. It denies

Hegel's thesis regarding both the Absolute Idea and the constitutive relation between the self and the state.

A further important difference between the account presented here and the Hegelian account is that Hegel does not see any tension between ethics and politics (in the same way that ethics and politics did not represent a tension for Aristotle). For him these collapse into one another, and we have seen that a consequence of this is his unfortunate views on the ethical significance of war. In addition to the customs, practices and laws of the state, there is for Hegel no remainder that is ethics. Ethics is for him completely described by politics. By contrast, on my account the development of the moral self is not exhausted by the socio-political arena as it is in Hegel.

Of course, if we reject Hegel's account of ethics and politics as collapsing into one another, with no tension between them, we are left with the need to offer an alternative account of the relationship between the ethical, on the one hand, and the political and social on the other. I do not think we have to opt for an absolute dualism here in order to avoid Hegel's conclusions regarding war.

I believe that we can extricate ourselves from the Hegelian legacy which sees the perspective of the state and its activities as exhausting the sphere of the ethical, and the ethical sphere as ruling out almost all forms of subjectivity. For we can point to an important area that is neglected by Hegel: the various practices that are involved in critical reflection on, and evaluation and re-assessment of, beliefs, values and ends. It is on these practices that my account has focused. These practices are not at all state-oriented, and we have seen that they encompass forms of subjectivity while at the same time being of great ethical import.

This book has presented a motivation to engage in these practices, and so a condition for the development of the moral self (which I conceive of as emerging in the context of these practices) as being a sense of justice, and I have claimed that this cannot be gained by acquiring certain pieces of knowledge. A central claim has been that virtue is not something teachable. A crucial point that emerges from my account is a reversal of the view of many moral theories that virtue is to be explained in terms of moral knowledge. In contrast to this view, moral understanding has been presented here as being explicable in terms of an agent's virtue. So a conclusion to be drawn from *The Moral Self* is that the ethical subject is not an object of knowledge. What we do know about the ethical subject is that she will always retain that measure of self-awareness and self-concern that will not permit the *content* of a belief or value to take over and determine her behaviour.

Despite virtue not being an object of knowledge, and so not something teachable, it has been presented here as something over which human agents have quite some control. It has been argued that the moral self values itself, not as the result of social and cultural forces over which it has little control, but rather for what it makes of itself. A person needs to have the psychic capacity to be able to avoid simply accommodating his self to the opinions and evaluations of others, and so to avoid valuing himself simply by means of a reflected image of his qualities and achievements, in order to have the capacity for virtue. As moral beings we esteem ourselves, not for how others see us, or for how our selves happen to have become constituted. Our moral self-constitution must be seen by us to be a manifestation of our own agency in order for it to be a source of what I have termed 'love of self'. As an infinitely refinable task (Murdoch), the development of the moral self is something for which we, individually, are to be held responsible:

> We are agents. Our constitution is put in our own power. We are charged with it; and therefore are accountable for any disorder or violation of it.
>
> (Butler 1969: 327)

Notes

CHAPTER I

1 Hume's account is gleaned from *A Treatise of Human Nature* and *An Enquiry Concerning the Principles of Morals*. References to these works will be abbreviated as T and E respectively.

2 Hume argues in Book One of the *Treatise* that reason is unable to disclose our personal identity since there is no metaphysical pure ego that reason can find. In Book Two he shows that our passions disclose personal identity: they disclose the self as possessor of certain qualities and attributes, the self for which we care and are concerned. This is the self of experience: the non-metaphysical self.

3 Primordial because it is (as we will see below) extremely primitive as well as pre-moral. It precedes the moral self which supersedes it.

4 Pride involves a reflex to another's pleasure – one where judgements concerning oneself are reinforced by others' esteem: one's own judgement and sentiment is not much use unless 'seconded by the opinions and sentiments of others' (T 316).

5 Thus Hume claims that animals can feel both pride and humility. See T 327–8 and Baier (1985).

6 For Hume's explanation of the relationship between impressions of reflexion and impressions of sensation see T 7–8.

7 Since 'ourself, independent of the perception of every other object is in reality nothing' (T 278), there is no such thing for Hume as unqualified pride in one's self as such. Pride always corresponds to a specific cause: some perception of a particular positive quality or attribute related to the self (Baier 1978: 36).

8 For a discussion of a number of objections to Hume's account of pride and the idea of the self, and some possible replies on Hume's behalf, see Rorty (1990).

9 Thus 'What is meant by saying that I am the object of pride, is that the feeling of pride is always and everywhere *followed* by the idea of myself' (Neu 1977: 8) is not quite right. My reconstruction of Hume's account will show that for him the idea of my self always accompanies pride: the idea of myself and my pride are simultaneous constructs. As we shall see more clearly below, we should say that the construction of pride and the construction of the idea of the self are systemic effects

199

which cannot be disentangled from each other or from the system of perceptions which gives rise to them. Neu writes:

> I have shown that one is forced (on pain of more immediate incoherencies) to understand Hume's notion of object in such a way that the object is not an effect either of the emotion [pride] itself or of the cause of the emotion, but rather is a cause of the emotion. That is, within Hume's system, the object collapses into the cause. And this is devastating to the whole system.

He continues:

> One must have the idea of self in contemplating the thing and its pleasant quality if one is to experience pride (rather than merely joy), so the idea of self is involved in the very idea of the subject or cause of pride. But if it is involved it is present, and if it is present it need not *arise*.... No new idea of self emerges as object. If the idea of self is still said to be the object of pride, the relation may still be said to be causal, but now the relation is seen to be reversed: the 'object' must be seen as a part of the cause of the pleasant sensation which is pride, and not its effect.

(1977: 28)

Neu looks for a non-Humean cause of pride in Hume's account, one which Hume successfully undermines, and points to incoherencies in it. We will see below that in his account of pride Hume successfully removes any metaphysical notion of 'cause' where pride would need to be presented as producing an effect (the idea of the self) which is independently describable from, and later than, pride. Self enters into both the cause and object of pride, and this is what has confused Hume's readers. We will see that for Hume, self can enter in an unproblematic way into the cause of pride, as well as be its object.

10 So my reconstruction only apparently goes against Hume's claim that pride produces the idea of the self. When we understand him to be getting rid of any metaphysical notion of 'cause', and asserting instead a relationship of mutual interaction and construction between pride and the idea of the self, we remove the confusions that philosophers have found in his account without needing to be at loggerheads with, or contradicting, anything Hume actually says.

It might be asked why Hume does not instead say that the self produces pride. Were Hume to have said this, it would look as though he were asserting a Cartesian order of things with the self there as a given. I take Hume's saying that pride produces the idea of the self to be a rhetorical way of undermining the view that the self is something given in experience. I thank Christopher Cordner for making me consider this question.

11 One must distinguish two things here. The first is the performer's misestimation of the degree of excellence of her performance; the second is the illusion that *she* has certain qualities. Both are caused by

what is given her in experience: the audience's pleasure. But, as we will see below, only the second involves a projective act.

12 I will show below that while proto-pride, on the Humean view, contributes towards the constitution of a primitive, pre-moral self, it is not sufficient to constitute the moral self and generate its ethical self-valuing.

13 In Freudian terms, this is the way in which the ego copes with reality: a reality that poses a constant threat of undermining it.

14 Gabriele Taylor thinks Hume regards such a person 'as uncommonly silly and so perhaps as not requiring serious attention' (1980: 388), an observation for which I can find little evidence in the *Treatise*. Hume's point is rather that the capacity to feel proud in virtue of 'an inconsiderable relation' such as 'being present at' is ours by nature, yet once we are social and moral beings convention restricts our pride to closer relations than this.

15 See also G. Taylor (1985: 23). Taylor wrongly accuses Hume of failing to appeal to the agent's beliefs. Hume's theory of the double relation between impressions and ideas (and the psychology this theory employs) can make perfectly good sense of Hume's boastful guest without any appeal to his beliefs, mistaken or otherwise.

16 Neu's claim that 'Hume's point *should* be: that *belief* in a relation to self is required if a thing or quality is to serve as a ground or source of pride' (Neu 1977: 37, my emphasis), is wrong in view of our capacity to feel proto-pride without the exercise of intellectual judgement or belief being necessary. See Baier (1978) for more on why Humean causes are not to be construed as reasons.

17 At T 295 Hume says that virtue is the most obvious cause of pride. Yet pride in what a person takes to be her virtue may be of no moral significance for Hume. If others' approval of her character and actions is not 'well-founded', her pride is not the kind that can constitute the moral self. See below where I consider the Humean moral self.

18 It is tempting here to draw an analogy between the Freudian demands of reality and the entrance of the Humean self into the moral domain. With proto-pride the Freudian pleasure principle, where perceptions are organised according to the dimensions of the perceiver's advantage, is being observed: for proto-pride, being a projected fantasy, is independent of the truth of sound judgement. The construction of proto-pride involves something akin to primary process thinking: a purely self-oriented, subjective, infantile thinking that suspends logic. With the attainment of moral personhood, it is required that the reality principle be observed since pride proper requires an exercise of true judgement. At this point secondary process thinking, which utilises the logic of objective assessment and judgement, is required.

19 The claim is not that the construction of the Humean moral self excludes pride in what many moral theorists would regard as evil qualities (where 'evil' is given by some determinate objective content such as harming, stealing or killing). For Hume, adjusting one's perspective to that of the party of humanity is to adjust one's perspective so that it is in line with that of trusted voices; it does not

mean that one's perspective is adjusted to conform with what is 'good' rather than 'evil', these being given by some determinate objective content. One might of course want to criticise Hume for the faith he had in the party of humanity.

20 Of course, for Hume, if I take a perspective that identifies with the party of mankind, I adopt a view that everyone can share, but not the completely impersonal view 'from nowhere'.

CHAPTER II

1 The distinction between these will be taken up below. I will follow Rousseau's usage and use the masculine pronoun throughout.

2 Many moral philosophers regard evil to be given by a determinate objective content such as killing or stealing.

3 The cost would not worry Rousseau. For Rousseau (implicitly) shares with Hume the view that the constitution of the moral self requires that it be on guard against allowing certain beliefs (regarding an objective content that describes good and evil) to be the ultimate determinant of action. In Chapter 8 we will see that my account is consistent with this view.

4 It has also been translated as 'self-respect' (Rousseau 1955a).

5 Rousseau writes that *amour de soi*, when 'guided in man by reason and modified by compassion, produces humanity and virtue' (1955a: 182).

6 *Amour-propre* has been variously translated as 'pride', 'selfishness', 'egoism' and 'vanity'. We will see below that Rousseau makes an extended use of this concept.

7 It is dependent on what contemporary self psychologists call 'mirroring selfobjects'. See Chapter 4.

8 It seems that Rousseau had himself not completely escaped *amour-propre*: one of the reasons why he wrote the *Confessions* was that he cared very much about others' opinions of him.

9 Jean Starobinski (1988: 13) refers to a state of 'transparency'.

10 The general will is the real will of every person *qua* citizen. It represents the form of law through which the force of the state could be exercised. Replacing private will with the general will involves a person in acting on principle. So this part of the cure actually presupposes what the cure is supposed to achieve: a self-legislating autonomous being guided by principle rather than passion (Rorty 1991).

11 Of course, Rousseau might not be happy with this option since acting in accordance with what he sees his civil duty to be might well involve overriding his private desires. As Rorty (1991: 423) points out, 'those desires can remain as a source of pain and ambivalence'. Rousseau could possibly reply that despite these desires remaining, the moral self of society is unified in virtue of its new collective identity: in basing its sentiment of existence on obedience to the general will, it only acts on a desire if it could will that everyone act on it, and so becomes a self of principle. This bestows a psychic unity despite the pull of contrary passions.

12 There would be no cost if private desires and interests could always coincide with those expressed by the general will. But Rousseau himself realises that 'each individual, as a man, may have a particular will contrary or dissimilar to the general will which he has as a citizen. His particular interest may speak to him quite differently from the common interest' (1955b: 15).

13 This 'something' is gleaned from our surmisings, not something encountered in our experience, since we cannot return to *amour de soi* in the state of nature.

14 There seems no clear-cut answer to the question of whether the three stages of Rousseau's account are supposed to present a temporal sequence.

15 In self psychological terms, a self that depends completely for a sense of its existence and worth on 'selfobject transferences' that others provide develops what analysts term a 'false self'. See Chapter 4.

16 Rousseau presents the self of *amour-propre* as being completely dependent on (not just as wanting) the praise and recognition of others, and so as lacking the self-sufficiency of the self in the state of nature, whose self-understanding is given by *amour de soi*. Since 'Dependence on men gives rise to every kind of vice' (Rousseau 1969: 49), the dependence of *amour-propre* rules out the possibility of it having a moral dimension in Rousseau's thought.

17 For more on this see Melzer (1990: Chapter 4).

18 Of course, for Kant the good will is purely rational whereas Rousseau recognised that a motivating force (the sentiments of *amour de soi* and *pitié*) other than mere rationality was needed.

19 We will see that on my account the moral self has the capacity to critically detach from those values and ends which are of crucial importance for self-identity.

20 This notion should be contrasted with Hume and Hegel, for whom the self is a social construction, being constituted in terms of some 'other'. In this respect my account will be seen to be closer to Rousseau's.

21 See Melzer (1990: 63) for more on this.

22 'Justice... springs up from below, as the spontaneous flow and expression of the collective will.... Where there is only a single "person" ruling itself, there can be no injustice' (Melzer 1990: 188–9).

CHAPTER III

1 I will follow Hegel's usage and employ the masculine pronoun throughout.

2 Robert Solomon (1983) takes *Geist* to be 'the human spirit'. This contrasts with Charles Taylor's interpretation (1975) of humanity being for Hegel a 'vehicle' for *Geist*. Taylor takes *Geist* as something other, or greater, than the human spirit, and understands Hegel as wanting to establish the 'Absolute' which would present a single, all-embracing system of philosophy. By contrast, Solomon sees an unresolved tension in Hegel between an 'historicist' and 'absolutist' point

of view and, wanting to salvage from Hegel what is most palatable, opts for the former alternative. I find much in Hegel that makes Solomon's interpretation difficult to accept, but I remain neutral regarding disputes about how we should interpret *Geist* since my discussion is not affected by these.

3 What the Hegelian agent values is not a particular or personal self but a self that achieves universal self-consciousness.

4 From an Hegelian point of view one might ask where this sense of justice and this desire for understanding come from, the point being that on the Hegelian view these are features of a subject that is *constituted* by the state, not the features of a *constituting* being. Chapter 8 will show why we must reject the Hegelian thesis that selves are totally constituted entities.

5 Hegel (1931) describes three moments of 'ethical substance', of which the state is the final one. The other two moments are the family and civil society. The state is for him the 'ethical substance' of self-conscious free individuals.

6 Hegel replaced Kant's formal rationality of consciousness and universality with the concrete manifestation of the rationality of state institutions, customs, and the social order. Rather than being an abstraction, for Hegel rationality makes certain ontological demands: there is for Hegelian rationality a certain external social and political reality which embodies and systematises universal laws and which must be actualised. Where for Kant rational activity is, at base, purely intellectual, for Hegel reason is teleological: it is aimed at unifying the members of the state.

7 One should ask whether Hegel has made a good case against Kant. Hegel did not seriously entertain the possibility that morality may indeed involve a formal element. It might be argued that morality requires that there be beings who know how to ask questions and initiate inquiry. There are good reasons for thinking that such beings are constitutive parts of the ethical.

8 From the social nature of the origins of a person's whole way of thinking and behaving, Hegel extrapolates that a person must align himself with the political state, rather than making the lesser claim that he ought to be faithful to the fellow human beings belonging to the state.

9 See Note 6 above.

10 For a different interpretation see Crittenden (1990: 250).

11 While it is not clear that a consequence of Hegel's account of the state is that what members might take to be unjust may be involved in morality, I will show in the final section of this chapter that this is a consequence of what he has to say about the ethical significance of war.

12 The moral self then is not for Hegel a particular or personal self. Individual self-fulfilment is one thing; the achievement of ethical life and the esteeming of the self as a moral being are quite another, even though the latter is impossible without the former. The particular or personal self is a stage on the way to universal self-consciousness and

must be transcended in order for unity with *Geist* and ethical life to be possible.

13 'Individuality' in the sense of what belongs to the singular, unique individual. I do not refer here to individuality in Hegel's sense: individuality that is realised when the self becomes conscious of itself as a mere moment in the life of *Geist*.

14 Readers who focus on Hegel's phenomenology rather than on his logic may regard this claim as being too strong. For Hegel's phenomenology searches for how we can find significance in our lives by being moral: it is by being moral (and so being part of a political state) that we realise our own individuality. Yet according to Hegel's logic, we are part of the Absolute, and the progress of history is something *necessary*. So according to his logic, we simply *cannot* oppose ourselves to the state: it is here that individuality must be surrendered. Hegel's belief that his phenomenology and his logic could be brought together seems to be mistaken; these cannot simply be regarded as two aspects of the same thing, but rather present the reader with contradictions that cannot be removed. I thank Janna Thompson for making me point this out.

15 See Hegel 1931, section entitled 'Society as a herd of individuals'.

16 One might here compare Strawson's contention (1959: Chapter 3) that only if one is prepared to ascribe person-predicates to others can one ascribe them to oneself.

17 He could not accept Rousseau's idea that all members of the state could play a part in determining the law, for freedom in the Hegelian sense may not be realised in a democratic state, which according to Hegel is unlikely to be a fully rational one.

18 'Death... plays a shockingly positive role in Hegel's philosophy, as the ultimate argument against the vanity of individualism' (Solomon 1983: 549). See also Lloyd (1986: 73–5).

19 The Hegelian view on war is not a mere historical aberration. The Hegelian thought involved here can be seen to underlie some modern movements. For example, certain kinds of radical feminists hold that the gendered self is completely constituted by patriarchy and that therefore there are certain kinds of activities that are good or healthy for gendered selves: conflict with the other gender, at the least. On the question of fairness or justice, a radical feminist answer may be that justice is something invented in order that we be able to live together, but that there are stakes far more important than this. Chapter 8 will show my opposition to this thought.

CHAPTER IV

1 Aristotle distinguishes two kinds of self-love (1168b15–1169a30). The first belongs to self-indulgent people who seek money, honour and physical pleasures, and is rightly reproached. The second belongs to virtuous people and is admirable. This second kind has as its object the self *qua* virtuous being. The object of love and concern is the moral self, yet it would be a bad misconstrual of Aristotle to take such

concern to be self-indulgent. Caring for the moral self is quite unlike caring for how others see one, or for the satisfactions that the self might accumulate. Aristotle's distinction makes it clear that caring and love for the moral self are the very antithesis of self-indulgence. Similarly, Socrates' advice to the Athenians to take care of their souls (*Apology*, 29d7–e3) is not an advice that they should become more self-centred, but that they should give attention to truth and understanding in order to make progress towards the achievement of goodness. Consistent with this advice, an Aristotelian lover of self wants to be guided, not by desires he happens to have, but by his understanding, which is what he, above all else, is (1166a22–4; 1169a1–2). This means that what motivates his acts is a desire for clear and just understanding of what is before him (he is anxious 'that he himself...should act justly, temperately, or in accordance with any other of the excellences', (1168b25–6)). His acts are not in any way self-indulgent, or even self-oriented, even though the significance of these acts has an important bearing on the self that performs them: they constitute the self as a self of a certain kind (i.e. as virtuous).

2 Aristotle does not use the term 'inner strength and resilience', but speaks instead of some people having love of self and of some people having 'nothing in them to love' (1166b25). While these terms are not interchangeable (a person with inner strength and resilience might choose to lead a selfish life, whereas I take love of self to be a sufficient condition for virtue), we will see below that having 'inner strength and resilience' and having 'something in them to love' are not unconnected.

3 This need not involve explicit self-consciousness. A self that is aware of its own virtue may know, for example, that there are certain sorts of things it would never do, no matter what the promised satisfactions.

4 We will see below that self psychology is able to account for the acquisition of this structure in terms of the right kind of care-givers and upbringing. Aristotle's account of the acquisition of virtue centrally involves the right kind of education and training for the young. We will see that what Aristotle takes to be needed regarding the acquisition of virtue is far more likely to be received by a child in the presence of what self psychology takes to be essential for the acquisition of psychic health. See also Note 15 below.

5 Compare Aristotle's discussion of the *megalopsychos*, the paradigm of virtue, at 1123a34–1125a16.

6 We will see below that the right kind of self-love excludes what self psychology calls pathological narcissism.

7 A relationship of dynamic interaction and mutual reinforcement exists between the nature of the self's psychic life and its relations to others. While for Aristotle virtue requires the right kind of self-love, the right kind of self-love can only develop in the presence of virtue. See also the last two sections of this chapter.

8 'The other' is not necessarily a person, but may be an object or activity.

9 Some examples of such behaviours are engagements in addictions, destructive relationships, or in any activities that provide excitement such as gambling, speeding, playing pinball machines, etc.

10 Kohut, like other classical psychoanalysts, would call these ego functions.

11 In the case of such failure, the self has not moved from relations with others in which selfobjects are desperately needed to shore up defects within the self to the internalisation of resources within the self that impart a sense of continuity and coherence. The clinical task for self psychology is to transform narcissism from its archaic to its mature forms, not to get rid of it, as Freud held.

12 Kohut (1977: 187) sees the cause of psychopathology as being chronic failure in empathy on the part of care-givers whose character pathology undermines the child's self development.

13 At the same time, some psychic strength and independence is needed for the development of virtue. See Note 7 above.

14 An infant's bad set of experiences can be compensated for to some extent in adult life through the right kind of therapeutic situation. Self psychology believes that the proper development of selfobject transferences makes it possible for psychic restructuralisation to take place via 'transmuting internalisation' (see the third section of this chapter).

15 This is not to suggest that a 'good-enough' parent is necessarily a virtuous person, but that a virtuous person is very likely to make a 'good-enough' parent.

16 It may be objected that while for Aristotle the psychic strength that goes hand-in-hand with the development of virtue is acquired by the kind of education and training that centrally involves modelling the virtues, for self psychology psychic strength is developed by the right kind of empathic responses on the part of care-givers, and that these requirements are quite different. Yet these requirements are importantly connected: a tutor who is empathic along Kohutian lines would make a far better educator of, and modeller for, virtue than an unempathic one.

17 There is, according to self psychology, a normal developmental line in grandiosity. A deficiency in grandiosity manifests itself in people who need to be constantly showing off in order to maintain self-esteem, in people who are masochistically humble ('Why should I try since I could never manage to do it?') and in people who are completely dependent on pride for a sense of self-worth.

18 See the final section of this chapter.

19 Chapters 6 and 7 will show why it is only through virtue that a person can develop love of self.

20 The defining marks when found in relation to the self *have priority*: one must have a certain kind of relation to one's own self in order to relate to one's friends in the way a virtuous person does. For example, regarding the first defining feature of character-friendship: to wish what is good for one's friend *qua* virtuous being, one must first understand the value of the virtues and want what is good for oneself *qua* virtuous being. It is inconceivable for Aristotle that one could understand the nature of goodness and yet not strive to be good oneself.

Notes

21 A negative variant of this is where the other is attributed all disvalue, and the person is able to 'feel real' only when he merges with the worthlessness of the other.

22 Cooper (1977: 640) writes that it could be claimed that only character-friends really love one another: only they concern themselves with the actual persons that their friends are. In a similar vein, Whiting (1991: 18) writes that only Aristotelian virtuous self-lovers love them*selves*, since non-virtuous self-lovers, in identifying with their appetites, 'make a mistake about *who* (or what) they are'.

23 On the development of a false self see Winnicott (1965b); Meares (1992).

24 Charles Taylor (1989) calls this kind of understanding 'correct vision'. Murdoch (1970) refers to such understanding as 'seeing things as they are' and 'accurate vision'.

25 See Vlastos (1981) and Whiting's discussion (1991) of Vlastos' views.

CHAPTER V

1 We will see that the rationality of significant action is grounded in its involving the important rational choice of what sort of person one should be. Significant action involves an *ontological* commitment because the choice of what sort of person one should be determines the kind of self that will be here constituted. This claim, together with a number of other claims, will be presented initially in a schematic way; they will be borne out later in this and the following chapters.

2 'Moral' should be taken here as contrasting with 'non-moral' and not with 'immoral'.

3 Assent must encompass understanding since it involves belief, and one cannot have a belief that one does not understand. And since one assents to the truth of a proposition, that to which one assents must be expressible in propositional form. A person's understanding of what she assents to is codifiable. But assent need not encompass what I here call a 'deepened' understanding; it need not encompass an understanding of the significance of acting or not acting in accordance with what one assents to. A deepened understanding may not be codifiable.

4 For Aristotle, to know what courage and justice (and indeed, the other virtues) are is to care about them, and to include them in one's concept of what a good life consists of: to know, to care, and to do this *is* what it is to be rational.

5 I refer here to Brandtian, Rawlsian and Bayesian conceptions of rationality. The Brandtian and Rawlsian conceptions are discussed below.

6 We might say that one gives notional but not real assent to the value. 'acts of Notional Assent...do not affect our conduct, and acts...of Real Assent do...affect it' (Newman 1985: 64).

7 Brandt might reply that he does not rule this out, but hold that this affective attitude has nothing at all to do with the rationality of what she does. This is precisely my point: I want to describe the account of a

philosopher who works in ethics with a concept of 'rationality' without its affective component.

8   One cannot construe Aristotle as holding such a conception since to be practically rational for him is to have a deepened understanding of the supreme good for man. According to Aristotle, an agent cannot be practically rational without possessing the virtues and having the capacity to derive a conception of what it would be good here and now for him to do from a conception of what is good for human beings as such. For Aristotle, to be practically rational one must have a deepened understanding of the nature of the values one wants to conserve: one must understand not merely how these values would be appropriate for one to pursue, but also the ways in which they are values which are important for humans as such. Given such understanding, the question of whether or not one should conserve them cannot intelligibly arise: it would be unintelligible for a person to have a deepened understanding of these values, but choose not to conserve them. Here, practical rationality encompasses ethical thought and action. By contrast, for Brandt, there is nothing unintelligible about our 'understanding' moral values but, given our desires and aversions, rationally rejecting the conservation of these values (Brandt 1979: 184).

9   In the rest of this chapter 'rational' and 'rationality' refer to this kind of narrow conception with which many philosophers work.

10 It also becomes clear that we need to distinguish between *akrasia*, where not being moved by one's values indicates a cognitive dysfunction, and an intermittent or permanent loss of grip – where one's values become unimportant to one. In this latter case we have an affective rather than a cognitive change or dysfunction.

11 I use the term 'non-significant' rather than 'insignificant' because the latter has connotations of unimportance or triviality. Non-significant action is not action that does not objectively matter. I employ 'non-significant' as a technical term that refers to action that is engaged in as though there were no significance for the agent.

12 We should contrast the case of the agent who, when she finds a different and easier way to impress the mother superior, chooses this other way rather than forgiveness.

13 I use the term 'affective attachment' to indicate that the commitment is more than a merely rational or intellectual one. A person is affectively attached to a value in virtue of what she understands about the meaning and significance of the value (i.e. in virtue of what she understands about its goodness) and what she understands is conveyed not merely by her intellect, but also by her emotions. An affective attachment incorporates the special moral understanding that the emotions provide. See also Stocker (1996: Chapter 3).

14 I discuss moral impossibility in Chapter 8.

15 So a significant action cannot be a merely prudential one where the agent saw, for example, that it would be a nuisance to have the other arriving and feeling guilty, and so decided to make tea for the other in order that she feel welcome. The reflection involved in this type of

thinking involves only reflection on how to cope with particular external circumstances.

16 MacIntyre (1982: 291–2) has pointed out that the questions 'How ought I to treat others?' and 'What shall I care about?' cannot be answered independently of providing an answer to that most fundamental of questions 'What sort of person am I to become?'. Browne (1990: 403) notes that 'the good is of benefit to the self because the self cares about the good'.

17 Compare Aristotle's discussion at 1169a18–1169b2 where self-sacrifice for one's friend, assigning to oneself 'the greater share in what is noble', has been wrongly interpreted by some commentators as self-centred. See for example Annas (1988).

18 Non-contingent values arise from an agent's own understanding of what it is to be a human being, and so are relativised to particular agents: not every agent will value the same things non-contingently. Whether an agent will value something non-contingently depends on her understanding of the human situation and of the particular circumstances in which she finds herself. This understanding does not arise in a social or cultural vacuum, but is informed by the concepts and teachings of the society and culture of which she is a part. Though there may not be agreement about the ultimate nature of non-contingent values, they are values that everyone can approach; they are discussable and shareable, and there can be agreement about their existence. They are not merely a matter of taste or preference.

19 So the account presented here should not be confused with that of Charles Taylor (1989), who wants no separation to be made between the empirical subject and the ethical subject. While I agree with Taylor that the subjects we empirically are are constructed from a commitment to and enactment of values that have been reflectively adopted, on my account we are not *qua* ethical subjects constructed merely from a commitment to certain values. Rather, the ethical subject emerges in the context of certain practices which may well involve a certain critical distancing from whatever has been constructed.

20 It would be inefficient to have to think through a whole logical line in order to discover what was good and valuable, or salient and significant, each time a choice or an action was contemplated. Much of this thinking is contained in the form of background assumptions about the world and oneself which have been inherited from one's culture and community. For Aristotle, a virtuous person has a whole history of deliberations and choosings behind him: he chooses virtuously as a result of many years of training and habituation. Thus Aristotle writes that it is the mark of a brave man to be fearless and undisturbed in sudden alarms, rather than to be so in those that are foreseen (1117a17–19). When there is no time for deliberation, a brave man's act flows from his character: 'at crucial moments of choice most of the business of choosing is already over...The moral life...is something that goes on continually, not something...switched off in between the occurrence of explicit moral choices' (Murdoch 1970: 37).

21 I do not confine significance or morality to the valuing of others or to the meeting of their needs. A man on a desert island can demonstrate his morality through his attitude to the blades of grass and the palm trees. Things other than people's needs can be understood and valued in such a way as to present the agent with significance.

22 It might be thought that this description is too intellectualist, relying too much on explicit articulation. Flanagan (1990: 46) has criticised Taylor's account of the relationship between moral goodness and strong evaluation, claiming that most of Tolstoy's noble peasants are inarticulate while being good people. What Flanagan does not point out is that Tolstoy's peasants talk a lot – they spend a lot of time telling each other stories – and that Tolstoy contrasts this wealth of story-telling (which is a rich source of contrastive characterisation) with the lives of the educated aristocrats in St Petersburg who spend much of their time simply striking poses. Tolstoy's peasants are not articulate in the way that Oxford dons are, but through their stories they are able to pay attention to (and also to reflect on) their own feelings, emotions, impulses, and their responses to the environment, allowing all their faculties play. This is not inarticulateness. 'Unschooled' does not mean 'inarticulate'.

Being an agent of significant action does not require sophisticated articulation, but rather a certain kind of civilised sensitivity to human values, one in which some of Tolstoy's aristocrats, as well as some of his peasants, are sorely lacking. The exercise of this civilised sensitivity involves both cognitive and affective elements. We should acknowledge that some affective component is already present in most cognition. I despair of the sharp distinction that is often drawn between affect and cognition, and I would want to argue that without affect, there would be no cognition. For example, in attending to something to find out about it, a person is already *interested in* or *cares about* doing so, otherwise we should want to know why she bothers. References to 'reflection', 'attention', and 'consideration being paid to', throughout *The Moral Self* should be taken as references to activities that are cognitive, or at least aided by cognitive understanding, but ones that are at the same time affectively motivated.

23 Only 'the possibility' of significant action, because freedom in Frankfurt's account (1971) is a necessary but not a sufficient condition for significance. Frankfurt's understanding of freedom in terms of having the desires and will that one wants does not take account of an agent's affective attachment to reasons, motives and values. Nor does it take account of the self-defining and self-affirming aspects of significance.

24 Courage is required because in performing significant action a person may need to risk changing their self.

25 Our conception of rationality can be broadened to accommodate ethical thought but, as previously stated, I use 'rationality' in its narrow sense, for example, as used by Brandt (1979). A person might focus on all the relevant and available information, arrive at the

rational thing to do, and do it without ever performing a significant act or entering the moral domain.

26 This is Lawrence Blum's term (1990). 'Action from a sense of role-responsibility' is used by Blum to delineate a response to another that does not fit the model either of the pursuit of individual good or that of response to impersonal moral demands. While I think that Blum's criticism of the strict dichotomy in the literature between personal good and impersonal morality is a much needed one, I am in disagreement with him over some crucial points. For example, I do not think, as Blum does, that being motivated to help by the require-ments of a particular role, for example those of a friend, can always be consistent with being motivated by the particular plight of a friend. On my view, what is seen to be *any friend's reason* needs to be made by a person into *her reason* in order for her to be motivated in the morally requisite way.

27 In changing his treatment of her, in this first description, the father may constitute his self as a self of a certain kind. But for action to be significant, it is not enough that a self of just any kind be constituted. Significant action does not merely reflect a structural relation. This will become clearer in the next two chapters. We will see that for action to be significant, the self being constituted must be a 'real' or 'true' self rather than a 'false' self.

28 A philosopher might interpret Murdoch's account as expressing a concern that the moral agent should pay attention to the truth. So paying attention to the daughter-in-law might be seen as a means to seeing the truth about her. I would argue that for Murdoch the Good is sovereign, not because it has a particular content, but because it guides us to see unselfishly, and that Murdoch's account expresses the concern that the moral agent overcome self-centredness, not that she perceive a moral truth or reality perceived by all other virtuous agents. For a different view see Platts (1979: Chapter 10).

29 Aristotle distinguishes between acts that are lawful and acts that are an expression of character (1136a9–25). Only the latter express the way in which an agent perceives the particulars.

30 This will be elaborated in Chapter 8.

CHAPTER VI

1 Since this relation centrally involves love, it is an affective relation. While a certain kind of critical evaluation is gone through in establish-ing this relation to the self, the critical evaluation involved is affectively motivated.

2 The modern conceptions and the external to internal direction will be discussed below.

3 In Chapter 2 we saw that for Rousseau the proper development of *amour de soi* was required for virtue.

4 For more on self-esteem see Sachs (1981). That there is some asym-metry between self-respect and respect for others is perceptively

acknowledged by Thomas Hill Jr (1982). But this asymmetry does not extend to self-esteem and esteem of others (Hill Jr 1986).

5   So it is not merely the structural direction (outer to inner) of the conventional conception of self-valuing that differentiates it from love of self, but also (and perhaps more importantly) the content of what goes into the assessment.

6   See Thomas (1978: 268, Note 16) and also Yanal (1987) who argues that 'good' self-esteem requires a person to judge the correct qualities, judge them correctly, and judge them himself.

7   Rawls has been much chastised for failing to distinguish self-esteem from self-respect.

8   Rawls' theory of the good requires that a person's plan of life be chosen in complete awareness of all the relevant facts (1972: 408).

9   Rawls introduces the Aristotelian principle into his account. Unless someone's plan of life calls

> upon his natural capacities in an interesting fashion... they are likely to seem dull and flat, and to give... no feeling of competence... A person tends to be more confident of his value when his abilities are both fully realised and organised in ways of suitable complexity and refinement.
>
> (1972: 440)

For a cynical view of Rawls' empirical generalisations see Nussbaum (1980).

10 We will see below that since love of self escapes all categorising in universal terms (there are no universal qualities or categories that underpin its development, and no objective criteria or yardsticks by which to judge how well one is doing with respect to its development), the Rawlsian 'making the same choice under the same conditions' is not applicable to it.

11 Page numbers appearing in parentheses refer to this edition.

12 David Norton (1976: 9) talks about 'foreign truths'.

13 The point is not merely that he failed to lead an autonomous life: in basing his life on a series of reactions to impingements, Illych formed a 'false self', becoming what he perceived the world to value and esteem. A false self's feelings of self-worth are vulnerable and fragile, particularly when the limited assets on which it bases its worth are threatened. The contingency of Illych's illness provided a threat to his sources of self-worth. See Chapter 4 for more on a 'false self'.

14 'In subordinating other ends to his rational agency, [a virtuous person] forms a stable self for which he has the proper sort of concern' (Irwin 1988: 384). 'A stable self for which he had the proper sort of concern' is precisely something that Illych failed to form.

15 Aristotle says that flourishing is an activity, something continuous, not like a piece of property that one might aim to possess (1169b28–1170a4). Similarly, what is important regarding love of self is not so much the *achievement* of possessing an authentic life, but rather the person's understanding and acknowledgement of the value and

importance of being true to the self, and her striving to be true to it. Love of self does not require the *achievement* of anything at all in particular.

16 In what follows, the ugly person who positively values and loves his self is not to be construed as one whose self-regard is grounded in self-assessments pertaining to other positive qualities and achievements possessed by him but not possessed by the beautiful person or by the ugly one who lacks positive self-regard. Let us imagine instead that the two ugly people and the beautiful one have otherwise almost identical qualities and attributes. The only apparent difference between them is their physical appearance.

17 The only exception to this is where he, for example, appropriately takes his ugliness as a reason to avoid entering a beauty contest. Since 'beauty' and 'ugliness' do not enter into the conception the man builds of himself, his avoidance of a beauty contest does not bear on his sense of self-worth.

18 Including self-assessments of one's own authenticity or autonomy. There are no external yardsticks by which to 'judge' the experience one has of oneself, so the inner reality to which love of self refers is not subject to the kind of assessment involved in self-esteem. Whiting (1996) argues that God is the standard against which an Aristotelian self-lover assesses himself. But while Whiting is right to say that in identifying with *nous* he will become more like God, more argument is needed to show why comparison and self-assessment are required.

19 This is not to deny that there are certain features of a person which facilitate the building of the kind of positive self-regard being referred to here. A discussion of these would need to refer to a story in psychology: we would need to look, for example, at the effects of early childhood experiences on particular psychic abilities.

20 Homiak (1981) develops an account of Aristotle that is largely consistent with mine.

21 Studies confirm a strong correlation between maternal sensitivity and an infant's later feelings of security and well-being manifested by social competence and higher self-esteem. See Ainsworth *et al.* (1978); Minde (1986: 48). Between a child's sixth and eighteenth month it 'needs to be looked at, smiled at, and approved of by an active, loving and responsive person. Without this emotional nurturance, the child experiences the world as persecutory and regards parts of his/her self as unacceptable' (Goldberg 1984: 518). So the self-making activity to which I refer involves a dynamic interaction, since causation goes in two directions: some inner strength and valuing of self is required for a person to acknowledge the need to make something of his self, and this activity of self-making serves to reinforce the already existing valuing of self. The circularity here is a beneficial one: the person who is given a sense of his own worth in infancy will be in a good position to develop more of it.

22 The motivation to attend carefully and justly to some reality external to the self is (at least partly) affective. Unless one first *cared* about careful and just understanding, it is difficult to see why one would bother about achieving it.

23 'The activities of the self-respecting man, to be worthy rather than merely lucky, must be chosen for good reasons, in awareness of their value... we will not call his actions fully good if he did not see them subjectively as such' (Nussbaum 1980: 403–4). The conversion of values into reasons to which I refer parallels Nussbaum's 'subjective seeing'. Actions which result from this conversion I regard to be 'fully good'. The possibility of a person 'subjectively seeing' and converting values into reasons for action, but thereby performing evil acts, will be addressed in Chapter 8.

24 The part of the soul that the Aristotelian lover of self loves more than any other is his understanding (1169a3). The desire for understanding is a deliberative desire (1113a9–12) which involves some more general desire regarding the good. In the case of our ugly man, this desire expresses his conception of what would constitute a good way to live a life.

25 Compare: 'this effort to understand is the primary and sole foundation of virtue, and... we do not endeavour to understand things for the sake of any end' (Spinoza 1949: 207). In Chapter 5 I pointed out that when the object of understanding is another person, the motivation to understand has its source in the agent's own sense of justice.

26 This remains neutral with respect to any substantive theory of ethics. A cognitivist will think that a cognitive mistake is involved.

27 We have here a man who wants to be guided, not by ignorance or inadequacies, but by values given by his own reflective evaluation and understanding: 'All reflective men might choose the same good life; but what makes each of them a *good man* is that he is the one who chooses it' (Nussbaum 1980: 423).

28 Being self-deceived is not consistent with the building of this kind of positive self-regard. For a person who self-deceives tells himself a lie which he then believes in order to hide from some truth related to himself. Such a person is sorely lacking in integrity. Indeed, a paradox revolves around the fact that a person who self-deceives, while aiming to eliminate inner conflict due to some unwelcome truth related to himself, and to restore a sense of integrity, is so easily able to embrace such conflict and unauthenticity within himself and so easily abandon the very integrity to which he so dearly wants to cling. While being quite consistent with pride, self-deception, rather than being consistent with love of self, is instead a form of self-degradation.

29 As was shown by Tolstoy in the case of Ivan Illych.

CHAPTER VII

1 All references to narcissism in this chapter refer to 'immature, archaic narcissism' as described by Kohut, and not to what he terms 'mature narcissism'. See Chapter 4 for this distinction.

2 Given that cultures vary, and impact upon self development, when I talk about self-creation and self-determination, I assume a cultural specificity. My account of love of self refers exclusively to the culture of

which I am a part. It may apply to other cultures (I take Aristotle's account to be quite consistent with mine) but I do not make any such claim here.

3 See Chapter 1.

4 Compare the self psychological account (Chapter 4), according to which some people depend for a sense of self on mirroring selfobject relationships.

5 A person may himself provide the external environment from which his pride is derived via the mechanism of the imagined audience. But love of self does not require the appreciation of any achievement, be it others' appreciation or one's own.

6 Such a self is in what Kohut calls a 'grandiose' state, not having transformed archaic narcissism into its more mature forms. See Chapter 4.

7 The narcissist is commonly thought of as simply experiencing a surfeit of self-love. The technical meaning is that of a preoccupation with and love of one's image. Narcissus fell in love not with himself but with his own image reflected in a pond. In human relations the mirror is replaced by the regard of others. 'Such selves need constant external feeding (feedback) to validate their presence. Without external feeding, the narcissistic self feels empty, cold, depersonalised and desperate' (Goldberg 1984: 519–20).

8 'Pride-dependency' is denoted by the technical term 'narcissism'.

9 For Hume pride requires specialness: we are not usually proud of things that we share with many others (Hume 1978: 291).

10 Narcissism excludes Aristotelian stable character, for a narcissistic self will keep moving indiscriminately to whatever will feed it, with an accompanying inconsistency of behaviour and judgement.

11 See Chapter 6.

12 This is not to say that a lover of self does not want or need the praise and recognition of others, or the guidance of a community. Without these a person's life is diminished. Yet while a lover of self may need and want these, she is *not dependent on them* for feelings of self-worth.

13 Research suggests that adolescents who have difficulty developing a secure and firm sense of identity are more dependent on external events and circumstances for self-attitudes. The mechanism of the imagined audience can compensate for the development of a positive self-perception (Toolan 1978).

14 We saw in Chapter 4 that Kohut relates selfobject needs to childhood experiences: a child needs care-givers who can provide adequate phase-appropriate mirroring so that the emerging aspects of the child's self are confirmed, so encouraging its omnipotence and autonomy (Kohut 1966; 1968; 1971). An adult who lacked adequate phase-appropriate mirroring in childhood is prone to developing a 'false self', trying to become what she perceives the world will praise and esteem.

15 Ivan Illych's rage and 'intolerable depression' on being passed over for a promotion suggest that his self-worth was based entirely on his perceived success and achievements (Tolstoy 1986: 243).

16 We should compare this with claims concerning excessive self-esteem. Philosophers take unduly high self-esteem to suggest egotism, and that ridding of such misconceptions is desirable (Yanal 1987: 378; Sachs 1981: 348).

17 Having securely held values does not mean that these values will always dictate behaviour no matter what the particular circumstances are. A lover of self retains the capacity to re-assess her values according to her own understanding of what the particular circumstances require.

18 Tolstoy (1954). Page numbers appearing in parentheses refer to this edition.

19 Compare what Aristotle says about a self-lover's response to events that 'bring pain with them and hinder many activities': 'Yet even in these nobility shines through when a man bears with resignation many great misfortunes, not through insensibility to pain but through nobility and greatness of soul' (1100b30–32).

20 Varenka had been jilted by a suitor in a similar way, but this had not affected her self-worth.

21 See Chapter 5.

22 'The main condition for the achievement of love is the overcoming of one's narcissism' (Fromm 1957: 85). Kitty's narcissism prevented her from loving those with whom she came into contact at the German springs.

23 'the things men have done on a rational principle are thought most properly their own acts. . . . That this is the man himself, then, or is so more than anything else, is plain, and also that the good man loves most this part of him' (Aristotle 1941: 1168b35–1169a3).

24 Neither love of self nor self-respect can be developed in a social vacuum: the evaluative conceptions that underlie the self-identifications involved emerge from a normative framework which is socially and culturally grounded. Nevertheless, both relations to the self are ones which the individual, *qua* individual, is able to influence and develop.

25 In Chapter 4 we saw that while love of self is not easily lost, the impact of great and sustained trauma – 'beyond human strength' (Aristotle 1941: 1115b8) – could damage love of self (see pp. 68–9). The murder of Hamlet's father and Hamlet's own damaged self-identity were, I suggest, subjectively experienced by Hamlet as traumas 'beyond human strength'. See the discussion below.

26 'The self as such' should be understood to include the moral self. The moral self is the particular entity towards which love of self is directed.

27 This realisation pertains to a deepened moral understanding of the significance of one's actions (or inactions).

28 See Charles Taylor (1989) for an account of the constitution of the psychological empirical self. Unlike my account, Taylor's draws no distinction between this self and the moral self.

29 These self-identifications should not be regarded as being necessarily held self-consciously, but can be seen to be part of what I have referred to as a person's 'background assumptions'. See Chapter 5.

30 A self psychologist would say that a loss of pride in such a person leaves her self function intact. See Chapter 4.

31 This will be illustrated in Chapter 8. While Kantian and utilitarian agents may reassess and re-order values, certain values (e.g. duty, happiness) cannot be subject to reassessment.

32 Aristotle's emphasis on the importance of the moral agent's perception of the particulars does leave room for the importance of such practices.

CHAPTER VIII

1 Hegel's ethics have no room for good and evil in the sense in which these concern most of us. Hegel's distinction between 'being there' and 'not yet being there' might be seen to replace our distinction between good and evil.

2 Someone might object that one need only point to the gas chambers, the crematoria, the mass graves, to know that evil has been done. Yet this description (of gas chambers, crematoria, mass graves) is loaded with the intentions and attitudes of subjects of understanding. This description of objective facts incorporates the structure of thinking and response to the world of those who designed, and put into operation, the most effective way of murdering and disposing of the remains of millions of innocent people.

3 Slote is not committed to denying this internal relationship. He might say that while at different periods and in different cultures the internal relationship remains, the moral views will subsequently be seen to be mistaken. I take it, though, that these 'mistaken' moral views would be taken by Slote to represent what was merely *thought* to be 'real moral growth', and that mistaken moral thinking would be regarded by him as indicating an absence of virtue.

4 I have in mind, in particular, Kantian and most utilitarian theories which locate the ethical in a set of fixed beliefs, propositions, values or ends. While Kant does emphasise the importance of the character of the moral self, and neither autonomy nor reason are 'objective' in the sense in which I am using this term, the 'objective determinate content' where Kantians locate the ethical refers to certain fixed beliefs regarding duty, consistency of the will, universal principle and the ends that reason puts forward. My critique can also be taken to be directed at all theories which focus moral thinking on *what should be done*, ignoring the moral importance of the meaning or significance of action. Many pluralist theories, Ross' intuitionism, and non-realist theories (e.g. J. J. C. Smart) are all *content oriented* in that they focus on *what should be done*, neglecting the fact that, even when moral thinking *is* concerned with what to do, moral seriousness shows itself in a concern with the meaning or significance of what might be done (Gaita 1991). My critique, in effect, is directed at normative theories. The term 'modern moral theories' refers to all theories that are normative or content-oriented, but does not refer to theories that

merely present a sociology or psychology of morality (Hume), or to meta-ethical theories such as emotive theories.

5 I am indebted here to Williams' discussion (1985: 144–5).

6 This is a moral rather than an historical point.

7 It is not available in the form of a determinate content, for example, propositions concerning universalisability, utility, reciprocity. Moral truth is available to a virtuous person because she has the capacity to distance herself from her own values and beliefs in order to reach a just understanding of the particular circumstances before her, and to judge what, in these particular circumstances, she must do.

8 Charles Taylor (1977; 1989) sometimes writes as though strong evaluation can guarantee ethical nobility. I make no such claim. Hitler engaged in some rather strong evaluations, but one could hardly claim that he was in possession of ethical nobility. There is no reason to think that engaging in a series of Taylor-like strong evaluations will yield love of self.

9 I target moral theory because while the objection to my account regarding evil need not necessarily be made from the perspective of some moral theory, it must share with many moral theories one of theory's basic presuppositions: that good and evil are given by some objective content. The focus of my attention in this chapter will be on Kantian and utilitarian theories. See also Note 4 above.

10 A moral theorist might say that when A understands x to be good or bad, moral theory T tells us *what it is* that A understands, although it may not tell us what it is *to* morally understand. T may hold that there is no special understanding involved since moral understanding is no different from other kinds of understanding. Later on in this chapter it will become clear that, on my account, moral understanding is quite unlike other kinds of understanding: for example, it is quite unlike understanding in science. If T sees no need, or is unable, to specify the way in which moral understanding is different from understanding in science, this is a serious failure on the part of T.

11 Kant writes that we have a duty to the self to establish in oneself principles and to strive to act in accordance with them (1963: 125). It may be thought that, for a Kantian, the moral understanding involved in doing this is prior to moral behaviour. It will become clear below that the understanding involved in the internalisation of principles that enables one to act from duty does not, on the conception invoked here, amount to *moral* understanding.

12 This suggestion is not new. See Murdoch 1970.

13 1949, Heinmann. Page numbers appearing in parentheses refer to this edition.

14 This will be discussed below.

15 Notice here the Hegelian idea that the world has a goal to which it needs to be led.

16 That Sonia thinks this will be made clear below.

17 Raskolnikov knew that the pawnbroker was a member of the species *homo sapiens*: a being with 'properties and capacities which are relevant to one's moral principles' (Gaita 1991: 168). But he was

missing a sense of what Gaita calls the 'reality' of another human being, leaving him an epistemic victim to evil. A lover of self cannot be that kind of victim: she has not ontological, but epistemic control over what she does. Dostoevsky uses utilitarianism as a device for showing what kind of self or mentality engages in the kind of thinking that leaves a person open to evil.

18   For Kant the ends that reason puts forward are the ones that must determine action: if an end is given by reason alone, it is valid for all rational beings (Kant 1969: 90).

19   Kantian imperfect duties leave room for *choice* of specific actions: the law here commands the adoption of a purpose rather than a specific action (Kant 1964).

20   It might be thought that a Kantian agent also has such self-awareness in view of the emphasis that Kant places on self-perfection. Yet the self-perfection of moral agents is for Kant crucially important because it enables them to pursue those ends that reason puts forward. Once put forward by reason, these ends are not subject to further review or revision. The moral law commands categorically. Where for Kant the self-awareness of a moral agent involves an awareness of being true to the aspirations that properly belong to a being whose inner life can be completely described without loss by its rationality, the self-awareness of my moral agent involves an awareness of being true to the aspirations of a self that has a far more substantial and richer inner life: one for which rationality is but one aspect. See also Note 40 below.

21   This is not to deny that utilitarian and Kantian agents adjust or revise beliefs and values. Yet there are certain beliefs and values (ones concerning utility, impartiality, universality) that they cannot revise without ceasing to be good agents.

22   We should contrast the Hegelian view that morality and moral obligation are both relative to a set of customs.

23   It might be claimed that the limits confronting the Kantian moral self are internal since it is unconditionally subject to the moral law in virtue of its own rational nature. The Kantian duties to the self, the required purity of Kantian moral motives, the good will as the only bearer of moral worth, and an agent's choice of *Gesinnung* (the 'ultimate subjective ground' of the adoption of maxims) as a precondition for moral development (Allison 1990: Chapter 7) may also be cited in support of this claim. Yet we will see below that, since an archetypal Kantian self, in order to successfully be 'subject only to law-giving reason' (Kant 1956: 118, 123) has an impoverished, contracted inner life, it is not one that is able to experience anything, including morality, as emanating from within.

Barbara Herman has suggested a model of deliberation and decision-making (the 'deliberative field' model) which she takes to be consistent with Kantian theory. This model internalises moral constraints so they become part of the self: the moral agent is 'someone who takes the fact of morality to be constitutive of herself... and for whom the normalisation of desires and interests [their being discounted in view of moral considerations] is a way of

Notes

making them her own' (Herman 1993: 201). She claims that moral requirement is not external to other motives such as attachment, love, friendship or desire. Moreover, Kant's claim about reason being the determining ground of the will is a claim about authority, not efficacy (Herman 1996). On this analysis, desire can be a legitimate Kantian moral motive. Yet Herman's Aristotelianised Kant speaks to us quite differently from the historical Kant, for whom desires are 'blind and slavish' (Kant 1956: 118, 123), and 'it must ... be the universal wish of every rational being to be free from them [inclinations]' (Kant 1969: 90). It is difficult to see how the moral motive could be, on Kant's view, internal to things blind and slavish, and from which rational beings wish to be free. Further, this neo-Kantian internalisation of moral constraints is still unable to escape the notion that a person's moral interests and concerns are completely separate from her interests and concerns of attachment. See Note 51 below.

24 The claim is that to understand the nature of the moral barrier is to understand that one *cannot* cross it.

25 For an Hegelian, this particular positive content of the mind is to be transcended.

26 I write 'possibly' because Raskolnikov is shown not to have been made free of moral anguish.

27 This difference would seem to undermine some recent attempts to reconcile ancient and modern ethical perspectives. Korsgaard (1996) is right that for both Aristotle and Kant human action must have endorsement of the agent's reason, that a conception of the action *qua* good must move the agent, while perception and judgement must play some role in the application of a principle. But where for Kant the categorical imperative must guide a moral agent's thinking, for Aristotle there is no relationship to any general principle that a person might have such that the principle could provide such a moral guide. For criticism of Herman's (1996) argument that Kant does not subordinate all values to principles of duty, see Schneewind (1996).

28 Compare Stocker's discussion (1996: 125–6) of the way an anti-semite's own hatred, contempt, loathing and disgust sustains his anti-semitism.

29 See Charles Taylor (1989) for an account of the constitution of the empirical substantive self.

30 A moral theorist might claim that had Raskolnikov understood the Principle of Utility or that he was bound by the Categorical Imperative, he would have had the moral understanding to desist from the murders. It should be clear that, on the account presented in this book, a good discursive understanding of the Categorical Imperative or the Principle of Utility does not amount to *moral* understanding. The experience of moral impossibility is given to a moral self, not by any principle, rule, or code of conduct, but by its own just understanding of the particular situation in which it finds itself: ethical truth is particular rather than absolute.

Barbara Herman's neo-Kantian internalisation of moral constraints may appear to transform Kantian ethics into an ethics where the moral subject's own moral understanding is what counts most. Yet her account is unable to eliminate the need to heed the Kantian rule that 'we are never to act on a maxim that we cannot will all rational beings to act on' (Herman 1993: 202). So if a particular agent understands the salient moral features before her in a way that is not consistent with duty (see the discussion of Sonia below), she must filter this understanding through 'the demands of moral requirement' (Herman 1993: 201) so that her subjective maxim is universalisable.

31 A Kantian might object that understanding is needed to apply the Categorical Imperative properly. It should be clear by now that, on the conception invoked here, the understanding of a Kantian agent that one must never act on a maxim that one cannot consistently will that everyone act on does not amount to *moral* understanding.

32 A Kantian might not be happy even with Sonia's behaviour, because it is far from clear that she acted from duty.

33 Kant would never have said this, but it is a possible position for a neo-Kantian. It might be claimed that, as a Kantian, Raskolnikov would have avoided the murder, because seeing other human beings as limits to the will is an essentially Kantian thought. Yet since a Kantian agent can fulfil the requirements of duty without caring about, or feeling anything for the people before him, he will fail to understand *the way in which* another human being is a limit to the will. See Gaita (1991: Chapter 9).

34 Someone might ask why she was not more horrified with what happened to the pawnbroker. Is not what happened to her the greatest evil of all? There is no doubt that Sonia *was* horrified at this: the point is that moral evil is not discovered by seeing a dead body.

35 For a discussion of these letters, see Langton (1992).

36 According to the criteria laid down by the *Diagnostic and Statistical Manual for Mental Disorders*, 1987.

37 For more on 'false self' see Chapter 4.

38 The borderline patient exists 'only on the basis of a continuity of reactions to impingements and of recoveries from such reactions' (Winnicott 1965a: 52).

39 For the same reason their own successes in the world bring them little or no satisfaction, since they do not experience their successes as emanating from their own selves.

40 Barbara Herman (1993: 203) claims that the Kantian conception of the autonomous agent does not elevate rationality to the only thing that really counts about persons, that Kantians need not view themselves, from the moral point of view, as 'essentially or even ideally rational' (207). I find it impossible to put this claim together with Kant's repeated stress on the need for moral agents to be ready to suppress inclination and be 'subject only to law-giving reason' (Kant 1956: 118, 123). Kant's ethical writings make it absolutely clear that what I morally am is to be identified with my rational nature. A condition of an uncorrupted polity (the kingdom of ends) is the identification of the self with reason.

41 For a discussion of a cohesive self for whom 'moral excellence is concerned with pleasures and pains' (Aristotle 1941: 1104b8) see

Chapter 4. Compare Kant's view (1963: 139–40) that right emotions are merely a moral accessory since they make the doing of duty easier. For the importance of emotions for moral understanding, see Stocker (1996).

42 I draw here on Gaita (1992: Chapter 4).

43 This is not to say that benevolence or acting from duty is not moral, but that benevolence and duty are not exhaustive of the moral.

44 It has been suggested to me that this makes the moral self seem like a self-indulgent navel-gazer whose prime concern is with its own or another's moral purity. Yet it must be remembered that it is only through a concern with justice that a person is concerned with the moral self. See Chapter 5.

45 Had she read Kant's *Lectures on Ethics* she would have found that 'A man who sells himself makes himself a thing as he has jettisoned his person' (Kant 1963: 124). Herman writes that 'the "worth beyond price" of the Kantian agent is in her autonomous will', and that this grounds 'the claim that persons are not to be valued only for use' (1996: 203). In turning to prostitution, Sonia did precisely that (valued her clients only for their use). Yet Dostoevsky presents her as a paradigm of moral goodness.

46 The suggestion is that justice *is* virtue or goodness: courage, loyalty, benevolence, temperance, etc., are, on this view, simply ways of being just. On this view, a person who appears as courageous, conscientious and loyal, but has racist views and acts in a racist way, does not display virtues of character at all since his courage, loyalty and conscientiousness are not motivated by justice. On this view, the virtues are inseparable.

47 See also Gaita's discussion (1992: 305–8).

48 So if the imagined objector wants some humanly implementable formula that will guarantee what kind of act a lover of self will perform, I reply, first, that this cannot be provided, and second, that the objector would do well to give up their philosophical will-o'-the-wisp quest for certainty. The kind of act a lover of self will perform cannot be guaranteed, but the objector can be assured that she will not be an epistemic victim to evil.

49 It is not being suggested that these constraints are morally equivalent. They are used merely to illustrate a certain structure of thinking.

50 As a Kantian agent she would have found that 'to be lord of oneself is to be independent of all things' (Kant 1963: 140), including, presumably, of one's family ties.

51 A human being is, ideally, a being for whom there is no split between her moral interests and her interests of attachment. It is such a split that Herman's neo-Kantian attempt to internalise the moral barrier so that it becomes part of the self is unable to avoid: 'If my child is among those who are at risk, I do not act for my child as a moral agent but as a mother...moral reasons...are out of place here' (Herman 1993: 189). Despite the attempted internalisation of the ethical that 'normalises' motives of connection, Herman (1993; 1996) is unable to escape the Kantian notion that the acts of a mother who cares for her

child do not belong to the moral domain. A Kantian cannot allow that a mother's caring act for her child is paradigmatically a *moral* act: 'virtue... is the conquest of inclination' (Kant 1963: 246). By contrast, Dostoevsky presents Sonia as an agent who in prostituting herself acted as a daughter and sister, but, in so doing, simultaneously gave expression to what she morally was. Her act was both an expression of her attachment to her family and an expression of her moral person-hood. Had her desires and interests been 'normalised' by Herman's (internalised) moral constraints, she would have been morally unable to save her family, because as Herman says, 'strength or intimacy of attachment alone does not provide grounds to rebut the demands of moral requirements' (1993: 201). Prostitution can never be acceptable for a Kantian since it uses both self and others only as a means, violating rational nature. As a Kantian agent, Sonia would have been unable to act in accordance with her own moral understanding of what she *had* to do. For moral constraints to be internal according to the conception invoked here, moral concerns must be integral to every encounter a person has with another, and are not something separable from her interests of attachment.

52 Nor should it be thought that self-respect ceased to be an important value for her. That Sonia chose to become a prostitute to save her family does not mean that this value ceased to attract her. The Aristotelian virtuous agent 'will have all the virtues (1145a2); though these cannot conflict essentially or in principle, contingent conflicts may arise.... Acting for certain ends may require the forfeiture... of other deeply valued commitments. The loss may be inescapable and not without trace' (Sherman 1989: 30–1).

53 'A given circumstance may have multiple descriptions, and yield competing ethical claims to equally virtuous individuals who simply see things differently as a result of having developed the virtues differently in their lives' (Sherman 1989: 29).

54 The Hegelian conception is also not able to come to terms with this thought. I have pointed out that Hegel has no room for good and evil as it concerns most of us.

CONCLUSION

1 This is not to say that *amour de soi* is not in any way akin to what I have termed love of self. Just as in the case of love of self, there are certain needs and desires from which a person who possesses *amour de soi* is immune. While the social self both needs and desires superiority, since it must constantly compare itself with others and gain their esteem in order to possess self-worth, the possession of *amour de soi* ensures that the self is free of this desire and need. Similarly, a lover of self is not one who desires or needs superiority in order to gain self-worth.

2 So the charge that the possibility appears to be left open in his account for an engagement in what many moral philosophers would regard as evil to be involved in the development of the moral self would not bother Rousseau. On his account, the domain of the ethical is given by the general will, and this does not have an objective determinant content.

Bibliography

Ainsworth, M., Blehan, M., Waters, E. and Walls, S. (1978) *Patterns of Attachment*, Hillsdale NJ: Erlbaum.

Allison, H. E. (1990) *Kant's Theory of Freedom*, Cambridge: Cambridge University Press.

Annas, J. (1988) 'Self-love in Aristotle', *The Southern Journal of Philosophy* (supplement) 27: 1–23.

Arendt, H. (1978) *The Life of the Mind*, vol. 1, London: Secker and Warburg.

Aristotle (1941) *Ethica Nicomachea*, trans. W. D. Ross, in R. McKeon (ed.) *The Basic Works of Aristotle*, New York: Random House.

Baier, A. (1978) 'Hume's analysis of pride', *The Journal of Philosophy*, 75: 27–40.

——(1980) 'Master Passions', in A. Rorty (ed.) *Explaining Emotions*, Berkeley CA: University of California Press.

——(1985) 'Knowing our place in the animal world', in *Postures of the Mind*, Minneapolis: University of Minnesota Press.

de Beauvoir, S. (1970) *The Ethics of Ambiguity*, New York: The Citadel Press.

Blum, L. (1990) 'Vocation, friendship, and community: limitations of the personal-impersonal framework', in O. Flanagan and A. Rorty (eds) *Identity, Character and Morality: Essays in Moral Psychology*, Cambridge MA: MIT Press.

Brandt, R. (1979) *A Theory of the Good and the Right*, Oxford: Clarendon Press.

Brink, D. (1986) 'Utilitarian morality and the personal point of view', *The Journal of Philosophy*, 83: 417–38.

Browne, D. (1990) 'Ethics without morality', *Australasian Journal of Philosophy*, 68: 395–412.

Buber, M. (1973) *Between Man and Man*, London: Fontana.

Butler, J. (1969) 'Fifteen sermons', in D. Raphael (ed.) *British Moralists* vol. 1, Oxford: Clarendon Press.

Carver, H. (1991) 'Aristotle's much maligned megalopsychos', *Australasian Journal of Philosophy*, 69: 131–51.

Cooper, J. (1977) 'Aristotle on the forms of friendship', *Review of Metaphysics*, 30: 619–48.

Bibliography

Crittenden, P. (1990) *Learning to be Moral: Philosophical Thoughts about Moral Development*, Atlantic Highlands NJ: Humanities Press International.

Darwall, S. (1977–8) 'Two kinds of respect', *Ethics*, 88: 36–49.

——(1983) *Impartial Reason*, Ithaca NY and London: Cornell University Press.

Dent, N. (1988) *Rousseau: an Introduction to his Psychological, Social, and Political Theory*, Oxford: Blackwell.

Devine, P. (1978) *The Ethics of Homicide*, Ithaca NY: Cornell University Press.

Diagnostic and Statistical Manual for Mental Disorders (1987) 3rd edn, revised, Washington DC: American Psychiatric Association.

Dostoevsky, F. (1948) 'Notes from underground', in *A Treasury of Russian Literature*, London: The Bodley Head.

——(1949) *Crime and Punishment*, trans. C. Garnett, London: Heinemann.

Engstrom, S. and Whiting, J. (eds) (1996) *Aristotle, Kant, and the Stoics*, New York: Cambridge University Press.

Flanagan, O. (1990) 'Identity and strong and weak evaluation', in O. Flanagan and A. Rorty (eds) *Identity, Character and Morality: Essays in Moral Psychology*, Cambridge MA: MIT Press.

Frankfurt, H. (1971) 'Freedom of the will and the concept of a person', *The Journal of Philosophy*, 67: 5–20.

——(1982) 'The importance of what we care about', *Synthese*, 53: 257–72.

Fromm, E. (1957) *The Art of Loving*, London: Unwin.

Gaita, R. (1991) *Good and Evil: an Absolute Conception*, London: Macmillan.

Goldberg, C. (1984) 'The role of the mirror in human suffering and in intimacy', *Journal of the American Academy of Psychoanalysis*, 12: 511–28.

Greenberg, J. and Mitchell, S. (1983) *Object Relations in Psychoanalytic Theory*, Cambridge MA: Harvard University Press.

Harsanyi, J. (1982) 'Morality and the theory of rational behaviour', in A. Sen and B. Williams (eds) *Utilitarianism and Beyond*, New York: Cambridge University Press.

Hartley, L. P. (1953) *The Go-Between*, London: Penguin.

Hegel, G. (1931) *The Phenomenology of Mind*, trans. J. Baillie, London: George Allen and Unwin.

——(1942) 'Philosophy of right', in *Hegel's Philosophy of Right*, trans. T. Knox, Oxford: Clarendon Press.

——(1944) *The Philosophy of History*, trans. J. Sibree, New York: Wiley.

——(1957) 'The philosophy of history', in J. Loewenberg (ed.) *Hegel: Selections*, New York: Scribner.

Herman, B. (1993) 'Agency, attachment and difference', in *The Practice of Moral Judgement*, Cambridge MA: Harvard University Press.

——(1996) 'Making room for character', in S. Engstom and J. Whiting (eds) *Aristotle, Kant, and the Stoics*, New York: Cambridge University Press.

Hill Jr, T. (1982) 'Self-respect reconsidered', *Tulane Studies in Philosophy*, 31: 129–37.

—— (1986) 'Darwall on practical reason', *Ethics*, 96: 604–19.

Homiak, M. (1981) 'Virtue and self-love in Aristotle's ethics', *The Canadian Journal of Philosophy*, 11: 633–51.

Hume, D. (1974) *An Enquiry Concerning the Principles of Morals*, ed. L. A. Selby-Bigge, Oxford: Oxford University Press.

—— (1978) *A Treatise of Human Nature*, ed. L. A. Selby-Bigge, Oxford: Clarendon Press.

Irwin, T. (1988) *Aristotle's First Principles*, Oxford: Clarendon Press.

James, W. (1890) *The Principles of Psychology*, vol. 1, New York: Dover.

Kant, I. (1956) *The Critique of Practical Reason*, trans. L. Beck, New York: Bobbs Merrill.

—— (1963) *Lectures on Ethics*, trans. L. Infield, New York: Harper and Row.

—— (1964) 'The doctrine of virtue', part II of *The Metaphysic of Morals*, trans. M. Gregor, New York: Harper and Row.

—— (1969) *Groundwork of the Metaphysic of Morals*, trans. H. Paton as *The Moral Law*, London: Hutchinson.

Kaufmann, W. (1972) 'The Hegel myth and its method' in A. MacIntyre (ed.) *Hegel: a Collection of Critical Essays*, New York: Doubleday.

Kohut, H. (1966) 'Forms and transformations of narcissism', *Journal of the American Psychoanalytic Association*, 14: 243–72.

—— (1968) 'The psychoanalytic treatment of narcissistic personality disorders', *The Psychoanalytic Study of the Child*, 23: 86–113.

—— (1971) *The Analysis of the Self*, New York: International Universities Press.

—— (1972) 'Thoughts on narcissism and narcissistic rage', *The Psychoanalytic Study of the Child*, 27: 360–400.

—— (1977) *The Restoration of the Self*, New York: International Universities Press.

—— (1984) *How Does Analysis Cure?*, Chicago IL: University of Chicago Press.

Korsgaard, C. (1996) 'From duty and for the sake of the noble: Kant and Aristotle on morally good action', in S. Engstom and J. Whiting (eds) *Aristotle, Kant, and the Stoics*, New York: Cambridge University Press.

Langton, R. (1992) 'Duty and desolation', *Philosophy*, 67: 481–505.

Lee, R. and Martin, J. (1991) *Psychotherapy after Kohut: a Textbook of Self Psychology*, Hillsdale NJ: Analytic Press.

Lichtenberg, J. (1983) *Psychoanalysis and Infant Research*, Hillsdale NJ: Analytic Press.

Lloyd, G. (1986) 'Selfhood, war and masculinity', in C. Pateman and E. Gross (eds) *Feminist Challenges: Social and Political Theory*, Sydney: Allen and Unwin.

Lycos, K. (1978) 'The amoralist', *Philosophical Papers*, 1: 6–17.

McDowell, J. (1978) 'Are moral requirements hypothetical imperatives?', *Proceedings of the Aristotelian Society*, supp. vol. 52: 13–29.

MacIntyre, A. (1982) 'Comments on Frankfurt', *Synthese*, 53: 291–94.

—— (1988) *Whose Justice? Which Rationality?*, Notre Dame IN: University of Notre Dame Press.

Bibliography

Meares, R. (1992) *The Metaphor of Play: on the Self, the Secret, and the Borderline Experience*, Melbourne: Hill of Content.

Melzer, A. (1990) *The Natural Goodness of Man: on the System of Rousseau's Thought*, Chicago IL: University of Chicago Press.

Minde, K. and Minde, R. (1986) *Infant Psychiatry*, Beverley Hills CA: Sage.

Monroe, K. *et al.* (1990) 'Altruism and the theory of rational action: rescuers of Jews in Nazi Germany', *Ethics*, 101: 103–22.

Murdoch, I. (1970) 'The idea of perfection', in *The Sovereignty of Good*, London: Routledge and Kegan Paul.

Nagel, T. (1970) *The Possibility of Altruism*, Princeton NJ: Princeton University Press.

——(1980) 'The limits of objectivity', in S. McMurrin (ed.) *The Tanner Lectures on Human Values*, Cambridge: Cambridge University Press.

——(1986) *The View from Nowhere*, Oxford: Oxford University Press.

Neu, J. (1977) *Emotion, Thought and Therapy*, London: Routledge and Kegan Paul.

Newman, J. (1985) *An Essay in Aid of a Grammar of Assent*, Oxford: Clarendon Press.

Norton, D. (1976) *Personal Destinies: a Philosophy of Ethical Individualism*, Princeton NJ: Princeton University Press.

Nussbaum, M. (1980) 'Shame, separateness and political unity: Aristotle's criticism of Plato', in A. Rorty (ed.) *Essays on Aristotle's Ethics*, Berkeley CA: University of California Press.

Parfit, D. (1984) *Reasons and Persons*, Oxford: Clarendon Press.

Passmore, J. (1968) *Hume's Intentions*, London: Duckworth.

Plato (1961a) 'Apology', trans. W. Woodhead, in E. Hamilton and H. Cairns (eds) *Plato: the Collected Dialogues*, New York: Random House.

——(1961b) 'Gorgias', trans. W. Woodhead, in E. Hamilton and H. Cairns (eds) *Plato: the Collected Dialogues*, New York: Random House.

——(1961c) 'Laws', trans. W. Woodhead, in E. Hamilton and H. Cairns (eds) *Plato: the Collected Dialogues*, New York: Random House.

——(1961d) 'Meno', trans. W. Woodhead, in E. Hamilton and H. Cairns (eds) *Plato: the Collected Dialogues*, New York: Random House.

——(1961e) 'Protagoras', trans. W. Woodhead, in E. Hamilton and H. Cairns (eds) *Plato: the Collected Dialogues*, New York: Random House.

——(1961f) 'Republic', trans. W. Woodhead, in E. Hamilton and H. Cairns (eds) *Plato: the Collected Dialogues*, New York: Random House.

Platts, M. (1979) *Ways of Meaning: an Introduction to a Philosophy of Language*, London: Routledge and Kegan Paul.

Popper, K. (1973) *The Open Society and its Enemies*, vol. 2, London: Routledge and Kegan Paul.

Railton, P. (1984) 'Alienation, consequentialism, and the demands of morality', *Philosophy and Public Affairs*, 13: 134–71.

Rawls, J. (1972) *A Theory of Justice*, Oxford: Clarendon Press.

Richard, R. (1988) 'Is humility a virtue?', *American Philosophical Quarterly*, 25: 253–9.

Rorty, A. (1990) 'Pride produces the idea of self: Hume on moral agency', *Australasian Journal of Philosophy*, 68: 255–69.

——(1991) 'Rousseau's therapeutic experiments', *Philosophy*, 66: 413–34.

Bibliography

Rousseau, J. (1955a) 'Discourse on the origin of inequality', in Rousseau, *The Social Contract and Discourses*, trans. J. Cole, London: Dent.

—— (1955b) 'The social contract', in Rousseau, *The Social Contract and Discourses*, trans. J. Cole, London: Dent.

—— (1955c) 'A discourse on political economy', in *The Social Contract and Discourses*, trans. J. Cole, London: Dent.

—— (1967) *The Confessions of Jean-Jacques Rousseau*, trans. J. Cohen, London: Chaucer Press.

—— (1969) *Emile*, trans. B. Foxley, London: Dent.

Sachs, D. (1981) 'How to distinguish self-respect from self-esteem', *Philosophy and Public Affairs*, 10: 346–60.

Scheffler, S. (1982) *The Rejection of Consequentialism*, Oxford: Clarendon Press.

—— (1986) 'Morality's demands and their limits', *The Journal of Philosophy*, 83: 531–7.

Schneewind, J. (1996) 'Kant and Stoic Ethics', in S. Engstom and J. Whiting (eds) *Aristotle, Kant, and the Stoics*, New York: Cambridge University Press.

Sherman, N. (1989) *The Fabric of Character*, Oxford: Clarendon Press.

Sidgwick, H. (1929) *The Methods of Ethics*, London: Macmillan.

Slote, M. (1987) 'Is virtue possible?', in R. Kruschwitz and R. Roberts (eds) *The Virtues: Contemporary Essays on Moral Character*, Belmont CA: Wadsworth.

Solomon, R. (1983) *In the Spirit of Hegel*, Oxford: Oxford University Press.

Spinoza, B. (1949) 'Ethics', in Spinoza, *Ethics and on the Improvement of the Understanding*, New York: Hafner.

Starobinski, J. (1988) *Jean-Jacques Rousseau: Transparency and Obstruction*, trans. A. Goldhammer, Chicago IL: University of Chicago Press.

Stocker, M. (1976) 'The schizophrenia of modern ethical theories', *The Journal of Philosophy*, 73: 453–66.

—— (1990) 'Friendship and duty: some difficult relations', in O. Flanagan and A. Rorty (eds) *Identity, Character and Morality: Essays in Moral Psychology*, Cambridge MA: MIT Press.

—— (1996) *Valuing Emotions*, Cambridge: Cambridge University Press.

Strawson, P. (1959) *Individuals*, London: Methuen.

Taylor, C. (1975) *Hegel*, Cambridge: Cambridge University Press.

—— (1977) 'What is human agency?', in T. Mischel (ed.) *The Self: Psychological and Philosophical Issues*, Oxford: Blackwell.

—— (1989) *Sources of the Self: the Making of the Modern Identity*, Cambridge MA: Harvard University Press.

Taylor, G. (1980) 'Pride', in A. Rorty (ed.) *Explaining Emotions*, Berkeley CA: University of California Press.

—— (1985) *Pride, Shame and Guilt: Emotions of Self-assessment*, Oxford: Clarendon Press.

Thomas, L. (1978) 'Morality and our self-concept', *Journal of Value Inquiry*, 12: 258–68.

Thompson, J. (1987) 'A rational world order: Hegel on international relations', *International Journal of Moral and Social Studies*, 2: 105–18.

Bibliography

——(1992) *Justice and World Order: a Philosophical Inquiry*, London: Routledge.

Tolstoy, L. (1954) *Anna Karenina*, trans. C. Garnett, London: Heinemann.

——(1986) 'The death of Ivan Illych', trans. L. and A. Maude, in *The Raid and Other Stories*, Oxford: Oxford University Press.

Toolan, J. (1978) 'Therapy of depressed and suicidal children', *American Journal of Psychotherapy*, 32: 243–51.

Vlastos, G. (1981) 'The individual as an object of love in Plato', *Platonic Studies*, Princeton NJ: Princeton University Press.

Walker, M. (1987) 'Moral particularity', *Metaphilosophy*, 18: 171–85.

Whiting, J. (1996) 'Self-love and authoritative virtue: prolegomenon to a Kantian reading of Eudemian ethics viii 3', in S. Engstom and J. Whiting (eds) *Aristotle, Kant, and the Stoics*, New York: Cambridge University Press.

——(1991) 'Impersonal friends', *Monist*, 74: 3–29.

Williams, B. (1973) 'A critique of utilitarianism', in J. Smart and B. Williams (eds) *Utilitarianism: For and Against*, New York: Cambridge University Press.

——(1981a) 'Moral luck', in Williams, *Moral Luck*, New York: Cambridge University Press.

——(1981b) 'Persons, character and morality', in Williams, *Moral Luck*, New York: Cambridge University Press.

——(1981c) 'Utilitarianism and moral self-indulgence', in Williams, *Moral Luck*, New York: Cambridge University Press.

——(1981d) 'Practical necessity', in Williams, *Moral Luck*, New York: Cambridge University Press.

——(1985) *Ethics and the Limits of Philosophy*, London: Fontana.

Winnicott, D. (1965a) 'The capacity to be alone', in *The Maturational Processes and the Facilitating Environment*, New York: International Universities Press.

——(1965b) 'Ego distinction in terms of true and false self', in *The Maturational Processes and the Facilitating Environment*, New York: International Universities Press.

Wolf, E. (1988) 'Basic concepts of self psychology', in *Treating the Self: Elements of Clinical Self Psychology*, New York: Guilford Press.

Wolf, S. (1982) 'Moral saints', *The Journal of Philosophy*, 79: 419–39.

Wong, D. (1984) *Moral Relativity*, Berkeley CA: University of California Press.

Yanal, R. (1987) 'Self-esteem', *Nous*, 21: 363–79.

Name Index

Ainsworth, M. 214n
Allison, H. 220n
Annas, J. 210n
Arendt, H. 186
Aristotle 4, 10, 11, 13, 62, 63–9,
    73–87, 112, 119, 120, 140, 151,
    154, 156, 157, 174, 192, 196, 197,
    205–6n, 207n, 208n, 209n, 210n,
    212n, 213n, 214n, 215n, 216n,
    217n, 218n, 221n, 222n, 224n

Baier, A. 199n, 201n
de Beauvoir, S. 134
Blum, L. 212n
Brandt, R. 91–2, 208n, 209n, 211n
Brink, D. 165
Browne, D. 210n
Buber, M. 135
Butler, J. 198

Campbell, J. ix
Carver, H. 85
Chazan, R. x
Cooper, J. 86, 208n
Cordner, C. ix, 200n
Crittenden, P. 204n

Darwall, S. 3, 112, 113, 114
Dent, N. 32, 38, 40–2, 44
Devine, P. 165
Dostoevsky, F. 163, 164, 165, 166,
    167, 172, 180, 188, 190, 191, 220n,
    223n, 224n

Eichmann, A. 186

Flanagan, O. 211n
Frankfurt, H. 125, 211n

Freud, S. 22, 72, 79
Fromm, E. 217n

Gaita, R. 155, 166, 172, 218n,
    219–20n, 222n, 223n
Goldberg, C. 214n, 216n
Greenberg, J. 74

Hare, R. M. 159
Harman, G. 159
Harsanyi, J. 92
Hartley, L. 88
Hegel, G. 9, 10, 11, 12, 13, 31, 33, 49,
    50–62, 88, 153, 154, 156, 157, 182,
    192, 195, 196, 197, 203–5n, 218n,
    224n
von Herbert, M. 182–3
Herman, B. 2, 220–1n, 221–2n, 223n
Hill Jr, T. 114, 213n
Hitler, A. 91, 161, 186, 219n
Homiak, M. 214n
Hume, D. 9, 10, 11, 13–30, 31, 33, 46,
    47, 55, 62, 88, 112, 127–8, 129,
    153, 156, 157, 182, 192, 193, 195,
    196, 199n, 200n, 201n, 202n,
    203n, 216n, 219n

Illych, I. 116–20, 130–1, 128, 150,
    215n, 216n
Irwin, T. 85, 127

James, W. 114, 115

Kant, I. 10, 46, 48, 52, 53, 58, 168,
    182, 183, 203n, 204n, 218n, 219n,
    220n, 221n, 222n, 223n, 224n
Kaufmann, W. 59

232

Subject Index

234

Subject index